For Don and Pat

READ THIS FIRST

It's frightening how some people, though adept at walking and scrambling, have none of the mountain sense usually learned through decades of mountain wandering, problem solving and familiarity with mountains in all weather.

Learn to read topo maps and be able to find a grid reference. Turn back if it looks too hard for you, if you can't handle loose rock, if the river is too high, if you can't hack a 10-hour day, or if the route-finding is out of your league. Turn back from a summit or ridge if a thunderstorm is approaching or if conditions are made dangerous by rain, snow or ice. *At all times use your own judgement.* The author and publisher are not responsible if you have a horrible day or you get yourself into a fix.

In this book there are no do's and don'ts. It is assumed that users of this book are caring, intelligent people who will respect the country they are travelling through.

Be aware that in Kananaskis Country, trails can change in an instant owing to logging and the search for oil and gas. Please notify me of any changes you find so I can make revisions in future editions. Use **Contact Us** under the **About** tab at kananaskistrails.com.

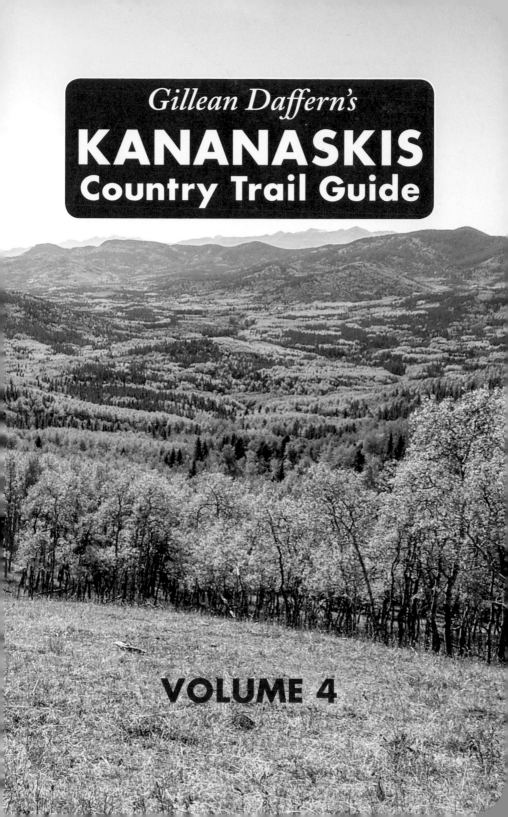

Gillean Daffern's
KANANASKIS
Country Trail Guide

VOLUME 4

Rocky Mountain Books
www.rmbooks.com

Library and Archives Canada Cataloguing in Publication

Daffern, Gillean, 1938-
    Gillean Daffern's Kananaskis Country trail guide. — 4th ed.

Includes bibliographical references and index.

Contents: v. 1. Kananaskis Valley — Kananaskis Lakes — Elk Lakes — The Smith-Dorrien —
    v. 2. West Bragg — The Elbow — The Jumpingpound —
    v. 3. Ghost, Bow Valley, Canmore, Spray —
    v. 4. Sheep, McLean Greek.

Issued also in electronic format.

ISBN 978-1-897522-76-9 (v. 1).—ISBN 978-1-897522-77-6 (v. 2)
ISBN 978-1-927330-03-6 (v. 3).—ISBN 978-1-927330-09-8 (v. 4)

1. Trails—Alberta—Kananaskis Country—Guidebooks.
2. Hiking—Alberta—Kananaskis Country—Guidebooks.
3. Kananaskis Country (Alta.)—Guidebooks.

I. Title. II. Title: Kananaskis Country trail guide.

GV199.44.C22K36 2010   796.51097123'32   C2009-907209-2

Book design and layout by Gillean Daffern
Cover design by Chyla Cardinal
Interior photographs by Gillean Daffern unless otherwise noted
Maps by Tony and Gillean Daffern
Topographical maps Her Majesty the Queen in right of Canada.

Printed in Canada

Rocky Mountain Books acknowledges the financial support for its publishing program from the Government of Canada through the Canada Book Fund (CBF), Canada Council for the Arts, and the province of British Columbia through the British Columbia Arts Council and the Book Publishing Tax Credit.

This book has been printed with FSC®-certified, acid-free papers, processed chlorine free and printed with vegetable based inks.

Disclaimer

The actions described in this book may be considered inherently dangerous activities. Individuals undertake these activities at their own risk. The information put forth in this guide has been collected from a variety of sources and is not guaranteed to be completely accurate or reliable. Many conditions and some information may change owing to weather and numerous other factors beyond the control of the authors and publishers. Individual climbers and/or hikers must determine the risks, use their own judgment, and take full responsibility for their actions. Do not depend on any information found in this book for your own personal safety. Your safety depends on your own good judgment based on your skills, education, and experience.

It is up to the users of this guidebook to acquire the necessary skills for safe experiences and to exercise caution in potentially hazardous areas. The authors and publishers of this guide accept no responsibility for your actions or the results that occur from another's actions, choices, or judgments. If you have any doubt as to your safety or your ability to attempt anything described in this guidebook, do not attempt it.

CONTENTS

TRAILS

Changes in the 4th edition

The big news is that the guide now extends to five volumes. The reasons are all advantageous to the reader: to keep the number of pages down (who wants to tote around a 1000-page guide book), to allow for a more user-friendly layout where trails are arranged by access road, to make room for more maps, and for ease of adding new trails and subtracting old ones.

There have been major changes to access roads, trails and trailheads. And as before, trails continue to be affected by logging, pipeline construction, the search for oil and gas and K Country management plans. Most notably the central portion of Gorge Creek Road has been permanently closed with barriers at Gorge Creek and Ware Creek trailheads, resulting in the loss of one trailhead. Official trails have been decommissioned, new trails have been built, and old and new trails have been rearranged with different names.

The Sheep, like other parts of K Country, has become a collection of parks: wildland parks, provincial parks, provincial recreation parks, Don Getty parks, ecological reserves, preservation zones, wildland zones, cultural and facility zones etc., each with a different level of protection and different sets of regulations. This makes things tricky for us guidebook writers. We have also been introduced to seasonal closures, permits, user fees and substantial fines for non-compliance. As if to sum it up, the word "ranger" has been replaced by the less friendly-sounding "conservation officer."

For up-to-date information visit our website at KananaskisTrails.com.

ACKNOWLEDGEMENTS

For this edition the following three people have been extremely helpful in the search for information over the years: Don Cockerton, Pat Ronald and Alf Skrastins. Thanks are also due to Avril Derbyshire, Tom and Phillis Gamble, Dewy Matthews, Jan Matthews, Julie Muller, Kathy Palese, Jon Rollins and the late Don King.

All photos are by the author unless credited otherwise. Most of all I want to thank Alf Skrastins for his generosity in opening up his entire photo collection. Other photos have been provided by Clayton Ditzler, Allan and Angélique Mandel, Jon Rollins, Derek Ryder and Jack Tannett.

PHOTO CAPTIONS

Front cover: #65A Threepoint Creek Gorge from the Hog's Back. Photo Allan and Angélique Mandel

Page 1: Inukshuk. Photo Alf Skrastins

Title page: #61 Aspen meadows of Ware Creek from Aspen Viewpoint.

Contents page: #9 Fall crossing of the Sheep River below Windy Point.

Page 17: #46A Mount Ware from the southwest spur.

Page 240: #64A Prayer flags below Mesa (Square) Butte.

Back cover: #51 The summit of Volcano.

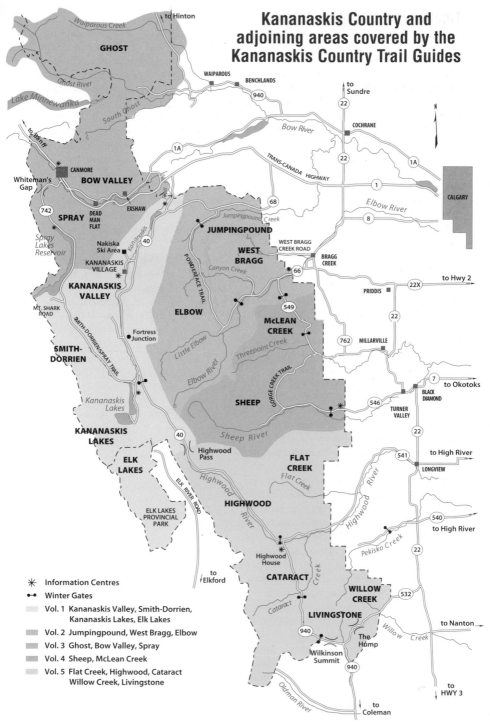

Kananaskis Country and adjoining areas covered by the Kananaskis Country Trail Guides

✳ Information Centres

•—• Winter Gates

Vol. 1 Kananaskis Valley, Smith-Dorrien, Kananaskis Lakes, Elk Lakes

Vol. 2 Jumpingpound, West Bragg, Elbow

Vol. 3 Ghost, Bow Valley, Spray

Vol. 4 Sheep, McLean Creek

Vol. 5 Flat Creek, Highwood, Cataract Willow Creek, Livingstone

KANANASKIS COUNTRY

It's kind of fun listening to Japanese tourists pronounce the name Kananaskis. The strange name dates back to 1858 when explorer John Palliser named the pass he was about to cross "Kananaskis Pass, after the name of an Indian, of whom there is a legend, giving an account of his most wonderful recovery from the blow of an axe which had stunned but had failed to kill him, and the river which flows through this gorge also bears his name." Possibly the Indian in question was the great Cree Koominakoos, who lost an eye and part of his scalp in a battle with the Blackfoot in the Willow Creek area but made a miraculous recovery and showed up at Fort Edmonton some weeks later "ready to take to the warpath again."

THE CONCEPT

Today the Kananaskis passes, Kananaskis Lakes and the Kananaskis River form the heart of Kananaskis Country (or K Country as it is more commonly called), a provincial recreation area established October 7, 1977, to "alleviate congestion in National Parks, and to provide greater recreation opportunities for Albertans."

Although former Alberta premier Peter Lougheed certainly deserves credit, it was actually Clarence Copithorne, rancher and MLA for Banff-Cochrane and Minister of Highways, who got the ball rolling with the reconstruction of Highway 40—the future Kananaskis Trail. Copithorne's vision for the Kananaskis Valley was one of strenuous physical outdoor activity accessible from a good road but with minimal services. As we all know, that simple idea turned into the grand plan called Kananaskis Country, encompassing a lot more country (over 4000 square kilometres) and a lot more development, namely interpretive centres, picnic areas, campgrounds, one alpine village, two Olympic venues, riverbeds refashioned for competition, and trails built for every conceivable sport.

LOCATION

K Country is located on the eastern slopes of the Canadian Rockies, west and south of the Olympic city of Calgary, Alberta. From the city outskirts the eastern boundary is only a 20-minute drive away.

The west boundary adjoins Banff National Park, then runs down the Continental Divide. The northern boundary is delineated by the Trans-Canada Highway and the fringe communities of Exshaw, Dead Man Flat and Canmore. The eastern boundary coincides neatly with the Bow-Crow Forest reserve boundary, while the southern boundary is marked by Highway 532 (Johnson Creek Trail).

GETTING THERE

Calgary is served by major airlines and several bus companies. That's it as far as public transportation goes. You need a car.

The area described in Volume 4 is usually accessed from the border towns of Black Diamond and Turner Valley on Hwys. 7 and 22 respectively. The towns can be reached from either Hwy. 2 south of Calgary, or via Hwy. 22 or Hwy. 762 south of Bragg Creek. To access the main thoroughfare, Hwy. 546 (Sheep River Trail), from Turner Valley follow Sunset Boulevard west up a hill and turn right at the top.

Since the last edition there has been a major change to Gorge Creek Trail, the road. Gorge Creek Road is now only accessed from Hwy. 546 and ends at Gorge Creek trailhead. Ware Creek Road (the northern portion of Gorge Creek Road) is accessed from Hwy. 549 and leads to Ware Creek trailhead. Note that road signs at the north end still read "Gorge Creek Trail." The middle portion of road has been permanently closed to vehicles and turned into Ware Creek trail.

Hwy. 549 (McLean Creek Trail, the road) on the eastern fringe is accessed from Hwy. 22 near Millarville or from Hwy. 762 south of Bragg Creek. You can also access it from the north via Hwy. 66 near the McLean Creek Recreation Area.

WHAT TO EXPECT

Volume 4 takes in the Sheep River (my favourite of all the eastern rivers) and all its tributaries, including Gorge Creek and Threepoint Creek, also known as the north fork.

The foothills are a mosaic of aspen, pine, spruce and meadows with sandstone and conglomerate outcrops. Two distinctive features of this area are its numerous rolling ridges and its celebrated black shale gorges — all of which make for grand walking country. As in the Elbow farther north, the foothills are criss-crossed by cutlines and logging roads, and in the far northeast by pipeline rights-of-way, and resource roads to sour gas wells. Both the McLean Creek OHV area off Hwy. 549 and the Sandy McNabb cross-country ski trails on both sides of Hwy. 546 near the field station utilize the leftover roads.

To the west, and delineating the western boundary, are the Highwood and Misty ranges of sedimentary limestones. Getting there usually entails waiting for the Sheep River to go down. It's a true explorer's paradise, featuring hidden waterfalls, alpine tarns and meadows. Scattered among its steep mountains — Gibraltar being the best known — are a few easy ascents and ridgewalks.

WEATHER TRENDS

Hiking season starts as early as March in the east and can continue until the end of November or beyond. As the snow clears, the areas farther west open up.

However, snow can fall in any month of the year, as campers well know. Just as likely, temperatures can rise to the mid-30s Celsius, leaving me and others who suffer from heat as limp as a dishrag. Rain most often falls in June or is associated with late-afternoon thunderstorms, which have accounted for a number of fatalities in K Country. Should it occur, the Indian summer can be glorious through October and even into November. Warm days, cold nights, no thunderstorms, no flies, no mosquitoes and no flowers, but then you can't have everything.

NATURAL HISTORY IN A NUTSHELL

I urge you to buy the appropriate field guides or Ben Gadd's all-in-one *Handbook of the Canadian Rockies.*

Mammals Most commonly seen in this area: bighorn sheep, cougars, feral horses, mule and whitetail deer, elk, moose, wolves, coyotes, black bears and grizzlies (which are more prevalent in the west). Having said that, the odd grizz does walk about in the foothills, forcing regular trail closures. At such times, conservation officers very properly rush out to close all trails in the immediate area with tape and notices.

Then there's the usual bevy of beavers and muskrats in every foothills valley, plus tree squirrels. Chipmunks, picas, marmots and porcupines are found more to the west.

The eastern slopes are a summer grazing area for cattle. Other animals you might see are pack horses, pack llamas, pack goats and sasquatch?

Notice at Mesa Butte campground.

Birds Most common: whisky jacks (the ones that gather around when you stop to eat), Clark's nutcracker, hummingbirds (wear red to attract them), ravens, crows, chickadees, kinglets, woodpeckers, northern flickers, flycatchers, warblers, owls, grouse, and birds of prey like the northern goshawk. Look for dippers and harlequin ducks on fast-moving rivers.

Fish Trout (cutthroat, rainbow, brown, bull) in small man-made ponds.

Vegetation Trees range from fire-succession lodgepole pine and aspen in the east to spruce and fir on north and east-facing slopes in the west with some larch at treeline on the eastern slopes of the Highwood Range. Look for limber pines on windy ridges. The Sheep is noted for its colourful aspens in the fall.

For flowers you'll need two field guides, one for the mountains and one for the prairies.

POSSIBLE HAZARDS

River crossings Large rivers like the Sheep are impassable during spring run-off and after prolonged rain. Schedule river crossing trips for mid-summer on. Another problematic river in spate is Threepoint Creek.

Caribbean water it is not: the water is often numbing even if it's only knee deep. Consider carrying neoprene booties.

Bears and other beasts At all times be aware of bears, but particularly in early spring, during berry season in August/September and during hunting season when the sound of a shot is like a clarion call for dinner. Often K Country will close a trail until a bear has moved out of the area, so be sure to read their trail report on the web before setting out. Carry a bear repellent and bear bangers where you can reach them in a hurry.

In the paranoia over predators we often forget that elk and moose should be given a wide berth as well, especially in spring when with young and in fall during mating season, when males get very ornery. Lately, cougars have become a year-round worry in this region.

Hunters Hunting is allowed everywhere except in provincial parks and provincial recreation areas. September to December is the time to dress in psychedelic shades of orange and pink. In November, hunting is allowed on Sundays. Before and after that month, Sunday is a "safe" day, but I wouldn't bet on it. Some hunters shoot at anything that rustles.

Ticks etc. Between about March and mid-June ticks are abroad and are found mainly in areas where there are lots of bighorn sheep. This applies particularly to Nash Meadows, Missinglink Mountain, Volcano Ridge, Allsmoke Mountain and the ridges and summits about Gorge Creek, particularly Mount Ware. While mosquitoes and horse flies can be a darn nuisance, they don't give you quite the same horrors.

Cattle East of the Front Ranges you'll run into herds of cattle. I would like to reassure visitors from Europe that bulls are quite placid; you can walk right past them without them budging an inch. Sometimes cows get panicky and run, often in the direction you are going. It requires strategy on your part to outmanoeuvre them.

Loose rock This refers mainly to the sedimentary limestone of the Highwood and Misty ranges. Of course there *is* firm limestone but it's safer to expect the worst. On scrambling pitches, develop the technique of pushing back handholds. Be extra careful of rockfall in gullies. On some routes you'll run into scree—lots of it. Use game trails, where the scree is more stabilized.

Logging trucks During logging be alert for trucks on logging roads AND on public roads. Hwy. 549 is particularly busy. Usually, there are warning signs.

Other users Very often you'll be sharing the trails with mountain bikers and with equestrians in particular; much less often with OHV users. You'll meet the occasional dirt bike rider on trails in Fisher Creek, Mount Barwell and Mount Quirk areas. Only occasionally is a trail slated for hikers only. Multi-use affects the trails, i.e., sections on soft ground become mud baths from equestrian use, while dirt bikes (and mountain bikes to some extent) make grooves which erode into gullies.

FACILITIES

Hwy. 546

The border towns of Turner Valley and Black Diamond provide all amenities: gas, eating places (western, Chinese, East Indian), campgrounds, B&Bs. In Turner Valley, Chuckwagon Restaurant on Sunset Boulevard does breakfast starting at 8 am. Breakfasts at Coyote Moon on the main street start at 7.30 on weekdays and 8 am on weekends. In Black Diamond, The Bakery & Coffee Shop does a full breakfast starting at 8 am, but is closed on Sundays. (It's a good place to pick up fresh baked goods for lunch.) If you get out of the mountains late when most eateries are closed, run to the historic Black Diamond Hotel, which stays open until 1 am and provides good food, entertainment on weekends and armchairs which weary hikers will find hard to get out of.

The Sheep River Provincial Park office, located on Sheep Station Road near the Sandy McNabb Campground, is open for information whenever someone is in residence; otherwise, phone the Elbow Valley Visitor Centre. In winter the campground road is plowed open to the skating rink. At such times, Group Camp A with picnic shelter doubles as a day-use area.

Hwy. 549

Millarville has a general store and gas station. Just west of town is the historic McKay Place restaurant (reservations recommended) which features a "regional ranch roadhouse menu" (open 11 am–9 pm on weekdays and 10 am–9 pm on weekends. Brunch on weekends.) At the north end of the highway is the Camper Centre that serves McLean Creek Campground.

Hwy. 22

Just north of Millarville is the cosy Corner House Cafe, which serves breakfast starting at 6.30 am and lunch. Closed on Mondays. In the winter months, approx. December to March, it is closed Sunday and Monday.

11

CAMPING

HIGHWAY-ACCESSIBLE CAMPING

Campgrounds fill up quickly in the summer. It's galling to find every site full of campers whose idea of exercise is the walk to the biffy, so book ahead if you can. After Labour Day the situation eases.

Use the phone numbers and email addresses to check on opening and closing dates, make reservations etc. Prices vary depending on amenities offered and the number of vehicles in your party. An RV and a tent count as one vehicle. Generally, Alberta seniors receive a discount.

Hwy. 546 (Sheep River Trail)

Sandy McNabb Campground has been enlarged and now features a comfort station at Loop D, amphitheatre at Loop D and plug ins at all sites. Open May 1 to mid-October. The equestrian campground is open April 1 to the end of October. The two group camps are open mid-June to mid-October.

When the campground is closed, you can vehicle camp in the Sandy McNabb day-use parking lot using self-registration.

Call Kananaskis Country Campgrounds 403-949-3132.

Bluerock, regular and equestrian, May 15 to the third week in September. In 2011 the regular campground sites were enlarged to accommodate larger RVs. Call Kananaskis Country Campgrounds 403-949-3132.

Hwy. 549 (McLean Creek Trail)

North Fork (Northfork) May 15 to the third week in September.
Mesa Butte equestrian May 15 to the third week in September.
Fisher Creek, year round. Call Kananaskis Country Campgrounds 403-949-3132.

For up-to-date specific info, pick up the *Explore Kananaskis Country* map and *Explore Alberta Parks* publication. Copies available at all information centres in K Country and Alberta.

BACKCOUNTRY CAMPING

Since the last edition, Wolf Creek backcountry campground has been closed. So now we are down to **Threepoint** in Volcano Creek (regular and equestrian), which is due for refurbishing in 2012: food lockers, new biffies, cattle fence.

For official sites you need permits costing $12 per person plus a $12 non-refundable reservation fee for all telephone and advance bookings. Children under 16 are free but still require a permit. Permits can be picked up from the Elbow Valley Visitor Information Centre, which is nowhere near the Sheep. The fastest and most hassle-free way is to phone 403-678-3136, give them your Visa or Mastercard number and ask them to fax the permit to you. In Alberta the number is toll free. Dial 310-0000 first. It will have occurred to you that camping at such sites can cost considerably more than highway-accessible camping.

Random camping is allowed almost anywhere except in provincial parks and provincial recreation areas and in a few areas that are broken down as follows: random permitted with permit, restricted random with no access April 15–Sept 30, no random camping and no access Dec 15–June 15, bivouac random April 15–Sept 30, bivouac random April 15–Sept 30 but with no access Dec 15–June 15. Contact the information centres for clarification.

Threepoint Campground.

INFO

SEASONAL ROAD CLOSURES

Hwy. 546 (Sheep River Trail) west of Sandy McNabb Recreation area is closed Dec 1–May 14. Walking and biking are allowed.

In winter Sandy McNabb Campground road is plowed to the skating rink.

Hwy. 549 (McLean Creek Trail) between McLean Creek Campground and Fisher Creek staging area and campground is closed Dec 1–April 30.

Gorge Creek Road to Gorge Creek trailhead is closed Dec 1–May 14.

Ware Creek Road to Ware Creek trailhead is closed Dec 1–May 14. NOTE Ware Creek Road is signed Gorge Creek Trail at the Hwy. 549 end.

A FEW RULES

- Respect seasonal trail closures.
- No registration is necessary for overnight trips. However, registration books are available at information centres and at some trailheads.
- Respect open-fire bans. Should you wish to report a fire, telephone numbers are listed on trailhead kiosks.
- Dogs must be on a leash.
- Anglers require an Alberta or BC fishing licence.
- There are some restrictions on backcountry camping. See "Backcountry Camping" page 12.
- There are some restrictions for mountain bikers. Read the trail description or contact an information centre.

FRIENDS OF KANANASKIS COUNTRY COOPERATING ASSOCIATION

This not-for-profit registered charity works to preserve "the ecological integrity of Kananaskis Country through educational programming, increased public awareness and leading by example." See www.kananaskis.org.

CHECK THE K COUNTRY WEBSITE

Check the K Country trail report for conditions. Especially useful are the "Important Notes," which among other things give warnings about bear or cougar sightings and temporary trail closures. See www.kananaskis-country.ca.

CHECK OUR BLOG

KananaskisTrails.com is a blog site maintained by Gillean and Tony Daffern. It covers all things Kananaskis, including notification of new trails, trail changes and trail issues.

CHECK THE WEB CAMS

The nearest web cam to this area is Bragg Creek, which features Moose Mountain.

ACRONYMS

- CMBA – Calgary Mountain Bike Alliance
- IMBA – International Mountain Biking Association
- DHS – Downhill Specific
- PRA – Provincial Recreation Area
- TPR – Tourism, Parks & Recreation

USING THE BOOK

ARRANGEMENT OF TRAILS

Trails are arranged by highway and are colour coded. Refer to map on page 16.

TYPES OF TRAILS

Official trails maintained by Kananaskis Country, Alberta Tourism, Parks & Recreation, and Alberta Sustainable Resources are a mix of new and old trails, logging and exploration roads, fire roads and cutlines. Expect parking lots at trailheads, biffies and the occasional picnic table. Junctions are marked with signage of the "You are here" variety. Some trails have directional arrows or coloured markers on trees or posts. Unless the trail is equestrian, expect bridges over creeks.

Unofficial trails are similar to the above, but sometimes have no obvious trailhead, are neither signposted nor marked in any way except perhaps for the occasional flagging, cairns or trimmed branches. Creek crossings are the norm. For the first time, this category includes trails demoted from official status.

Routes either have no trails or have long trail-less sections where you have to navigate from one intermittent game trail to another. Often there is some bushwhacking.

Scrambles can have official or unofficial trails or be routes. They range from ridge walks to gruelling uphill flogs in excess of 1000 m to the top of a mountain. You can be sure of scree, and possibly a pitch or two of easy scrambling. There may be mild exposure. Special equipment is unnecessary in optimum conditions when the mountain is devoid of snow and the weather is good.

HEIGHTS, HEIGHT GAINS

are given in both metric and imperial.

RATING TRAILS

No attempt has been made to classify trails. What's difficult for one person is easy for another. It's all relative. Also coming into play are the length of a trail, its gradient, its remoteness from a trailhead, conditions underfoot and so on. Read the introductory description carefully. If you're having a horrible time, it's up to you to turn back and try something easier.

RATING TIMES

Times are dependent on too many variables—everybody chugs along at a different rate. Some will be carrying heavy packs; some people, like me, want to make frequent flower stops. And then there are the underfoot conditions to consider, the weather and so on.

- Half-day, up to 3 hours.
- Day, up to 6 hours.
- Long-day, up to 10 hours plus. (Take headlamps.)
- Backpack, overnight camping.

Some of the trips are designated "bike 'n' hike" and "bike 'n' scramble." Biking the first part of the trail can cut down the time considerably. In this way I've often squeezed a weekend trip into one day.

DISTANCES

Distances are given in kilometres. Distances shown between each segment of trail are not cumulative; they show the distance of that segment only.

TRAIL DESCRIPTIONS

Trail descriptions are arranged according to the character of the trail. Most trails lead to a single destination. But sometimes the destination is the springboard for further options under headings like "going farther," "side trip," "optional descent route" etc. I sometimes describe the same mountain with different ways up and down, or an area with a number of trails or peaks radiating out from the same access. Occasionally loop trails can be extended into longer loops. Long-distance trails, rarely hiked in their entirety, are described by segment.

DIRECTIONS

Left and right refer to the direction of travel. Skier's left/right refers to descent, climber's left/right to ascent.

GRID REFERENCES AND
GPS RECEIVERS

Where I give grid references, you can follow along on your topo map.

Maps have blue grid lines running east–west and north–south. Each line is numbered. The first two numbers indicate the grid line forming the west boundary of the kilometre square in which your point is located, and the third number the estimated number of tenths of a kilometre your point is east of that line. The fourth and fifth numbers indicate the south boundary of the square, and the last number is the estimated number of tenths of a kilometre your point is north of that line.

GPS receivers are useful when bushwhacking or for finding your way back to a trail or a trailhead. Use NAD 83 datum.

MAPS IN BOOK

Sketch maps in the text are not always to scale and serve only to clarify complex areas where you might go wrong. Maps at the back of the book are based on today's topo maps, which come in a mix of imperial and metric. Therefore, the contour intervals vary. There are also errors like missing creeks, lakes, mountains and glaciers. Because of this these maps are intended as a guide only. Still, trails and routes are marked as accurately as possible.

- Red line: a trail, official or unofficial.
- Red dash: a route.
- Black line: trail in other volumes, or trail not used.
- Dashed black line: route in other volumes of this series.

BUYING MAPS

Maps in the back of this book are for reference only. You need to carry a bona fide topo map. The latest editions of Gem Trek maps come close to being the perfect maps for the area, with contour intervals of 25 m. They show grid lines, up-to-date road alignments, official trails, some unofficial trails, and major powerlines.

Government topo maps, depending on the edition, are in both imperial and metric, with contour lines at 100-ft. intervals and 40-m intervals respectively (not so good). Occasionally, features like small lakes, streams, glaciers and even mountains are omitted, which leads to exciting discoveries. Generally, road alignments are corrected on maps newer than 1983.

Provincial Resource Base Maps from Alberta Energy are updated fairly regularly and show what the other maps don't: all cutlines, all powerlines and exploration and logging roads. Unfortunately, the reality is sometimes nothing like what is shown on the map.

MAPS FOR VOLUME 4
Gem Trek

- Bragg Creek and Sheep Valley: scale 1:50,000, contour interval 25 m.
- Highwood and Cataract Creek: scale 1:50,000, contour interval 25 m.

Government topo maps
Scale 1:50,000
- 82 J/9 Turner Valley
- 82 J/10 Mount Rae
- 82 J/15 Bragg Creek

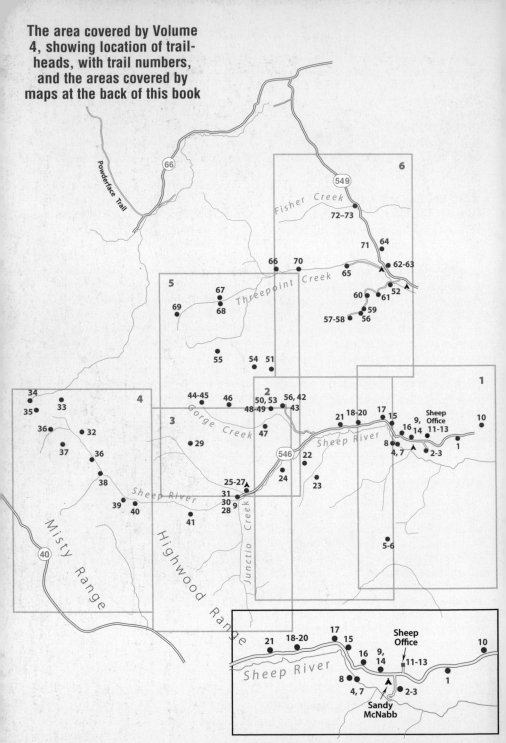

The area covered by Volume 4, showing location of trail-heads, with trail numbers, and the areas covered by maps at the back of this book

Close-up of trails near Sandy McNabb Recreation area

TRAIL DESCRIPTIONS

1 HIGH NOON HILLS — map 1

Half-day, short-day hikes
Unofficial trails, routes
Map 82 J/9 Turner Valley

Access Hwy. 546 (Sheep River Trail).
1. From the K Country boundary, drive 1.9 km to near the top of the hill and park off-road on the verge.
2. 600 m west of the K Country boundary at 788132, park at the side of the highway
Also accessible via #3B from Sandy McNabb Hills.

High Noon Hills refers to a wedge of land south of Hwy. 546 delimited to the east by the K Country boundary and to the west by Long Prairie Creek near its confluence with the Sheep River. Within it lie a couple of foothills at 785124 and 794124. Their grassy, southwest-facing slopes shed snow early, so naturally they're good choices for early spring. Some people, like Steve, make them their annual fall pilgrimage to enjoy the colourful aspens.

#1A Nearing the top of Hill 785124.

In summer you're contending with cattle for the trails, but also enjoying meadows crammed with prairie flowers.

Most people just do A from access 1 and return the same way. B takes you to the Sheep River for lunch with an option on the way back of ascending the second hill more easily than flogging up its west slope. Access 2, used mainly by riders from nearby Anchor D Guiding & Outfitting, offers a faster route to B. Yet another option is to connect these hills with Sandy McNabb Hills to make a longer day trip which requires two vehicles or a plod back along the ski trails and some road bashing. See the sketch map on page 24.

NAMING NOTE Mike Potter named these hills after the ranch to the east. Prior to this they were nameless according to Gary Thompson, who rides with the Sheep River Cattlemen's Association.

MAP NOTE These hills are not shown on the Gem Trek map.

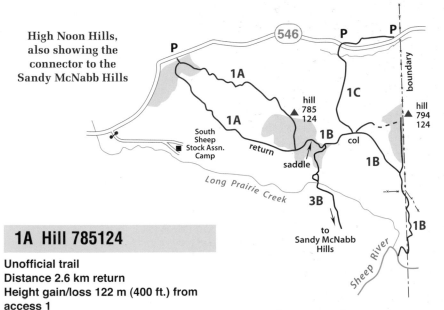

High Noon Hills, also showing the connector to the Sandy McNabb Hills

1A Hill 785124

Unofficial trail
Distance 2.6 km return
Height gain/loss 122 m (400 ft.) from access 1
High point 1518 m (4980 ft.)

The most popular trip from access 1.

To summit 1.3 km

Mount the small bank on the south side of the highway and pass through a gate in a fence, Immediately turn left, shortly cutting right through a narrow belt of trees into a large southwest-facing meadow. The trail follows the left edge of the meadow to the northwest ridge, then swings right through a few aspens into the pines.

Much clearer now, the trail undulates along the northwest ridge through pines, aspen woodland and aspen meadows (yes, there is a difference) to the grassy summit. Meadows sweep down to the south and west, allowing panoramic views of Front Range peaks between mounts Head and Glasgow. To the east rises Hill 7941245 on the K Country boundary. Down below in Long Prairie Creek, you can just spot the old shack of the South Sheep Stock Association camp where cattle have been rounded up from the forest reserve since 1918 by such people as Harry Sinnot and Bob Carry.

Optional return 1.8 km

Descend the grassy south ridge for 300 m to an intersection with a well-defined cow/horse trail and turn right. (To left B rises to a saddle.)

The cow/horse trail returns you to the big meadow you started out on without dropping to Long Prairie Creek Valley bottom. It's all very painless: after a spot of step-over aspen deadfall, you descend and join another trail in a meadow. Turn right. Go straight through alternating meadows and patches of small trees. At the end of meadow no. 3, continue along a grassy avenue scarcely recognizable as an old track. (En route a narrower side track to left leads to the corral at the South Sheep Stock Assn. Camp.)

Just after the avenue starts turning right, continue ahead on one of several trails through a strip of pine forest into the big southwest facing meadow you started out on. Preferably take the third trail that passes a salt lick in the trees and can be traced for some distance across the meadow, aiming to the left of prominent brown deadfall. Here you are just metres away from the gate in the fence and the highway.

GOING FARTHER

1B Sheep River, Hill 794124

Distance from saddle 4.5 km return
Height gain extra
Height loss extra
High point 1542 m (5060 ft.)

To the Sheep River 2.25 km
From Hill 785124 head down the south ridge to a cow/horse trail and turn left.

The trail winds uphill onto a saddle where you meet the connecting trail from Sandy McNabb Hills—it's the trail running parallel on your right.

Keep left and descend to a T-junction on the col at 789123 between the two hills. This is where the trail from access 2 joins in from the left. Turn right.

Almost straightaway ignore a faint trail climbing the hillside to left (it doesn't lead to the summit of Hill 794124) and continue straight on the main trail that drops a little then traverses the southwest slope of the hill to the K Country boundary fence at 794121.

Turn right and follow the fenceline trail downhill and through a gate where another fence comes in from the right at right-angles. After the boundary fence wanders off to the left, continue on the trail that shortly winds in dramatic fash-

ion down to the Sheep River, reached at the bend just downstream of the confluence with Long Prairie Creek.

Hill 794124 add on 0.5 km
Return the same way to 794121. Continue to climb the fenceline trail to the summit area of Hill 794125 for a slightly better view westwards (possibly because Hill 785124 is also included in the view).

Bushwhack down the steeper west slope to the col between the two hills at 789123. Return to the saddle below the south ridge.

ALTERNATIVE START

1C from access 2

Distance to Col 789123 0.9 km
Height gain to col 52 m (170 ft.)

At 788132 pick up the horse trail where it crosses the highway after paralleling it from the K Country boundary.

Heading south, the trail descends through a gap in a fence to Macabee Creek. Cross on culvert. Enter mixed forest and enjoy a gentle climb with variations to the col. Just before reaching the T-junction with B, the trail descends slightly, a point to note for the return.

#1B Winding down to the Sheep River.

#1B The summit of Hill 794124, looking toward Hill 785124.

#2 Sandy McNabb interpretive trail. View from the return leg of the Sheep River, the day use area and Mount McNabb.

2 SANDY McNABB interpretive trail—map 1

Hour hike
Official trail
Distance 1.9 km loop
Height gain/loss 24 m (80 ft.)
Map 82 J/10 Mount Rae

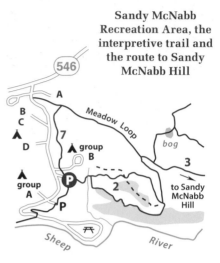

Sandy McNabb
Recreation Area, the
interpretive trail and
the route to Sandy
McNabb Hill

Access Hwy. 546 (Sheep River Trail) in the Sandy McNabb Recreation Area. Turn left just before the winter gate and drive 740 m to the Sandy McNabb interpretive trail parking lot access road on the left side. Access road is open year-round.
Also accessible from #7 Price Camp trail.

A short forest loop that takes in a viewpoint. The prerequisite to #3 Sandy McNabb Hill.

NAMING NOTE The trail, campground and everything else around is named after Alexander "Sandy" McNabb who came to Dewinton from Scotland with his three brothers and worked for the Royalite Oil Company during the boon years. He was largely instrumental in founding Turner Valley's Fish and Game Association and it was they who called Sandy's favourite fishing spot Sandy McNabb's (fishing) Camp. That's the flat down in the day use area

On the return leg beyond the bank top.

To Sandy McNabb Hill junction 900 m
From the parking lot head east on a trail that crosses a gate in the cattle fence. Shortly it circles left across a spring to a junction. Loop left.

The trail wanders through aspen and pine forest, crossing a track and then the Sandy McNabb Loop ski trail at sign 4. Between signs 5 and 6 it intersects Sandy McNabb ski trail for the second time. Go straight across a bridge. (Ski trail to left climbing up the hillside is the route to Sandy McNabb Hill.)

Bank top leg 1 km
Arrive at the edge of the high bank falling to the Sheep River. Here the trail curves right and follows the bank edge through flowery aspen meadows where you'll find benches and a spate of interpretive signs looking out over the Sheep River, the day use area and Mount McNabb.

Gradually the trail moves away from the bank top and climbs a little through aspens back to the junction. En route look for Spotted coral root orchids at a creek crossing. At the T-junction turn left to get back to the parking lot.

3 SANDY McNABB HILL — map 1

The ridge between the summits.

Half-day hike
Official, unofficial trails
Distance 2.1 km one way
Height gain ~97 m (320 ft.)
High point ~1500 m (4921 ft.)
Map 82 J/9 Turner Valley,
82 J/10 Mount Rae

Access Hwy. 546 (Sheep River Trail) in the Sandy McNabb Recreation Area. Turn left just before the winter gate and drive 740 m to the Sandy McNabb interpretive trail parking lot access road on the left. Access road is open year-round.
Also accessible from #7 Price Camp trail.

This is the hill that doesn't exist. For some strange reason several editions of the government topo map have mislaid a few contour lines, while the hill is missing completely from Gem Trek's Highwood map. You have to go back to pretechnology days to find it, i.e., A.O. Wheeler's map of 1895 and subsequent maps through the 1940s. There's a lot to be said for research from the ground up.

It lies east of the recreation area access road at 760115 and can be seen very well from Group Camp A's picnic shelter. A good well-used trail runs up its west ridge, so lots of gasping people can testify that it is, actually, a hill. And one with a fine view.

In this description I have combined the hill with the walkers only Sandy McNabb interpretive trail. It can also be accessed via Meadow Loop (nee Alder) from equestrian campground A, or from the Sheep River Provincial Park office parking lot via the ski trails (nee logging roads) of Loggers Loop. Know that these trails, though flat, are often wet and muddy in summer. No fun at all.

Two options exist to turn the half-day hike into a day hike:

1. Continue over Sandy McNabb Hill East and return via the north bank connector. See GOING FARTHER A.

2. Follow B to High Noon Hills, having parked a second vehicle or bikes at access 1. Alternatively, walk back along the road and ski trails. See the sketch maps on pages 22 and 24.

Interpretive trail and Meadow Loop ski trail 1.5 km

Set out on the interpretive trail. Keep left at the loop junction. Where it intersects Sandy McNabb Loop ski trail for the second time between signs 5 and 6 turn left.

Climb to a junction with map. Turn right onto Meadow Loop ski trail. A short distance along at a post with a green arrow, turn right onto a faint trail.

To summit 600 m

The trail soon becomes clear and climbs about 70 vertical m up the west ridge of your hill, between forest on the left and grassy slopes rolling away on the right. Arrive at the first top which looks over the Sheep River Valley to such recognizable peaks as Windy Point Ridge, Bluerock Mountain and Gibraltar.

Walk the summit ridge to a second top—a superior viewpoint because it also takes in the view to the east of Sandy McNabb Hill East and the High Noon Hills. The surprise here is the southeast slope that plummets in cliffs and rubble all the way down to the Sheep River, so thwarting any attempt to "get along the bank." See NOTE in next section.

Return to the interpretive trail.

Interpretive Trail Finish 1 km

On reaching the interpretive trail keep left and follow the trail to the banktop above the Sheep River and from there back to the parking lot.

NOTE If you want to view the cliff below the hill, start from the banktop and descend grass to a wide grassy bench. Turn left and walk past posts to the Sheep River.

Return the same way. (There are more cliffs lying in wait between the bench and the campground access road.)

GOING FARTHER

3A Sandy McNabb Hill East

Short-day hike
Unofficial trails & route
Add on 4.3 km return to hill
Add 207 m (680 ft.) height gain/loss return to hill
High point 1512 m (4960 ft.)

Tacking on the slightly higher hill to the east and returning via the north bank connector is a logical loop.

The trail over Sandy McNabb Hills and the north bank connector to High Noon Hills

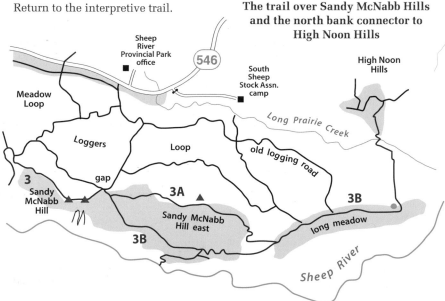

To the Gap 380 m
From the summit of Sandy McNabb Hill
the trail continues down the east ridge.
On meeting a fence, keep left of the fence
on the trail and descend to the bottom of
the hill. Turn right on Loggers Loop ski
trail, pass through the fence and arrive
at the very obvious gap between Sandy
McNabb Hill and a nubbin to the east. At
a post turn right off the ski trail onto the
narrower north bank connector.

**Over the tops to the north bank
connector 1.8 km**
Shortly, leave the connector trail and on
a bit trail ascend the steep grassy nubbin
on your left. Descend the far side to a col.
    From here an intermittent trail climbs
much less steeply up the west ridge to the
highest part of Sandy McNabb Hill East,
which has no sharply defined summit.
The trail stays mainly in the trees, aspens
low down, then pines. But of course the
great temptation is to walk at the top of
the south-facing meadow which sweeps
down to the Sheep River and is the main
characteristic of this hill.
    From just over the top a more defined
trail heads down the east ridge on grass.
After zigging to the right down a south
ridge a way, it again heads east descending
through aspen woodland—keep left, then
right at questionable junctions—reaching
the north bank connector at the start of the
long meadow (flagging at ~778112).

The return 2.1 km to hill
Turn right and follow the north bank connector across meadows and through aspen
copses back to the gap.
    Instead of climbing Sandy McNabb
Hill all over again, there is the option of
using Loggers Loop and Meadow Loop ski
trails (née logging roads) that sneak along
the north base of the hill. This idea is not
as good as it looks on the ski brochure!
Apart from muddy patches, the east end of
Meadow is an impassable slough, forcing
a bushwhack around one side or the other.
The distance is almost the same.

*#3A Looking west from the summit of the east
hill to Sandy McNabb Hill.*

3B to High Noon Hills

Short-day hike
Unofficial trail, creek crossing
Distance from hill 4.5 km
Add 91 m (300 ft.) height gain from hill
Height loss 144 m (471 ft.) from hill

The north bank connector joins Sandy
McNabb Hills to High Noon Hills and is
primarily a meadow walk with one crossing of Long Prairie Creek.

**To Sandy McNabb Hill East trail junc-
tion 2.1 km**
From Sandy McNabb Hill descend to the
gap as per A and turn right onto north
bank connector.
    This delightful trail traverses sun-
baked south-facing meadows between
Sandy McNabb Hill East and the Sheep
River. Look south across the Sheep River
to Channel Ridge, Blue Ridge and little
Mount Dyson in line with the rocky mouth
of Wolf Creek.
    (DETOUR Near the end of this section
just before the trail crosses a couple of

shallow draws, you'll note a parallel trail lower down the slope and a faint trail leading down to it. Should you follow this trail back west, you'll discover it zigs down a steep shaley bank to the Sheep River at about 769109. A picnic table shaded by spruce is a heavenly spot on a hot day.)

But back to the main trail. After it enters aspen woodland, flagging on the left indicates the trail up Sandy McNabb Hill East at 778112. This occurs at the start of the long meadow.

To High Noon Hills 2.4 km
The long meadow, easily picked out on Google Earth, is a long strip of grass extending almost to Long Prairie Creek. The trail follows the left forest edge all the way, crossing the odd intersecting game trail. In case you are wondering, the prominent ridge off to the southeast is Okotoks Mountain.

Near meadow's end, the trail turns sharp left past a seasonal pond into pine forest. Cross a gate in a drift fence (usually open) and descend to Long Prairie Creek upstream of steep shaley banks. Head upstream a short way past the bear tree, then cross the creek onto south-facing hillsides of grass and aspens.

The trail climbs into a grassy draw and follows it below the south ridge of Hill 785124 to the left. Higher up, past a side draw to the right, minor trails lead onto the south ridge, but the main trail itself winds upward to the right and joins B trail on a saddle between the south ridge and the col at 789123.

For access 1 turn left; for access 2 turn right and descend to the col.

Top: #3B The Sheep River near the picnic table.
See DETOUR.
Bottom: #3B The long meadow, looking west.

4 WOLF CREEK—map 1

Long-day hike, backpack
Unofficial trail, possibly with red
markers, major river crossing, creek
crossings
Distance 11.2 km from river
Height gain 305 m (1000 ft.)
High point 1661 m (5450 ft.)
Map 82 J/10 Mount Rae

Access Hwy. 546 (Sheep River Trail) at Sandy
McNabb Recreation Area. Turn left at the
winter gate and drive down the access road.
1. In 850 m, opposite group camp A, turn left
into a parking area.
2. Drive all the way down the road to the day-
use area by the Sheep River.
Also accessible from the eastern terminus of
#7 Price Camp trail, the southern terminus of
#6 Phone Line and the eastern terminus of #5
Junction Mountain from Coal Creek.

The Wolf Creek trail heads over the watershed to Coal Creek, then carries on to
the unsigned intersection with Junction
Lookout from Coal Creek and Phone Line
trails. The scenery is pine forest and
meadows, the route an amalgamation of
exploration road, cutline and trail. Not too
exciting, one would think, but it does have
a huge surprise in store as you'll discover.

During runoff or after steady rain, high
water in the fast-flowing Sheep River
makes this trail inaccessible unless you
can hitch a crossing on a horse.

TRAIL NOTE In the third edition this
was an official trail with red markers and
signposts at junctions. In 2007 the trail

*The big meadow between the Sheep River
and the west fork option.*

beyond the pass was undesignated. Then
the Sheep management plan of 2008
determined that the remainder of the
trail be undesignated despite opposition.
After all, it was a pretty popular trail and
improvements had been made just prior
to the decision. (Unfortunately, the ongoing removal of culverts means a return to
mud.) Also decommissioned is Wolf Creek
backcountry campground. You can still
camp there, you just won't have a picnic
table and will have to go behind a bush.

Ironically, while all this decommissioning was going on, equestrians under
GT were secretly improving a side trail up
the west fork so they could make a loop
around Mount Dyson. See OPTION A.

See also OPTION B for the ascent of
Mount Dyson from the main trail.

To Sheep River crossing ~450 m
From access no. 1, pick up Price Camp
trail just beyond the parking area and wind
down a grassy slope to the access road.
Cross it and continue to the bank of the
Sheep River. From access no. 2, walk back
along the road to the intersecting trail and
turn left. A red marker indicates the best
crossing place.

Wade the Sheep to another marker
(possibly removed) DOWNSTREAM of
Coal Creek. If water levels are iffy the Price
Camp crossing upstream of Coal Creek is
easier, which means, of course, that you
also have to wade Coal Creek.

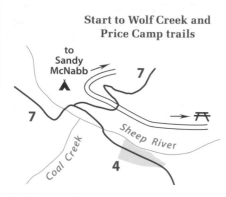

**Start to Wolf Creek and
Price Camp trails**

To West Fork junction 4.3 km

On the far bank, Wolf Creek trail heads downstream through a meadow, then climbs steeply up the bank. A more gradual uphill leads to a gate in a drift fence. A long flat stretch with boggy bits has been fixed up by the use of culverts and built-up sections of trail with rails on both sides. At last trees before the big meadow, a faint trail to right leads to a grave marker.

The big meadow is gorgeous, the trail winding around the left perimeter of it below a big grassy hill. A view of Blue Ridge ahead—the pleated forest ridge—gives

Coal Creek gorge from the viewpoint.

you some idea of how far you have to go to the pass, which is located another 2 km beyond it. Re-enter trees. You are now walking on the banktop above Wolf Creek Valley, seen down below to your left. The second grassy track heading right (the one with tread) is A, the west fork trail. The junction is at 752086 at the top of a steep downhill.

To the pass 3.7 km

The main trail descends and crosses the west fork. Climb out of the dip and in about 800 m join a NE–SW cutline. Turn right. That there is a junction here is no longer obvious, but years ago, two Calgary women, having successfully navigated across the foothills from Flat Creek, crossed Wolf Creek as shown on an early edition of a K Country map and were lost in the cutlines for three days!

On the cutline, pass through a drift fence into the inner fastness of Wolf Creek between Blue Ridge (formerly Whaleback) and Mount Dyson. At a cutline split, keep right on what looks more like a trail. A little farther on, a small meadow on the left side marks the taking off place for Mount Dyson. Pass through another drift fence.

Shortly the trail turns right up a steep hill into a tributary valley. You cross the tributary, then climb steadily to an unsigned 4-way junction at about 729065. To right is the blazed west fork trail. Straight on is the official trail. To left is a shortcut I like to take because it is flat. Beyond the shortcut, the trail makes a final climb to the pass.

Grassy south-facing slopes allow a view of foothills and far-off mountains. But wait. Follow the trail through the meadow, and where it veers left head right to a bench and horse rail. In a countryside of low relief, it comes as a huge shock when the ground suddenly opens up into a savage, black-shale gorge—the greatest moment of the day. Although short, the Coal Creek version is just as impressive as its better-known counterparts, particularly if you can persuade a passing mountain biker to pose on the edge.

To Coal Creek 3.2 km

Back on the trail, descend an open draw, cross the NE–SW cutline and pick up the cutline access road that takes you down the hill to Coal Creek Valley. A lovely stretch through riverside meadows takes you past the site of Wolf Creek backcountry campground (where noises in the night were likely cows) to the creek. The trail crosses to the north bank, recrosses the cutline, then recrosses the creek to the unsigned junction on the south bank at 717046 with Phone Line (right) and Junction Lookout from Coal Creek (straight).

OPTIONS

4A West fork trail

Unofficial trail
Distance 4.3 km
Height gain N–S 168 m (550 ft.)

This trail, a mix of logging road, cow trail and equestrian trail allows you to make a loop around Mount Dyson. The going is easy through meadows and pine forest,

NORTH TO SOUTH

At 752086 on Wolf Creek trail, turn right onto a grassy track with tread. This heads along the right bank of the west fork, shortly passing through a drift fence into meadows. In lush grass, the trail is sometimes hard to follow as it traverses large interlinked meadows just above the banktop. At one point it dips steeply to cross a side creek. On entering trees, the trail once again becomes clear.

The valley narrows and turns southwest. Enjoy a flat stretch alongside the creek below flowery banks. Do not cross the creek on side roads. At the valley head the creek divides, the trail following the right-hand fork. Shortly you cross the creek below the spring and follow a tight, twisty draw that unfolds before you reach a pass in the pines at 727073.

Descend the far side into more open woods. When it seems the trail is aiming for Coal Creek gorge, it turns sharp left up along the left bank of a tributary, gradually climbing over a low ridge to intersect Wolf Creek trail at the 4-way junction at about 729065, not far below the pass.

#4A The west fork trail in the draw.

Monarda meadows on the east ridge, looking back down to the southeast ridge and across Wolf Creek to Blue Ridge.

4B Mount Dyson

Route
Distance 1.4 km from Wolf Creek trail
Height gain 305 m (1000 ft.)
High point 1826 m (5990 ft.)

This low (some might say lowly) foothill has meadows secreted away on the southeastern slope that are only visible from Blue Ridge opposite. This is the way of ascent, a sometimes steep climb through a thousand feet of flowers.

NAMING & HISTORY NOTE Its first ascent was on August 13, 1896, and on September 2 and 3, 1897, during the Irrigation Survey. A.O. Wheeler named the camera station and hence the hill after his assistant Dyson.

"Why," my friend wanted to know, "is Mount Dyson miles away from Dyson Creek?" That's because Coal Creek was called Dyson Creek on Wheeler's map of 1895 and on all subsequent maps until coal was discovered at the mouth of the creek and some government department went and changed the name in 1951.

Leave Wolf Creek trail at about 743068 opposite a small meadow on the left side.

After a preliminary push through trees, climb steep open hillside to the right of a small side valley. Gain the southeast ridge which ultimately turns left and becomes an east ridge leading directly and ever more steeply to the summit. You follow the demarcation of trees and grass with frequent forays into the meadow to look at flowers that on an August long weekend were a kaleidoscope of yellows and purples, the beautiful wild bergamot (*Monarda*) and lupin predominate.

On gaining the flat summit ridge, which is covered in pines, turn right (north) and walk along it to the "summit," distinguished solely by a few piled-up rocks. For a summit view, continue north about 50 m, then descend the left (west) flank a short way to a large rectangular-shaped meadow which gives an unobstructed view to the west.

Return via the southeast face and small side valley out to Wolf Creek trail.

5 JUNCTION LOOKOUT from Coal Creek—map 2

Backpack
Unofficial trail, creek crossings
Distance 7.5 km
Height gain 667 m (2190 ft.)
High point 2240 m (7350 ft.)
Map 82 J/10 Mount Rae

East access At the 3-way junction of #6 Phone Line and #4 Wolf Creek trails.
West access #22 Junction Lookout fire road just north of the lookout.
Also accessible from Sullivan Pass to Coal Creek (Volume 5).

The trail along scenic upper Coal Creek is a much more pleasing route to Junction Lookout than route #22 up the fire road, despite a steep climb at the end and umpteen creek crossings for which you need Tevas. Even in fall.

Combine with other trails like Wolf Creek, Phone Line, Junction Mountain, Green Mountain, Mount McNabb and Price Camp to make a terrific three-day weekend backpack.

TRAIL NOTE So when the trail was undesignated in 2007, the news was naturally received with much perplexity.

FROM EAST ACCESS
To Sullivan Creek junction 1.1 km
At the 3-way junction head southwest along the riverbank. Join a cutline access road that's come in across Coal Creek and turn left. A short way on, at a right-hand curve, a NW–SE cutline to left is the soggy route to Sullivan Creek. Continue on road and cross an ENE–WSW cutline. Emerge from trees into a tiny meadow identified on the right side by two extra large spruce with a stump in between. This is where the cutline access road turns left to Sullivan Creek in the Highwood. (See Volume 5.)

To the lookout 6.4 km
Keep right on a trail that continues up the flat and rather beautiful valley of upper

Coal Creek with its meadows and mixed forest. The sides close in and you cross the creek seven times, encountering a drift fence between crossings 2 and 3. After no. 5 the east ridge return option joins in from the right.

After crossing no. 7, you come in sight of the lookout, which appears impossibly high up on a grassy ridge. The trail climbs toward it, taking a STRAIGHT line through trees and three longitudinal meadows. En route, ignore an equally good cow trail heading right between meadows 1 and 2.

After meadow no. 3, the trail turns left and crosses a tiny creek marking the start of an arduous 12-zig climb up the east face of a south ridge. Pine forest yields to flowery grasses by the time you reach the south ridge (post minus red marker). Head right for the lookout. But stymied by a rockband, you are forced to traverse left instead, following cairns to gain the fire road between two large cairns. Turn right and walk up to the lookout building.

The lookout from the meadows of upper Coal Creek.

OPTIONAL DESCENT

5A The east ridge

Scramble route, then unofficial trail
Distance add on 500 m to return
Height gain 61 m (200 ft.)
Height loss to creek 579 m (1900 ft.)

Anyone who loves ridge walks will be off like a shot along this grassy ridge with three separate tops. Amazingly, the whole route into Coal Creek unravels beautifully. Expect no trail until the very end.

HISTORY NOTE Somewhere along this ridge is where the Irrigation Survey in the fall of 1897 and 1898 set up a camera station, erroneously calling it Highwood River Divide. In all they made six climbs to the ridge from upper Coal Creek and each time noted the cold, blustery weather.

From the lookout head east past the word "Junction" spelled out in rocks painted white. Straightaway the east ridge is rocky and, unguessed at, has two narrows if you decide to be sporting and keep to the crest. At top no. 1 (cairn) the ridge turns southeast and you descend a long grass slope to a col.

Climb top no. 2 via a rising bench on the right side, then work your way up through rocky outcrops. The way down to the next col is not totally straightforward. Veer left and start down the rocky rib. Before the rib erupts in pinnacles, step off left into trees and connect up little openings.

The third top features a free-standing wall of rock on the west side. Either go over the top, or traverse below the rockband as we did (cheaters!) to the third col. This is where you leave the ridge.

Below the col on the west side is a very convenient grassy avenue between the pines. Follow it down a long way, past springs, to a large meadow with amoeba-like fingers extending farther down the slope to left and right. Carry on down the left-hand finger to its end in a belt of fine-looking spruce.

Hereabouts starts a small creek heading left. An excellent cow trail runs along the creek's left bank and can be followed all the way out to Coal Creek. At the very end, head farther left into a meadow where you join the Coal Creek trail between creek crossings 5 and 6.

#5A Looking along the east ridge toward top no. 1 (left) and top no. 2 (right).

6 PHONE LINE — maps 1 & 2

Long-day hike, backpack
Unofficial trail, creek crossings
Distance 7.8 km
Height gain S–N 180 m (590 ft.)
Height loss S–N 228 m (748 ft.)
High point 1673 m (5490 ft.)
Map 82 J/10 Mount Rae

South access The 3-way junction of #4 Wolf Creek and #5 Junction Lookout from Coal Creek.
North access The 3-way junction of #23 Green Mountain trail and #8 Mount McNabb trails at 694091 in North Coal Creek.

This undulating forest trail cuts across the grain of the country, connecting Wolf Creek trail and Junction Lookout from Coal Creek with Green Mountain and Mount McNabb trails.

TRAIL NOTE Since the third edition, this historic trail has been undesignated, a casualty of the 2008 Sheep River management plan.

HISTORY NOTE The route more or less follows the old telephone trail between Sentinel ranger station in the Highwood and Bighorn ranger station in the Sheep. As you hike this trail you can picture the scene back in 1915. A string of pack horses, each carrying two rolls of #9 gauge wire, stopping every 60 m or so to drop off a coil. The construction crew coming along behind would stretch the wire, and with the aid of spurs, climb 5 m up a suitable tree, tie the porcelain insulators onto the wire, then attach the insulator to the tree with a large staple, so that if the tree toppled, the staple would pull out and allow the line to sag but not break. Insulator trees can be recognized by trimmed branches. When no trees could be found, tripods were built from deadfall. As you hike, be on the lookout for about a dozen wooden tripods nearly 100 years old!

SOUTH TO NORTH
Straightaway Phone Line crosses South Coal Creek to north bank meadows. Head upstream a little, then turn right up a side valley to a wooded pass at 706053 where the trail teams up with a cutline access road that has come in from your left. The road dips into a tributary of Coal Creek (crossing at the same place as the N–S cutline), then swings away right, then left over a broad ridge of lodgepole pines. This is the first place to look for tripods.

Just over the height of land, a trail circumvents the road's foray into a bog (birthplace of a small creek), so when you see the road suddenly turning left into a "meadow," keep straight, following red markers (if they still exist) to the N–S cutline. Here, SIDE TRIP A turns off to the right.

Phone Line crosses the N–S cutline, then swings right along the bank of the bog stream, finally crossing it by bridge and doubling back to the road.

Turn right and on road cross two low ridges well endowed with tripods, ultimately dropping into the valley of North Coal Creek. Walk downstream for about 400 m and ford the creek. Wind upward to a T-junction with a NE–SW cutline on the north bank with #22B and turn right.

Follow the cutline a short way, then on trail turn off left and jump a tiny tributary. Cross meadow to the 3-way junction (sign removed) under Spaulding Point.

SIDE TRIP

6A to Hidden Lake

The not so little Hidden Lake is only five minutes walk away from the trail. Where you intersect the N–S cutline turn right (north) and descend to the first berm. Turn right onto a game trail leading through a grassy draw to the reedy shoreline.

#6 Nearing the "junction" with Green Mountain
and Mount McNabb trails below Spaulding Point.

#6 A tripod on Phone Line.

#7 Price Camp. The remains of Mr. Price's logging camp in the meadow.

7 PRICE CAMP TRAIL — map 1

Day hike, backpack
Official trail with signposts & red markers, major river & creek crossings
Distance 5.7 km from access 1.
Height gain E–W 152 m (500 ft.)
Height loss E–W 61 m (200 ft.)
High point 1509 m (4950 ft.)
Map 82 J/10 Mount Rae

Access Hwy. 546 (Sheep River Trail) at Sandy McNabb Recreation Area. Turn left at the winter gate and drive down the access road.
1. In 850 m, opposite group camp A, turn left into a parking area.
2. Drive all the way down the access road to the day-use area by the Sheep River.
Also accessible from #9 Sheep trail east and the northern terminus of #8 Mount McNabb.

This forested trail with a meadow in the middle connects Sandy McNabb Recreation Area to Sheep trail via a route along the southwest side of the Sheep River. NOTE After rain and during runoff, high water in the fast-flowing Sheep River makes this trail inaccessible.

ACCESS NOTE Price Camp starts from the equestrian campground and can be picked up en route near Group Camp B and the interpretive trail parking lot.

To Sheep River crossing ~450 m
From access no. 1, pick up Price Camp trail beyond the parking area and wind down a grassy slope to the access road. Cross it and continue to the bank of the Sheep River. From access no. 2, walk back along the road to the intersecting trail and turn left.

A red marker indicates the crossing place. It's important to wade the Sheep River UPSTREAM of Coal Creek. See the sketch map for #4 Wolf Creek on page 28.

To Mount McNabb trail, 2.5 km
On the southwest bank, the trail heads upstream through aspen meadows below Mount McNabb. Entering darker forest, it climbs to a terrace where it intersects a cutline and a drift fence. Traverse a steep slope above the river, then climb some more to an even higher terrace where the trail levels off and moves inland. At 720124 come to the T-junction with Mount McNabb trail. Keep straight.

To Sheep trail east 2.7 km
The trail wanders through pine forest, crossing a NE–SW cutline (see A) and a bit later on, little March Creek. On the far bank turn left and follow the north bank upstream to a very large meadow, the site of Mr. Price's logging camp of nearly a century ago. Today all that's left are foundation logs and pieces of rusted metal.

Here the trail turns right and crosses a low ridge into trees. Descend steeply at first to a major NE–SW cutline. Cross and a few minutes later arrive at a T-junction with Sheep trail east.

Turn left for Indian Oils trailhead, right for Windy Point parking lot.

7A Shortcut to Sheep trail

Distance 1.1 km

A well-used shortcut that saves 2 km for anyone bound for Windy Point parking lot.

The shortcut starts from Price Camp trail between Mount McNabb trail junction and March Creek crossing and basically follows the NNE–SSW cutline. Initially, a trail descends the bank to March Creek a little west of the cutline, then climbs up the far bank to join the cutline just before its intersection with a game trail that runs along the banktop.

After this, simply follow the grassy cutline. A gradual downhill leads into a boggy flat (bypass trail to right), below which is a steeper hill with runout to Sheep trail. Turn right for Windy Point.

8 MOUNT McNABB TRAIL — map 1

Long-day hike, backpack
Official trail with signposts & red markers, creek crossings
Distance 7.5 km
Height gain N–S 183 m (600 ft.)
Height loss N–S 122 m (400 ft.)
High point 1570 m (5150 ft.)
Map 82 J/10 Mount Rae

North access Via #7 Price Camp trail at 720124.
South access At the northern terminus of #6 Phone Line and the eastern terminus of #23 Green Mountain trail in North Coal Creek.

This trail connects Price Camp trail to Phone Line and Green Mountain trails in North Coal Creek. Discounting the steep hill at the north end, this is a thoroughly enjoyable walk through the meadows of North Coal Creek.

FUTURE NOTE Within the next year or two this trail will become part of #23 Green Mountain trail.

NORTH TO SOUTH

After a muddy flat you're into a muddy steep-twisting climb of 122 vertical m (400 ft.) to a pass a long way west of Mount McNabb at 715119.

The descent of the dry, gently angled south slope is much more enjoyable. About halfway down, keep left at a puzzling junction. A final downhill and the trail enters a side valley of Coal Creek and crosses it a little upstream of where you came in. Look for red markers. An uphill stint through forest leads into a meadow at the head of another side valley. Careful! Do NOT follow the obvious game trail ahead. Look for a red marker waaaay down the grassy draw to the left.

As you descend the velvety smooth trough of close-cropped grass, the trail picks up and is followed *almost* to North Coal Creek, at the last moment turning right and crossing the side creek back

into trees. A short climb and you top out into meadows. After another side creek crossing the trail turns west into the breathtakingly beautiful meadows above North Coal Creek. Far off to the west, the pointy peaks of the Highwood Range poke up above low, forested foothills. Junction Mountain fire lookout is visible to the left, while closer in to the right is Green Mountain, the prominent point at its left end known as Spaulding Point.

When you arrive at the top of a little downhill above side creek 707097 a decision must be made. Which trail to follow around the upcoming bends in the creek? The realigned official trail that has reduced the five creek crossings to two, or the bypass trail which has no creek crossings at all. The decision is easily made. North Coal Creek, which arises from many springs in the dark, forested north slope below Junction Lookout is a lively stream that must always be waded.

So follow the bypass trail that starts off in the angle between the official trail and a grassy cutline heading right. The trails unite just before a red marker on a post. See sketch map below.

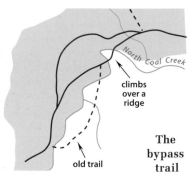

The **bypass trail**

The trail continues through meadow, almost touching the creek, then climbs away again and rounds a corner to the 3-way junction (sign removed) with Phone Line and Green Mountain trails at 694091.

Mount McNabb trail in North Coal Creek, looking toward Spaulding Point on Green Mountain.

9 SHEEP TRAIL EAST—maps 1, 2 & 3

Day hikes, backpack
Official trail with signposts & red markers, major river crossings
Total distance 19.7 km
Map 82 J/10 Mount Rae

The first section of trail runs above the canyon of the Sheep River. In the background rises Windy Point Ridge.

Highway access Hwy. 546 (Sheep River Trail). NOTE The highway west of Sandy McNabb Recreation Area is closed Dec 1– May 15.
1. At the winter gate at the Sandy McNabb Recreation Area, turn right and drive to the day-use parking lot.
2. 1.6 km west of the winter gate is a pullout on the right (north) side of the highway.
3. 3.3 km west of the winter gate is a pullout on the left (west) side of the highway. Then via #15 Windy Point trail heading south.
4. Indian Oils day-use area. Cross the bridge over the Sheep River at Tiger Jaws Falls.
5. Bluerock campground. Start from the west end of the campground near site #30 (also the start to Bluerock Creek interpretive trail) and descend steps to the highway.
6. EQUESTRIANS ONLY Bluerock equestrian campground and parking lot.
7. Terminus of hwy. at Junction Creek day-use area. Use the lower parking lots.

Also accessible via #14 Death Valley trail, #16 Foran Grade Ridge, #15 Windy Point trail, #7 Price Camp trail, #22 Junction Lookout fire road, #25 Indian Oils trail and #28 Bluerock Creek trail.

This is a long-distance trail which, from its beginning at Sandy McNabb Recreation Area on the eastern fringe of the foothills, follows the Sheep River Valley through some spectacular Front Range scenery over a pass to the Elbow River Valley. No one ever follows the whole trail in one go. So Sheep trail has been split up into two logical sections: Sheep trail east between Sandy McNabb Recreation Area and Junction Creek day-use area, and Sheep trail west between Junction Creek day-use area and Big Elbow trail, which is described on page 111.

Sheep trail east is a mixed bag of disused exploration and logging roads, cutlines, fire roads and trails, most often used in combination with other trails to make loops.

NOTE There is only one bridge across the Sheep River in this stretch, and that's at access 4. After rain and during runoff, high water makes wading the fast-flowing Sheep a chancy business.

EAST TO WEST
Sandy McNabb to Windy Point
Distance 3.6 km
Height gain NA
Height loss 36 m (120 ft.)
High point 1433 m (4700 ft.)

Highway access 1, 2 & 3.
Also accessible from #14 Death Valley trail, #16 Foran Grade Ridge, #15 Windy Point trail.

A walk above the Sheep River that parallels the highway.

FROM ACCESS 1
A connecting trail leaves the parking lot access road at a sign and cuts through to Death Valley trail. Turn left, cross Hwy. 546 and the rec area boundary fence to a T-junction south of the road. Turn right. (The trail to left offers alternative access from Sandy McNabb Campground access road. See the sketch map.)

Enjoy a kilometre-long stretch of aspen meadows with views across the Sheep River Valley to dark-forested Mount McNabb. Recross the rec area boundary fence and then a drift fence to a junction with a trail that comes in across the highway from access 2.

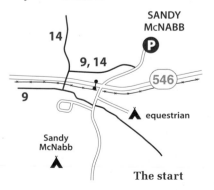

The main trail veers left and in meadow drops 30 m. Near the bottom of the meadow turn right and traverse to an aspen-treed corner close below the highway. Out of the trees, enjoy a scenic traverse above a canyon of the Sheep River—a place to hold on to the kids. Ahead is a view of Windy Point Ridge showing the ascent route up the left-hand skyline ridge.

A descent signals the approach to a T-junction in a meadow where a hiker was once threatened by a cougar. At the sign Sheep trail turns left down the hill. (Windy Point trail ahead rises to access 3.)

Windy Point to Indian Oils
Distance 12.4 km
Height gain 320 m (1050 ft.)
Height loss 198 m (650 ft.)
High point 1646 m (5400 ft.)

Highway access 3, 4.
Also accessible from #15 Windy Point trail, #7 Price Camp trail and #22 Junction Lookout fire road.

The boring nature of this section improves with the proliferation of meadows and views as you near Dyson Creek. Right off the bat the unbridged crossing of the Sheep River can spell FAILURE during times of high water.

To Price Camp trail 2.2 km
Turn left. Wind down aspen meadow to the Sheep River at the point where the black shale walls of the canyon break down momentarily. Wade the river on the diagonal via an underwater shelf.

On the west bank the trail climbs up left and through a drift fence to a terrace, site of John Lineham's lower logging camp. On the terrace, bear right and cross a NNE–SSW cutline which is a shortcut to Price Camp trail. (See #8A.)

A few metres farther on turn left up an NE–SW cutline and climb a hill, but before starting up a second, steeper hill, turn right onto a trail. The trail parallels the cutline lower down the slope to a T-junction with Price Camp trail. This occurs just before a small glade. Keep straight.

To Junction Lookout fire road 6.7 km
The trail continues running parallel with the cutline, sometimes using the cutline itself, many kilometres of boring plodding under the pines. On cutline ford Dyson Creek and climb to a 4-way junction with the Teskey Road. See OPTIONAL EXIT A.

Turn left and follow the Teskey Road through increasingly open country to an unsigned T-junction above Dyson Creek meadows. If headed for Green Mountain trail or Junction Mountain lookout turn left down the bank on Teskey Road continued. Otherwise, stay right and in another half kilometre come to a signed junction at 660100 with a fire road. Turn right. (To left is Junction Lookout fire road that meets Teskey Road in a V at Dyson Creek crossing. If detouring to Dyson Falls for lunch, why not make use of both these roads?)

To Mount Hoffmann trail 2 km
Keep right as you climb gradually to a wide pass on the Dyson–Sheep watershed. To your left the lower slopes of Mount Hoffmann have been thoroughly logged, but here the meadows are the real thing, and for the next kilometre sweep up the right hillside to the hilltop at 648098, which I've climbed a couple of times for the view.

Re-enter forest and cross tiny Hoffmann Creek. At the top of the hill following, at 642099, the logging road to left is the route up Mount Hoffmann. (See #24.)

To Indian Oils bridge 1.5 km
The fire road descends in stony waves to the Sheep River. The roar of Tiger Jaws Fall is heard long before you arrive at a T-junction on the bank. Turn left for the next section of Sheep trail. (Turn right across the bridge for access 4 at the top of the hill close to Hwy. 546. See SIDE TRIP B to look at Tiger Jaws Fall.)

OPTIONAL EXIT

9A The Teskey Road

Distance 2.5 km
Height gain/loss 97 m (320 ft.)

South access Via #9 Sheep trail east.
North access Hwy. 546 at Gorge Creek confluence with the Sheep River. Just east of the bridge over Gorge Creek, turn north onto the R.B. Miller Station access road. Shortly keep left on a road ending at Gorge Creek. Park here.

When we first went to Green Mountain and Junction Lookout we took the Teskey Road to Dyson Creek. That is what this old logging road is useful for: as a shortcut between Sheep trail and Hwy. 546 at Gorge Creek. It has one drawback: you have to wade the Sheep River.

It was likely built by Benjamin Teskey in the 1940s to access his sawmill and camp at Dyson Creek. For eight years Bighorn Lumber Company ran trucks up and down this road as did other logging companies working in the area. I bet Teskey never imagined that one day his granddaughter Laureen would be the wife of Canada's 22nd prime minister, Stephen Harper.

SOUTH TO NORTH
At the 4-way junction turn right (north) if approaching from the east, straight if coming from the west. The road runs across country to the lip of the high bank above the Sheep River. The descent is thrilling. Almost straightaway you're into the infamous hairpin bend with its vertiginous view into the black shale gorge. I haven't checked the river bed below, but it appears there was never an incident of brakes failing at Hell's Fire Pass as it was called. From here the road heads right downhill, then turns sharp left toward the river. Emerge opposite Gorge Creek confluence. Wade across to the bridge on Hwy. 546.

If travelling in the opposite direction, finding the road will require a brief search at the forest edge.

#9B Tiger Jaws, showing the original, more exciting bridge that was used by logging trucks.

#9B The Devil's Elbow below Tiger Jaws.

#9 Sheep Falls from the southeast bank. Shunga-la-she in the background.

SIDE TRIP

Looking northwest through the pass on the Dyson–Sheep watershed.

9B Tiger Jaws Fall

Below the bridge is Tiger Jaws Fall as it was named back in the 1920s. Check out the outrageously rough piece of river below the bridge as it squeezes through Devil's Elbow. This has to be my favourite piece of the Sheep River and it pays to wander even farther downstream to the awesome Triple Falls (class V), known in the 1920s as the Blue Shoots.

Indian Oils to Junction Creek via Bluerock Creek
Distance 3.7 km
Height gain 61 m (200 ft.)
High point 1615 m (5300 ft.)

Highway access 4, 5, 6 & 7.
Also accessible from #25 Indian Oils and #28 Bluerock Creek.

The trail follows the forested southeast bank of the Sheep River initially, then crosses to the northwest bank for the final stretch to Junction Creek trailhead.

The only tricky part is the river crossing, which is entirely dependent on water level and speed of flow.

See the sketch map on page 112.

On the southeast bank of the Sheep River turn left, or straight if joining in from access 4.

A side trail to right is the defunct equestrian cutoff to Indian Oils trailhead. (Nowadays the horses cross the bridge.) Straightaway after this junction the trail turns left and climbs up three terraces to the trail's high point. The following flat is the place to head for Sheep Falls. Strangely there is no good side trail to this important feature. And given that the river is much farther away than you think, there are many pieces of trail made by people groping their way there and back through the bush.

A short descent brings you to the T-junction with Indian Oils' west leg equestrian trail that crosses the river—a bad crossing for two-legged humans.

The trail swings away again for a long stint below the west ridge of Mount Hoffmann. Up there to your left is what some of us believe to be the most magnificent feathermoss forest in all of K Country, now protected within a Wildland Provincial Park. But back to the trail that edges closer to the river. While out of sight of the water, you are not out of earshot, and here and there people hearing the roar of a rapid have decided to "go and have a look" and have made trails.

Turn a left-hand bend and ford the river just west of the highway bridge over Bluerock Creek. On the far bank is a junction. What you do next depends on your destination.

1. To access 5, Bluerock campground

Go straight and climb up to Hwy. 546. Turn right and walk the road to the bridge over Bluerock Creek. At the trail sign on the east bank, climb steps to the far west end of the campground loop road.

2. To access 6, Bluerock equestrian parking lot and campground

Go straight and climb up to Hwy. 546. Cross. The trail continues up a steep bank (crossing the old road twice), making a beeline for the equestrian campground loop road. Turn right for the campground, left across a 4-way intersection for the day parking lot.

3. To Junction Creek day-use area 500 m

Sheep trail turns left and climb steps to the banktop opposite the equestrian campground access road. Walk a narrow strip of land 'twixt the highway and the Sheep River now closeted in a canyon, rapids and deep pools following one another without variance. Nearing Junction Creek day-use area and loop road you cross a meadow and arrive among picnic tables. Keep straight (Junction Creek interpretive trail crosses the loop road to right), following the lower leg of the interpretive trail, past an interpretive sign about log drives, to a T-junction. For the lower loop road parking lots turn right.

For the upper loop parking lot, turn left on the Junction Creek logging road. Turn next right and follow the trail along the banktop above a viewpoint and up a hill to the upper loop road parking lot near the start of Sheep trail west.

The canyon near Junction Creek day-use area.

10 CARRY RIDGE—map 1

Short-day, day hikes
Unofficial trail, creek crossings
Distance 10.7 usual loop
Height gain/loss 465 m (1525 ft.) return
from end of ridge
High point 1536 m (5040 ft.)
Maps 82 J/9 Turner Valley,
82 J/10 Mount Rae

Access Hwy. 546 (Sheep River Trail) at the Kananaskis Country boundary sign. There's room for a few vehicles.

Carry Ridge is a low-level, ruler-straight ridge running SE–NW between Anchor D Ranch on Hwy. 546 and Ware Creek. You can see the grassy south end of it behind Anchor D on the drive in. A trail runs all along the crest to the far north end. Side trails peeling off its west flank onto the west fork trail of Mud Springs Creek allow loops to be made. There are also longer return options written up under B and C.

While enjoyable for early- and late-season hikes, the ridge is most beautiful in early summer when white geraniums brighten the aspen forest floor and a great variety of sun-loving flowers, including the silky blue lupin, add colour to the many meadows.

ACCESS NOTE Don't bother looking for public access onto the north end of the ridge or to Mud Springs Creek from 338 Avenue South in Ware Creek. "No Trespassing" notices are everywhere.

NAMING NOTE According to Dewy Matthews, the ridge is known locally as Carry Ridge after Bob Carry, who in 1912 homesteaded on the site of Anchor D and was a main player in the South Sheep Stock Association.

MAP NOTE These ridges are not shown on a Gem Trek map.

Getting to the ridge 1.3 km

Every time I start this trail I groan inwardly, because it would be so much easier to

The ridge north of the summit.

just walk around the bottom of the ridge east of the K Country boundary fence and trespass through Anchor D land. But strangely, the boundary crosses the ridge about 46 m (150 ft.) up from the flat, forcing an unnecessary climb, which you'll surely appreciate on the return!

Start up the shaley trail behind the K Country sign. Keep right and traverse toward the boundary fence. Here turn left and climb meadow paralleling the fence to the ridge crest. Pass through a wire gate. To avoid the steep drop on the north side, traverse left on a trail to a track and follow its zigs down into the west fork meadow of Heel Creek. See inset map.

Head diagonally left across grass and cross the creek via a culvert. Then make your way back right on a trail that parallels the boundary fence up a hill below the gable end of Muley Ridge. In spruce forest the trail becomes track and veers

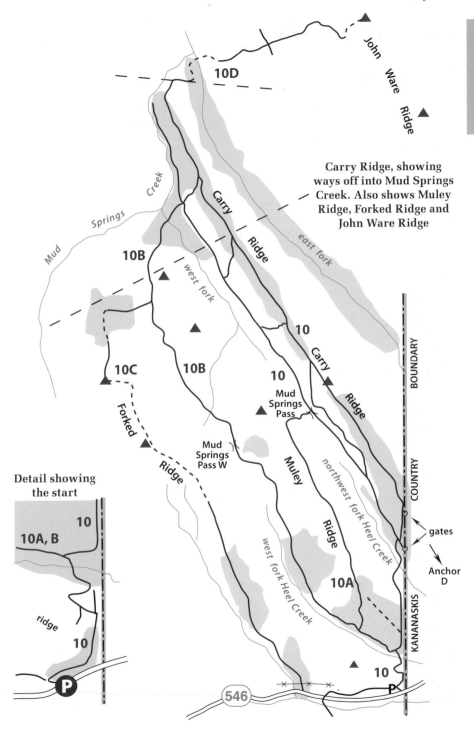

John Ware Ridge

10D

Carry Ridge, showing
ways off into Mud Springs
Creek. Also shows Muley
Ridge, Forked Ridge and
John Ware Ridge

Creek

Springs

Mud

Carry

Ridge

west fork

east fork

10B

10C

10B

Forked

10

Carry

10

Mud
Springs
Pass

Mud
Springs
Pass W

Ridge

Muley

Ridge

northwest fork Heel Creek

10

Ridge

BOUNDARY

COUNTRY

gates

Anchor
D

KANANASKIS

west fork Heel Creek

10A

Detail showing
the start

10

10A, B

ridge

10

P

10

546

P

45

left to avoid bog near the fenceline. At the end of this section it reverts to trail and crosses the northwest fork of Heel Creek into a longitudinal meadow. NOTE If the main crossing is too deep in mud from cow trampling, head left upstream on the detour trail that crosses the creek above a split. Make a note of where you emerge from trees for the return.

In the meadow you intersect a good horse trail that has come in from Anchor D through a gate to your right. Ahead rises the grassy slopes of Carry Ridge. Trail to left leads up the northwest fork of Heel Creek over a low pass into Mud Springs Creek and is your return route and also route 1 onto the ridge.

Carry Ridge ~4 km

There are two good routes onto Carry Ridge. Route 1, the "west slope trail," is a gradual ascent onto the ridge just north of the summit. It's worth noting that the lower half of the trail offers a drier and more pleasing route to/from Mud Springs Pass. Route 2 features a steep climb, but takes in the south end of the ridge and the summit. Both routes can be combined to make a leisurely half-day trip of 7.4 km.

1. West slope 2.2 km Turn left, following the valley trail through meadows mainly. In 880 m at 679153 turn right. After a short initial climb the trail traverses the west side of the ridge through meadows and aspens to Mud Springs Pass above the salt lick. Stay on the trail that traverses meadows to gain Carry Ridge at 784164. The summit is just up to the right.

2. South end of ridge 2.3 km Cross the valley trail and on occasionally steep trail climb diagonally up left by the side of boundary fence to the ridgetop. At the T-junction near another gate turn left (north).

The uphill work is done, leaving you to enjoy an easy rolling ridge walk on grass. Reaching the high point, you realize just how low this ridge really is, overlooked by John Ware Ridge to the east and by Muley

and the forked ridge to the west. Descend a stony hill, keeping left to where route 1 joins in from the left at 784164.

Head north along the slightly undulating but downward trending ridge through alternating meadows and aspen woods. Whenever you decide you've gone far enough, choose from one of the good side trails that descend left into the valley of Mud Springs Creek's west fork. The cutline access road crossed at 777174 is one such descent route. The usual way off, or if returning via Mud Springs Pass West or the forked ridge, is the second cutline access road, at 773180.

I like carrying on to the very north end, at 770187, where the ridge rises in a last hurrah in long waving grasses. To reach the west fork trail from here, simply walk down the flowery west slope.

Return via Mud Springs Pass 4.1+ km

Having arrived in the west fork of Mud Springs Creek by whatever route, turn left and head south on a good horse trail. The north end runs through meadows

The very north end of Carry Ridge.

alongside the creek with crumbling mud banks. Level with a confluence of creeks, the cutline access road joins in off the ridge and leaves a few metres farther on at Y-junction 772178 with B. Keep straight.

Meadows lessen in number (watch for where the trail climbs a shade more steeply through spruce forest to the pass between Carry and Muley ridges (salt lick).

It then makes a very gradual descent down the northwest fork of Heel Creek 'twixt aspen woods and mixed forest with wet and muddy sections. An alternative route from the pass follows the drier ground of the "west slope trail."

Both alternatives join for the final stretch through meadow to the Anchor D gate at the K Country boundary fence. Before you get there, turn right and return the same way you came.

Alternative returns

From the very north end, a fainter trail carries on down the ridge under the aspens and intersects a grassy NE–SW cutline. Should you descend right into the east fork of Mud Springs Creek, getting back

Trail in the west fork of Mud Springs Creek.

into the west fork by rounding the north end of the ridge is doable with a little bushwhacking.

But what about the east fork valley that lures with meadows? A good trail runs high up along the east side of it, offering fast progress to the pass with Heel Creek at "No Trespassing" signs, forcing you to follow the K Country boundary fence, with all its bogs and foibles, back to Carry Ridge.

OPTION

10A Muley Ridge

Unofficial trail
Distance 2.7 km to pass
Height gain 168 m (550 ft.)
Height loss 46 m (150 ft.)
High point 1560 m (5120 ft.)

Muley, one ridge over to the west from Carry, has an attractive meadow start, then is eclipsed in trees. However, it provides an optional route to Mud Springs pass that can be combined with Carry Ridge to make a short loop. Best in this direction.

SOUTH TO NORTH

Follow Carry Ridge trail to the west fork of Heel Creek.

After crossing the culvert, head left on a trail through grass that joins another trail from the fence. Turn left and follow the trail up the west fork below the open slopes of Muley Ridge. In 350 m at 790138 is a T-junction. Turn right. (Straight on leads to West Mud Springs Pass.) The trail climbs a sub-ridge onto the main ridge of Muley. (NOTE that some people reach this point by climbing up the open ridge directly from the boundary fence. More flowers that way.)

Veering left, it continues along the broad, gently rising ridge through alternating aspen and spruce woods. Before reaching the high point, it hops over the right side of the ridge and as a DHS horse trail twists down the steep east flank to Mud Springs pass.

#10A Muley Ridge. Photo Alf Skrastins

#10B In the west fork of Heel Creek, where meadows reach up the hillside to Muley Ridge.

OPTIONAL RETURNS

10B West Mud Springs Pass

Unofficial trail, creek crossing
Distance 5.7 km
Height gain 122 m (400 ft.)
Height loss 107 m (350 ft.)
High point 1486 m (4875 ft.)

A longer return option taking in the pass between Muley Ridge and the forked ridge. Though the going is easy, this is a very wet trail in spring. Save it for the fall.

To the pass 2.9 km
At 772178 in Mud Springs Creek, head toward the creek on a track (cutline access road) that can be traced in the grass. Cross the creek, then grass, making for the continuation of the track that can be seen rising into some trees. Grassy at first, the track upgrades to dirt road where it turns right into forest and curls left behind a grassy knoll to a salt lick on a col at 769169.

A trail carries on from the col, heading southeast through mixed forest below the steep east face of the forked ridge. Keep right at a split and cross two small creeks. A dry section through aspens ends at another creek crossing. The next section is soggy, especially in spring when a jillion upwelling springs stream down the hillside and across the trail. Cross another side creek. From here it's a short climb up and right to the pass.

West fork of Heel Creek 2.8 km
On the other side is aspen meadow and a salt lick. The trail descends very gradually into the west fork of Heel Creek, its upper part occasionally muddy in spruce forest. Lower down is dry grass below beautiful meadows sweeping up the west slope of Muley Ridge. At 790138 come to a T-junction. Go straight. (Trail to left is the horse trail climbing onto Muley.)

Shortly you near the boundary fence and the culvert crossing of west Heel Creek. Return the same way you came.

10C "Forked Ridge"

Unofficial trails & route
Distance 6 km from 10B back to
parking area at boundary
Height gain 251 m (825 ft.)
Height loss 290 m (950 ft.)
High point 1661 m (5450 ft.)

A longer return option via the N–S ridge between the Mud Springs and Macabee Creek drainages, which is higher than all the neighbouring ridges of Carry, Muley and Pine. Navigation is tricky in a couple of places, so you need to be an experienced off-trail hiker.

To the ridge crest 540 m
Take B West Mud Springs Pass to the col at 769169 where there is a salt lick.

The main climb of the day starts here—the 122-vertical-m (400-ft.) climb onto the ridge crest. Head west through open forest, the terrain steepening into a wide rib of grass with aspens. A narrow trail runs all the way up it onto the grassy north shoulder of the ridge proper. Look across the valley to Pine Ridge.

The ridge 5.4 km to parking
Turn left. The upcoming climb through open forest to the highest top at 766159 is made easy by a trail.

Enter pine forest and turn left slightly downhill. This is tricky bit no. 1 where the eastern escarpment turns left, then right, before getting back on a straight line. Just follow the edge around and intersect a NE–SW cutline. The next time, you may feel confident enough to cut across the dogleg from the top to the cutline.

From the cutline, the way ahead is obvious: a slight descent followed by a slight climb to the treed lower top at 770154.

Continue south. A little way down the other side, the ridge forks, both heading to the SSE—tricky bit no. 2. You're aiming for the left-hand ridge, so as you descend pine forest continue to keep the eastern escarpment on your left side. Emergence into aspen meadows tells you you're on the right ridge. (The parallel ridge to the west is all forest.)

The trail reappears and can be followed all the way down through alternating aspen woods and meadows, giving the day's best views looking south and southwest toward the Front Ranges.

A last steep grass slope deposits you in a side valley of Macabee Creek. A trail on the left side of the little creek takes you out through a gate in a fence to Hwy. 546.

Turn left and walk 1 km back to your starting point.

#10C Descending the lower ridge, looking south beyond High Noon Hills to Okotoks Mtn.

GOING FARTHER

10D John Ware Ridge

Long-day hike
Unofficial trail & route, creek crossing
Distance 8 km one way from trailhead
Height gain to north end 244 m (800 ft.)
from east fork of Mud Springs Creek
High point north top 1545 m (5070 ft.)

The energetic can add in John Ware Ridge, which is the easternmost of the parallel ridges north of the highway. Only the north summit lies within K Country, so getting to it requires following Carry Ridge all the way to its north end first. The route is cutline access road that is revegetating (as is its cutline), so you need to be an observant route finder.

NAMING & HISTORY NOTE Originally known as Nigger John, the ridge was renamed to be politically correct in 1970. The first recorded climb to the north end of it was on August 23, 1895, by the Irrigation Survey. A.O. Wheeler was up again the following August 11, and bivvied on the summit waiting for better weather in the morning.

To the north top 2.7 km
Follow Carry Ridge to the grassy north end. Continue down the aspen ridge on a fainter trail that delivers you to a grassy NE–SW cutline. Turn right down the cutline into the valley of Mud Springs Creek's east fork. In lieu of the grown-in cutline access road, head left to the confluence with the west fork, cross the east fork and walk up grass toward the tree edge.

At ~774192 pick up a trail (remnant of access road) that soon veers left between aspens as a grassy avenue. Follow it up through a shallow draw to its intersection with a wide grassy swath used as a thoroughfare by the east fork trail.

Cross the swath and east fork trail. In just a few metres you cross a side creek, beyond which the road is readily identifiable (doubling as a creekbed perhaps) as it climbs uphill, eventually curving right to join its "cutline" on a saddle.

From anywhere on the level, beyond a bit of deadfall, turn left and climb an ever steepening slope through a drift fence and up grass to the summit. The panoramic view of Front Range peaks extending far to the south of K Country is astonishing for such a low level ridge.

Return the same way or bushwhack round the north end of Carry Ridge onto the west fork trail.

Going farther. Add 1.3 km one way
Walking south along the ridge crest to the highest point at 794186 would be simple if it weren't for all the barbed-wire fences in between.

The north end of the ridge is covered in roses.

11 LONG PRAIRIE RIDGE—map 1

Half-day hike
Official trails with signposts & red markers
Distance 5.4 km loop
Height gain/loss 131 m (430 ft.)
High point 1542 m (5060 ft.)
Map 82 J/10 Mount Rae

Access Hwy. 546 (Sheep River Trail).
3 km west of the K Country boundary, turn right on Sheep Station Road into the Sheep River Provincial Park office parking lot.
Also accessible from #14 Death Valley and from various Sandy McNabb ski trails. See the sketch map.

The trail along Long Prairie Ridge in the midst of the Sandy McNabb Ski Trails is an easy and enjoyable walk along a grassy ridgetop with views. Combined with Long Prairie Loop, it is sure to become a popular walk with novice hikers, especially in the spring and fall.

TRAIL NOTE The ridge trail was built in 2009 with the help of the Alberta Equestrian Federation as primarily an equestrian trail, part of what the equestrians call the Long Prairie Ridge Loop, which heads south across Hwy. 546 on the Meadow connector to Meadow Loop based out of the equestrian campground at Sandy McNabb. For hikers, this bigger trek is totally unnatural, involving as it

Heading southeast along Long Prairie Ridge near the high point. Photo Alf Skrastins

does two crossings of Hwy. 546. I recommend starting from the office parking lot and taking in just the cream of the loop as marked in red on the sketch map.

FUTURE ACCESS NOTE In 2012 a short connector trail is due to be built from Sandy McNabb day-use parking lot to the south leg of the loop.

ANTICLOCKWISE
Ridge section 2.7 km
From the head of the parking lot at a sign "No horses" walk out on Pine Ridge Loop trail to a wooden fence alongside Long Prairie Creek and turn left. Following the fence, you pass through a gate to a T-junction outside the station compound. Turn left onto Long Prairie Loop.

The trail (nee Easy Out) climbs to a junction. Go straight. (Return leg to left.)

Cross a NE–SW cutline and continue climbing up the ridge at an easy gradient through aspen forest with a grassy floor. Then follows a long, undulating section with a steeper pull across a side hill. Enter a big meadow gently sloping down the left flank and walk around the top of it at the demarcation of pines to the ridge's high point at a bend.

This meadow marks the start of panoramic views to the west that continue to be enjoyed the rest of the way because the ridge is now predominantly grass. A red marker precedes the T-junction with Death Valley trail. Turn left.

Return via Long Prairie Loop 2.7 km

Wind down the west slope between aspens as high as my ankles when I first knew them. At a T-junction with Long Prairie Loop keep left. Just down the hill is another T-junction. Turn left. (Right is Death Valley trail, an optional return route to the day use parking lot.)

The south leg of Long Prairie Loop traverses the lower west slope of the ridge below aspens and meadow. At one point you can look up to the summit.

On entering pine forest, recross the NE–SW cutline and either traverse on splinter trails or descend a little to a gate in the fence. Do not go through the gate, but continue on trail slightly uphill to join the splinters. (Beyond the gate is Meadow connector that leads past the meadow plot to Hwy. 546 and crosses it to Meadow Loop.)

Your trail soon joins your outgoing route at a T-junction. Turn right twice and return to the parking lot.

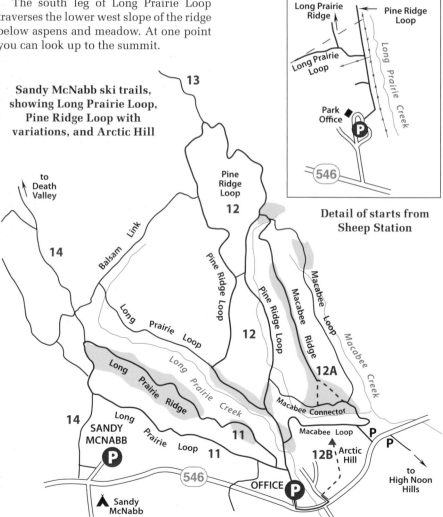

Sandy McNabb ski trails, showing Long Prairie Loop, Pine Ridge Loop with variations, and Arctic Hill

Detail of starts from Sheep Station

12 PINE RIDGE LOOP — map 1

Short-day hike
Official trails, signposts, ski markers,
creek crossings
Distance 8 km
Height gain 223 m (730 ft.)
High point 1630 m (5350 ft.)
Maps 82 J/9 Turner Valley,
82 J/10 Mount Rae

Access Hwy. 546 (Sheep River Trail).
1. Official 3 km west of the K Country boundary, turn right on Station Road into the Sheep River Park office parking lot.
2. Casual 2.1 km west of the K Country boundary, park off road. On the north side of the hwy. a track heads through an open gate and down alongside a fence to Macabee Loop.
Also accessible from #13 and various Sandy McNabb ski trails.

A longer circuit of the Sandy McNabb Ski Trails on the north side of Hwy. 546. Theoretically, any of the ski trails shown on the sketch map can be walked, but in practice, some are too wet or muddy, particularly after snow melt and during June rains. Cattle plodding along the trails to get to meadows and salt licks doesn't help either. Fall is generally the best time.

Pine Ridge Loop takes in the highest pine-covered hill. I also describe two open ridges in the area that have the advantage of views and dry ground. See the sketch map for the previous entry.

ACCESS NOTE Access 2 is a fast way to Macabee Ridge.

ANTICLOCKWISE FROM ACCESS 1
To Macabee Loop 500 m
From the head of the parking lot at a sign "No Horses," walk out on Pine Ridge Loop to a wooden fence alongside Long Prairie Creek and turn left. Following the fence, you pass through a gate to a T-junction outside the station compound. Go straight into meadow. (Trail to left is Long Prairie Loop, south leg.)

Pine Ridge

Cross Long Prairie Creek. Almost straightaway, Macabee Loop (née Arctic Hill) turns off to the right up a hill and through a fence. Pine Ridge Loop stays in the grassy valley bottom.

To Macabee Connector 600 m
In 310 m turn right at a T-junction (trail ahead is your return route) and climb through aspen meadow to a low ridge crest. On the far side of a drift fence is a junction. Keep straight. (Trail to right is Macabee connector that rounds the south end of Macabee Ridge.)

To Pine Ridge connector 900 m
Descend and cross the west fork of Macabee Creek by culvert. After a stretch along the east bank below the aspen slopes of Macabee Ridge, the trail recrosses the creek (culvert) to a T-junction. Keep straight. (Pine Ridge connector to left is a shortcut to the return leg of Pine Ridge.)

53

To Macabee Loop 580 m

Climb slightly as you head north to a T-junction in a meadow. Go straight on Pine Ridge trail. (Trail to right crossing the soggy meadow is the east leg of Macabee Loop, which is not at all recommended as a summer trail.)

To #13, 1.4 km

The trail heads north as if aiming for the gap between Pine Ridge and the forked ridge. Instead it turns left, winds uphill onto Pine Ridge, turns right, and still climbing arrives at viewpoint no. 1 with picnic table. The view is of Mesa Butte and the Quirk Creek gas plant. Possibly this is the loop's high point at the edge of the northeastern escarpment.

Continue to viewpoint no. 2 with bench and view of Calgary. At a T-junction at 758157 keep left. (Trail to right is #13 to Death Valley. This point is almost equidistant from both legs of Pine Ridge Loop.)

To Balsam Link 800 m

Initially descend, then wind and undulate around the ridge in the pines to the next T-junction. Go straight. (Trail to right is Balsam Link. If you want to lengthen the loop you can follow Balsam down a long hill beside the infant Long Prairie Creek to Long Prairie Loop, then either return via the north leg or the south leg or via Long Prairie Ridge.)

To Long Prairie Loop 1.8 km

The trail descends all the way (one steep hill) to a T-junction with Pine Ridge Connector. Turn right and descend much more gradually on a trail that used to be called Wolftree, after full-branched spruce trees lining the trail. In Long Prairie Creek valley bottom is a T-junction. Turn left.

Back to station 1.4 km

A flat stretch through the meadows of the valley bottom leads in 630 m to the junction with your outgoing trail. Go straight and return the same way you came.

#12A Typical view along Macabee Ridge.

OPTIONS

12A Macabee Ridge

Half-day hike
Official trails, route, unofficial trail
Distance 6.3 km loop
Height gain S–N 183 m (600 ft.)
Height loss S–N 69 m (225 ft.)
High point 1576 m (5170 ft.)

The low ridge between the forks of Macabee Creek can be combined with Pine Ridge Loop to make a very pleasant half-day hike from access 1. Starting from access 2 is about a kilometre shorter.

SOUTH TO NORTH
Getting to the ridge 1.8 km

From the head of the parking lot at a sign "No Horses," walk out on Pine Ridge Loop to a wooden fence alongside Long Prairie Creek and turn left. Following the fence, you pass through a gate to a

T-junction outside the station compound. Keep straight into meadow and cross Long Prairie Creek. Almost straightaway, turn right onto Macabee Loop (née Arctic Hill).

Beyond the fence the trail winds uphill to an E–W cutline and turns left, gradually descending to a T-junction with a track come in from Hwy. 546 (access 2). Continue ahead on track and wind down left to Macabee Creek's west fork. Cross and continue to a T-junction with Macabee connector below the grassy south end of Macabee Ridge.

The ridge 1.9 km
Climb south slopes of moderately steep grass to the ridgetop and head north on a developing trail. While the ridge crest lacks the attractive openness of Long Prairie Ridge, it offers delightful walking on grass under the aspens.

From the high point the trail descends slightly into pine forest. Continue on trail up to the north point. The getting off trail is a little sketchy. Basically, it descends left, then circles around to the right and descends on the diagonal to the west fork of Macabee Creek, which is enclosed in deep mud banks. Cross the creek and wet meadow to Macabee Loop east leg. Turn left and reach the junction with Pine Ridge in a minute or two.

Turn left to return on Pine Ridge Loop east leg. Read #12 in reverse.

12B Arctic Hill

Route
Distance 2 km return
Height gain 122 m (400 ft.)
High point 1533 m (5030 ft.)

A small grass and aspen hill rising above the highway at 770128.

NAMING NOTE The name "Arctic Hill" refers neither to the ski trail nor to this hill, but to the section of the highway just east of the hill that retains the snow in winter. The name was coined back in 1921 when the road was first hacked out with pickaxes.

This hill is girdled by barb-wire fences you can squirm under—but why not use the gate? From access 1 walk out to the highway and turn left. In 300 m turn left onto a service road. Immediately after crossing the texas gate, turn right and follow the fence to a gate in another fence at right angles. (Be sure to close it to keep the horses corralled.)

Continue alongside the first fence a way, then turn left and climb the mostly grassy south ridge to the summit. The summit is viewless (aspens, some fallen you can sit on), but just below is a fine viewpoint for the Sandy McNabb and High Noon Hills.

#12B Near the summit of Arctic Hill.

13 PINE RIDGE to Death Valley—map 1

View across Death Valley to the Front Ranges.

Long-day hike
Official trail
Distance 3.9 km
Height gain S–N 61 m (200 ft.)
Height loss S–N 290 m (950 ft.)
High point 1625 m (5330 ft.)
Map 82 J/10 Mount Rae

South access Via #12 Pine Ridge Loop at the second viewpoint at 758157.
North access Via #14 Death Valley just south of the junction with Windy Point trail at 736173.

A new trail made in the fall of 2010 connects Pine Ridge Loop to Death Valley over the ridgetops—viewpoint detours inclusive. Most obviously you can loop with Death Valley and the ski trails, 17 km being the smallest available loop. Or you can point to point with #15 Windy Point trail.

SOUTH TO NORTH

From Pine Ridge Loop, the trail heads northwest along a ridge crest through mixed forest. At a viewpoint sign step right for a view looking north along a fork of Mudsprings Creek to Carry Ridge. Another great view opens up to the left a bit farther on where the ridgetop is grassy.

Shortly after, the trail swings left and begins a long, winding descent down the west slope into Death Valley. You're mainly under pines or aspens the whole way, so it pays to take the side trail to a second official viewpoint where you look down on Death Valley from a grassy hillock.

The trail reaches Death Valley trail just south of the T-junction with Windy Point trail at 736173. Turn left to get back to your starting point.

14 DEATH VALLEY — maps 1 & 6

Day hike, backpack
Official trail with signposts & red markers, creek crossings
Distance 10.7 km
Height gain S–N 256 m (840 ft.)
Height loss S–N 332 m (1090 ft.)
High point 1539 m (5050 ft.)
Map 82 J/10 Mount Rae

Access Hwy. 546 (Sheep River Trail). Drive to the winter gate at Sandy McNabb Recreation Area. At the 4-way intersection turn right and drive to the hikers day-use parking lot (biffy, picnic table).
Also accessible from #9 Sheep Trail east, the northern terminus of #15 Windy Point trail, the eastern terminus of #56 Ware Creek trail, the southern terminus of #62 9999 trail and the northern terminus of #13 Pine Ridge to Death Valley.

Although an important link between the Sheep River and Threepoint Creek trail systems — it joins 9999 and Ware Creek trails at the north end — 90 per cent of people use it to make a loop with #13, or an even longer loop, or point to point with Windy Point trail, Foran Grade and Sheep trail east.

Though the terrain couldn't be easier, go after a dry spell. Anything less and you'll spend more time figuring out how to dodge mud than paying attention to your surroundings, which, though lacking the drama of crags and steep slopes, have the friendly charm of meadows and aspen woodlands.

NAMING NOTE The name, therefore, is intriguing, and why this particular valley should be the site of several deaths and disappearances right up to the present day is a huge mystery. Rumour has it a band of horses died in the valley in the 1800s during a bad winter. The most likely explanation for the name arises from the finding of a skeleton believed to be that of a trapper who had gone into the valley some years earlier and disappeared. The body was respectfully buried where it was found and the skull taken back to the Fisher Ranch, where it was placed on a fence post and used as a football.

Typical early spring view in mid-valley, looking toward Gleason Ridge.

SOUTH TO NORTH
To Long Prairie Ridge 1.6 km
A signed trail leaves the parking lot access road just before the lot and cuts through forest to intersect the equestrian's start to Death Valley trail just north of where it crosses the highway from Sheep trail east. Turn right.

The going is easy through pine forest. You cross a fence (gate) and make a gradually rising beeline for the T-junction with Long Prairie Loop below the grassy west slope of Long Prairie Ridge. Turn left.

At the next signed T-junction keep right. (To left is a ski trail.)

Lined with aspens, the trail curves up the west slope onto the ridgetop. At the T-junction in the meadow wend left. (To right is Long Prairie Ridge.)

To Windy Point trail S junction 4.3 km
Shortly, come to a 4-way junction. To left and right is Long Prairie Loop ski trail. Go straight on the combo Death Valley trail/ Death Valley Loop ski trail. The trail descends into Death Valley's drainage. In fact, the stream you cross in the middle of a mud bath is the infant Death Creek. On its far bank is a T-junction. Turn right up the hill and leave the ski trails far behind. Over the next 2 km the trail makes a slow descent to valley bottom, crossing aspen hillsides and two side creeks that are bridged. En route keep right just before the second bridge.

It's an enjoyable walk through valley bottom meadows thronged with cattle to two T-junctions within a very short distance of one another at 736173. The first is Pine Ridge to Death Valley trail that turns off to the right. Across the little side creek, Windy Point trail east fork turns off to the left and fords Death Valley Creek (no bridge). Keep straight ahead.

To Windy Point trail N junction 1.4 km
The going is straightforward to 732185 where Windy Point trail north fork comes in from the left across Death Valley Creek. This is opposite a side valley to the west.

To Ware Creek 3.4 km
Enter a narrows between high grassy banks where the trail is forced back and forth across the creek. Opposite the second side valley to the west, the trail recrosses the creek and starts up the left bank of the tributary.

After the trail crosses to the right bank, detour up the grassy right-hand slope to a flat meadow with a wonderful vista of the valley to the west. You can hardly miss the metre-high aluminum cross glittering in the sun, the summer flowers rising halfway up the shaft. Here lies Muriel Dixon, a Stoney from Eden Valley Reserve, who was just 23 when she died some 50 years ago. I finally found the exact location thanks to Avril Derbyshire, who some of you may remember as houseparent of the Bragg Creek Hostel that burned down in the spring of 1984. She rides there often "to keep Muriel company for a while."

Return to the trail which crosses the right fork of the tributary and follows it around to the right, i.e., back north. (Any trails you see heading left are first-generation Death Valley trails. A wide grassy track starting from the far right side of the right fork offers a direct route through the aspens to the Dixon cross meadow.)

Cross a low, forested ridge, en route crossing a NE–SW cutline and then a fence (gate). At the next intersecting NE–SW cutline turn right onto it and follow it a way, watching for where the trail turns off to the left and in soggy meadows crosses a tributary of Ware Creek.

Climb to a T-junction and turn left. Cross another (aspen) ridge, en route intersecting another NE–SW cutline. A gradual descent above a small creek ends with short, steep zigs into the large meadow above Ware Creek.

Cross the meadow, at 717221 noting the old Ware Creek trail to left. Continue on down to the fording place. On the far (north) bank is a 3-way junction with the latest Ware Creek trail to left and 9999 trail to right at 715224.

#14 The cross in Death Valley at about 731189.

#15 Windy Point trail, looking back down Swanson's Draw from near the pass.

#15 Windy Point trail in Death Valley.

15 WINDY POINT TRAIL — map 1

Half-day, day hike
Official trail with signposts & red markers
Distance 5 km via 1., 5.9 km via 2.
Height gain S–N 160 m (525 ft.)
Height loss S–N 206 m (675 ft.)
High point 1600 m (5250 ft.) at pass
Map 82 J/10 Mount Rae

Usual access Hwy. 546 (Sheep River Trail). 3.3 km west of the winter gate at Sandy McNabb Recreation Area is a pullout on the left side of the road. Walk 100 m farther west along Hwy. 546 to where Windy Point trail crosses the road. NOTE This section of Hwy. 546 is closed Dec 1–May 15.

South access #9 Sheep trail east at the junction 200 m downslope and south of the usual access.

North access #14 Death Valley trail at 732181.

Also accessible via the northern terminus of #16 Foran Grade Ridge at the pass.

Travelling mainly through meadows and aspen forests, this trail offers an alternative way into or out of Death Valley. Combine with Death Valley trail and Sheep trail to make a 15 km loop from Sandy McNabb day parking lot. More often the southern section is used in conjunction with Foran Grade Ridge and Sheep trail to make an extremely popular half-day loop of 6.6 km.

TRAIL NOTE Since the last edition you'll be happy to learn the muddy mess of the old trail has been circumvented by a new trail.

HISTORY NOTE This area of the highway just east of Windy Point by the draw was once known as Frank's Cabin, after Frank Swanson, who built a cabin there pre-1920. He held a coal lease to Windy Point and starting from the rock face above the "road" he sank a shaft 100 feet into the ridge. Nowadays its existence is unguessed at, but before it was filled in you could scrabble up the scree for a look-see.

FROM SOUTH & USUAL ACCESSES

To the pass 1.4 km
From the signpost at south access, the trail climbs the grassy slope to Hwy. 546 just west of the usual parking lot access. En route pass two wonderfully situated seats dedicated to Don Lineham and Charles and Effie Conibear.

The trail crosses the highway and climbs in short bursts through meadow and aspen clumps up Swanson's Draw. A final straight leads to the pass between Foran Grade Ridge to right and Windy Point Ridge to left at the demarcation of meadow and trees. Here is a crossroads of sorts. Turn right. (The old trail ahead has been decommissioned.)

Death Valley 3.6 km via 1., 4.5 km via 2.
In a few metres turn left (route #16 ahead) to begin the long-drawn-out descent into Death Valley. Initially you follow the east bank of a tributary. After crossing the tributary and a drift fence, the trail traverses aspen hillsides. Lower down in mixed forest, the old trail, famous for mud the width of the Trans-Canada Hwy., has been replaced by a trail farther to the left that joins the original trail just before it enters the big meadow in Death Valley. Make for a raised island of aspens with red marker where the trail curves left and crosses a creeklet. Come to a junction, both forks leading to Death Valley trail.

1. Heading east and south Turn right on the east fork and ford Death Valley Creek to a signed T-junction with Death Valley trail at 736173 just north of the intersection with the trail from Pine Ridge, #13.

2. Heading north Continue ahead on the north fork, moving onto a forested rib of higher ground before dropping to a tributary. Here the trail turns right and fords Death Valley Creek to a second T-junction with Death Valley trail at 732185.

16 FORAN GRADE RIDGE—map 1

Half-day hike
Official trail with signposts & red markers
Distance 3.3 km
Height gain S–N 229 m (750 ft.)
Height loss S–N 91 m (300 ft.)
High point 1685 m (5530 ft.)
Map 82 J/10 Mount Rae

Access Hwy. 546 (Sheep River Trail). 1.6 km west of the winter gate at Sandy McNabb Recreation Area is a pullout on the right (north) side of the highway. NOTE This section of Hwy. 546 is closed Dec 1–May 15.
Also accessible from #9 Sheep trail east and #15 Windy Point trail at the pass.

This easy ridge is a favourite half-day walk for novice hikers and is usually combined with Windy Point trail and Sheep trail east to make a 6.6 km loop back to the pullout. When the highway is closed, biking to the pullout from the winter gate is no sweat. (The road is flat.) Alternatively, at such times you can make a longer, 10.8-km loop with Sheep trail east from Sandy McNabb day-use parking lot.

NAMING NOTE As Gregg Foran kindly pointed out to me, Foran Grade Ridge is named after his grandfather Bill who was a foreman at Lineham's logging camps in the Sheep and the Highwood, ranger at Bighorn Ranger Station and, by default, foreman of the road-building crew around Windy Point.

Not far from the pullout, the trail crosses a fence into a very large meadow with views of Long Prairie Ridge rising above the trees to your right. You wend left, aiming for the forested eastern aspect of Foran Grade Ridge, its south end soon reached by easy uphill windings in the trees.

The easy going continues as you follow the crest northwards through pines and aspens, clearings at many points allowing stunning views of the Sheep River wind-

Foran Grade Ridge from the big meadow near the start.

ing past Nash Meadow into the heart of the mountains. The square block of Gibraltar is instantly recognizable, while to its left the big mountain with concertina strata is Mist Mountain. This is also an excellent place to inspect Windy Point Ridge and the normal route up it that follows the left-hand skyline.

Shortly after the high point is passed, the trail winds down west-slope meadows to the pass between Foran Grade and Windy Point ridges, and it's here where you join Windy Point trail just before the trail sign. To complete the popular loop keep left.

Turn right for Death Valley before you get to the sign. The game trail straight on from the pass starts bushwhackers off up the steep east face of Windy Point Ridge.

#16 Foran Grade Ridge, looking west from the ridge to Windy Point Ridge (first top at left) and the pass on Windy Point trail.

#17 Windy Point Ridge. View from the first top looking down the ascent ridge. In the background are the mountains of the Highwood, including Junction Mountain.

17 WINDY POINT RIDGE — map 1

Climbing the south ridge to the first top.

Half-day hike
Unofficial route & trail
Distance 1.4 km
Height gain 296 m (970 ft.)
High point 1752 m (5750 ft.)
Map 82 J/10 Mount Rae

Access Hwy. 546 (Sheep River Trail). 4.5 km west of the winter closure gate at Sandy McNabb Recreation Area, stop in a small pullout on the left side of the highway below the ridge. NOTE This section of Hwy. 546 is closed Dec 1–May 15.
Also accessible from #18 East Canyon Creek.

Who can resist the grassy ridge rising above a section of highway known as Windy Point? Most people just go to the first top: a short, steep pull offering a panoramic view of foothills and mountains to the south and west. I particularly love coming up here on a blue-sky day in spring when the grass is green and yellow with dandelion and buffalo bean, yet the mountains are still plastered in snow.

HISTORY NOTE The lower slopes were used as a camera station in 1895

and 1896 by C.S.W. Barwell of the Irrigation Survey. He called the camera station "Lower Camp" after Lineham's lower logging camp that was located immediately below on the opposite bank of the Sheep River.

Of course, back then only a trail existed around Windy Point. It was later widened to take horses pulling wagons. So naturally, come the 1920s when Model-T Fords tried to get along the same track, there were problems, particularly during winter chinooks when seepages from the hillside above froze all over the track. At such times, ruts would have to be cut in the ice to prevent cars from sliding over the edge into the Sheep River. I'm told the passengers usually got out and walked.

To first top 900 m
Walk a little farther west along the highway to the texas gate sign where a trail climbs the right bank to a swing gate in the fence. Climb the first steepest step of the grassy south ridge above. After a second grassy step you reach the edge of a rising line of cliffs that feature a textbook anticline.

A trail appears and in multiple strands threads its way up a third step in scree and gravel. All that's left is an easy walk along the edge 'twixt trees and drop-off to the first top—a pocket handkerchief of grass. During raptor migrations you'll likely be sharing a cramped summit with birders who've staggered up the ridge with tripods, binoculars, spotting scopes and cameras equipped with heavy telephoto lenses.

To the summit 500 m

Continue to follow the trail, which turns left down a hill to a col. Keep straight up a grassy ridge into the pines, where the trail traverses left to a small meadow marking the summit at 715150. The new view is to the north and northwest.

GOING FARTHER

17A Gleason Ridge

Day hike
Mainly route, game trails
Distance loop 9 km
Height gain 140 m (460 ft.)
Height loss to #18 323 m (1060 ft.)
High point 1759 m (5770 ft.)

The section known as Windy Point Ridge refers to the south end of the very long S–N ridge extending to Ware Creek. The north end was named Gleason by the Irrigation Survey in 1895, so that's the name I'm using when describing the ridge north of the usual stopping place. The high point lies two-thirds of the way along at 697186.

Most people looking to extend the walk from Windy Point Ridge follow the ridge over several tops of the meadow and pine variety, then drop down to #18 East Canyon Creek to the west and return via the horse trail, so avoiding the uninteresting northern half that is all in trees.

In grass, a fainter trail continues down the other side and up over top no. 3. From the col beyond at 712153, is an escape route left into a tributary of Canyon Creek's east fork, that has a 5-star cow trail running along the left bank.

On the climb to top no. 4 stay in the ridgeline pines. The top is indeterminate and you have to stay alert so as not to end up in Death Valley. Watch for flagging indicating a LEFT jog down to the col at 708162 and up onto the continuation of the ridge to the west.

On open ridge again, head north over minor top no. 5 and on up to top no. 6, which is cluttered by windfall. Descend the far side to intersect a NE–SW cutline.

Drop left down the sometimes steep cutline. Low down at 696169 look for a trail on the left side between two blazed trees. This is East Canyon Creek trail. Now read #18.

View from the high point of Windy Point Ridge of Gleason Ridge, showing tops no. 3 (ahead) and no. 4 (at far right),

18 EAST CANYON CREEK—maps 1 & 2

Short-day hike
Unofficial trails
Distance 4.9 km
Height gain S–N 113 m (370 ft.)
High point 1570 m (5150 ft.)
Map 82 J/10 Mount Rae

Access Hwy. 546 (Sheep River Trail) 4.5 km west of the winter closure gate at Sandy McNabb Recreation Area, stop at a small pull-out on the left side of the highway below Windy Point Ridge. NOTE This section of Hwy. 546 is closed Dec 1–May 15.
Also accessible from #19 Missinglink, #20 Missinglink–Canyon Connector and #17A Gleason Ridge in a couple of places.

A trail made by range riders and cows runs all the way along this valley and connects with Missinglink trail at the pass, so making possible a loop with #19 and #20. You also connect with routes off Gleason Ridge #17A.

Like its west fork, Canyon Creek's east fork is wide and flat, typically foothills with its mix of pines, aspens and meadows. So anyone walking down it will think "where the heck IS this canyon?" So, on to the next paragraph.

NAMING NOTE Canyon Creek was named way back in the 1920s for the small canyon at the south end that was spanned by a log bridge. Nowadays, motorists zoom across a meadow without realizing they are crossing infill above a culvert. Such a pity. Because all unseen the creek pours out of the culvert and plunges down a rocky gully to the Sheep River below. To look at this sizeable waterfall, which is spectacular in spate, head down the grassy left bank as you look out from the highway, but take care at the cliff edge. For many years a cross marked the site of a fatality here in 2005.

Canyon Creek waterfall below the highway.

To NE–SW cutline 4 km
The first part is shared with #20 Missinglink–Canyon Connector, finish 1.

Walk west for 340 m along the highway, en route crossing the texas gate. After the second white post on the right, turn right up the bank on a trail. At the top the trail reverts to old road (track). Follow it through a gate in a fence, then across meadows sweeping down to the canyon. A little farther on, the track dips steeply to cross a side creek at a left-hand bend. At the top of the far bank is a meadow. This is where you leave the road. (The continuing track is the Missinglink–Canyon Connector).

Cross the meadow to the edge of the aspens and locate a good trail heading up-valley. At a split keep right. Come

The upper section of the trail in the Canyon–Link watershed meadow. Photo Alf Skrastins

to a major side creek in a dip and cross. (Running along the right bank of the side creek is an excellent cow trail that can be followed almost to Gleason Ridge at the col at 712153.)

The main valley trail runs through mixed forest and then crosses a large meadow. Shortly after re-entering trees, keep left, cross a tiny side creek and veer right to a salt lick where the cut trail ends.

Pushing away a few branches, continue along the trail. Keep right all the way, noting occasional blazes. Immediately after a second area of deadfall is a questionable junction. Possibly the left-hand trail intersects the NE–SW cutline at 695166. The blazed trail, however, goes right past a pile of bones and climbs into drier pine forest before reaching the cutline a little farther east at 696169. This cutline is the descent route off Gleason Ridge.

To Missinglink trail 900 m

Walk left along the slightly soggy cutline and cross the valley creek in a dip. Just past another salt lick enter meadows at mid-valley. Leave the cutline and turn right on a trail that dekes through a few

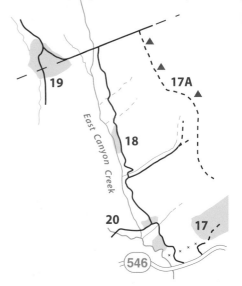

East Canyon Creek, showing ways off Gleason Ridge and the connection with Missinglink trail

trees to the watershed meadow with Link Creek. Here intersect the very much larger Missinglink trail.

Turn left to return to Hwy. 546 via #19 Missinglink trail; keep straight if northbound for Ware Creek trail.

19 MISSINGLINK TRAIL — maps 1 & 6

Short-day, day hike, backpack
Equestrian
Unofficial trail, creek crossings
Distance 8.1 km
Height gain S–N 143 m (470 ft.)
Height loss S–N 198 m (650 ft.)
High point 1615 m (5300 ft.)
Map 82 J/10 Mount Rae

Access Hwy. 546 (Sheep River Trail). Since the last edition the parking lot and its access road was plowed under. You must now park on the shoulder of the hwy. at 688138, or use the Bighorn parking lot 500 m to the west. NOTE This section of Hwy. 546 is closed Dec 1–May 15.
Also accessible from #56 Ware Creek trail at 677207, #18 East Canyon Creek at the pass.

A foothills trail that connects Hwy. 546 to #56 Ware Creek via the Canyon–Link watershed. The sunnier south end is where most of the meadows are and it's here that the options present themselves. The north end between Missinglink Mountain and Gleason Ridge is "a boring old trail" following cutlines and cutline access roads in the lodgepoles. Should the official red markers ever be taken down, this is where you would get lost and I would have to draw a map.

TRAIL NOTE Since the last edition the trail has been undesignated, and while not the most beautiful of trails, it is, nevertheless, still a useful connector between the trails about Hwy. 546 and the Ware Creek road (alias former Gorge Creek road), one of only two connectors to the northern trails of the Sheep. (The northern stretch of Death Valley was almost a goner, too, until its value as the only official connector left was realized at the last moment!)

SOUTH TO NORTH
To the forks 1.6 km
From Hwy. 546 walk to the site of the former parking lot, from where a trail cuts across to a gate in a drift fence. You're now on a track making for the west fork of Canyon Creek. En route go either way at a

The trail south of the watershed, crossing the first side creek into the meadows.

split, then stay left where the track makes a bigger split. (Right leads to the Missing-link–Canyon connector.) Wind downhill to a second T-junction with the split, also #20. Go left and down a hill to a side creek.

Cross and enjoy the next half kilometre of riverside meadows overlooked by a rocky bluff on the far side of Canyon Creek's west fork. Ford the main west fork just upstream of a confluence with a north tributary. At the top of the meadow is an indistinct Y-junction. Keep straight at the red marker. (Track to left is #21B Missing-link Mountain from the south.)

To the watershed 2 km
In forest, start up a steepening N–S cutline. Before the top of the hill is reached you turn right onto a trail that descends and crosses the north tributary. Since removal of the culvert, which still languishes on the west bank, the crossing point features bottomless black mud from extra water. Find another place to cross.

After this the trail follows the tributary's right bank at an easy angle to an intersecting NE–SW cutline. Cross the cutline. (Cutline to left is a way onto the northern escarpment of Missinglink Mountain.) Rejoin the N–S cutline briefly, then cut away right and descend slightly to the watershed, a longitudinal meadow sweeping through the gap from Link Creek on your left into Canyon Creek's east fork on your right. Cross the meadow to an unmarked junction with the narrower East Canyon Creek trail coming in from the right.

Link Creek 4.5 km
Keep left here and on cutline access road cross a drift fence en route to the day's high point. This is a viewpoint for Missinglink Mountain. Whereas its south and west slopes present exciting meadows and cliffs dotted with Bighorns, the back side is miles and miles of unappealing forest.

A steep descent of alder alley, followed by a up-down sidehill bash brings you to strips of meadow alongside the south fork of Link Creek.

For a while the going is pleasant, but far too soon the access road turns away from the creek and crosses a major N–S cutline, resuming its northward direction to the right (east) of the cutline as a trail. Twice it touches on the cutline before breaking away left toward the creek. Just in time, too. Rearing up ahead is the hill we skied pre K Country by kicking steps up and down it.

On the following straight-through meadow, you cross three tiny side creeks. Go right at the first split, then either way at a second split—one is as deep as the other. Regain the N–S cutline and turn left.

Cross a side creek, small meadow and tree ribbon to a large meadow sloping down to the confluence of the south and southwest forks of Link Creek. Ahead is a view of the upper Ware Creek Valley. Follow the posts down to Link Creek and wade. (Alternatively, jump both forks upstream of the confluence.) Climb the far bank to a post with red marker in Gleason's Meadow.

For Link trail (#56A) keep left on the good trail that heads up-meadow. For Ware Creek trail (#56) cross the meadow on a narrower trail that splits before climbing up to the old road at 677207.

The meadow descent to Link Creek crossing. Gleason's Meadow in view ahead.

20 MISSINGLINK–CANYON CONNECTOR — maps 1 & 2

Half-day, day hike in combo
Unofficial trails
Distance 3.3 km via finish 1
Height gain W–E 12 m (40 ft.)
Height loss W–E 36 m (120 ft.)
High point 1509 m (4950 ft.)
Map 82 J/10 Mount Rae

Access Hwy. 546 (Sheep River Trail).
1. Via #19 Missinglink trail in the west fork of Canyon Creek.
2. Via #18 East Canyon Creek.

Connecting trails and old roads are best used for making an anticlockwise 10.7 km loop with East Canyon Creek and the southern section of Missinglink.

MISSINGLINK TO CANYON CREEK

Let's assume you're heading south on Missinglink trail in the drainage of West Canyon Creek and have crossed the north tributary, the main fork and the side creek. At the top of the hill above the side creek turn left at the split in the track. Do not follow the track back to Missinglink trail, At the bend at 694143 continue straight on a narrow but good trail heading southeast through open mixed forest. At a junction wend left and soon reach an E–W cutline and fence at yellow flagging. Turn left and walk the cutline alongside the fence.

Finish 1 longest 3.3 km
If you're a purist turn left on the old road that leaves the left side of the cutline. It descends ever more steeply to Canyon Creek, a hill I first skied up in the dark a very long time ago. Nowadays the road is infiltrated with alder, with thin trails leading through it or around it. Low down at the confluence of the east and west forks, the road has been totally lost to willow bush. Go right along the riverbank into a meadow where the road can be seen crossing the creek upstream of a bend. Thereafter the road is in good shape.

An easy uphill connects with East Canyon Creek trail at a right-hand bend. Stay on the road, which crosses a side creek, then sidles above the canyon to a gate in a fence. A trail takes you out to the highway 340 m west of the Windy Point Ridge parking area.

Finish 2 easier 3 km
The easy cop-out. Carry on along the cutline to where it ends above the canyon of Canyon Creek. Here turn right, slip through a gap in the fence and descend to the highway. Turn left and walk the highway for 740 m to the Windy Point pullout. En route, take the opportunity to look at the waterfall below the Canyon Creek culvert.

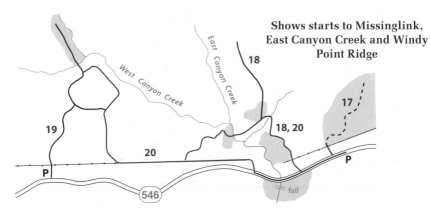

Shows starts to Missinglink, East Canyon Creek and Windy Point Ridge

21 MISSINGLINK MOUNTAIN from the south—map 2

Summit view of Mount Ware, Bluerock Mountain, Mt. Rose, Threepoint Mountain and Surveyor's Ridge.

Day hikes
Unofficial trails & routes
High point 1945 m (6380 ft.)
Map 82 J/10 Mount Rae

Access Hwy. 546 (Sheep River trail). NOTE This section of hwy. is closed Dec 1–May 15.
1. Nash Meadows, either a small pullout on the west side of the texas gate or a small pullout at the interpretive sign farther east.
2. Via #19 Missinglink trail at the 1.6 km (second) creek crossing.

The short, popular way to the summit is from Gorge Creek Road. See #42. Other people, lured by the steep grassy south ridge of Dot Mountain (so named by researchers from the R.B. Miller Station) follow the west escarpment and then bushwhack the rest of the way. (Route not described, nor the dreadful valley to its east.)

Two reasonable routes exist from Hwy. 546 from the south. They are longer, of course, and mostly forested, but have trails for the most part. So while there is no beating through dense bush, be prepared for a little route-finding by compass, GPS or ESP right at the end.

Both routes can be linked to make a loop of about 12.5 km. If looping, start from Bighorn Sheep Lookout parking lot and use the highway as a connector both ways.

Why bother climbing a low, sprawling, forested foothill, you ask? Well, apart from the attraction of its having an intriguing name, the summit is a very fine viewpoint. Also, I'm glad to report the whole area is now part of Sheep River Provincial Park, which means that all animals, including humans, are safe from hunters.

NAMING NOTE The name "Missinglink" is not named after the well-known sausage factory in Calgary. It was first used in A.O. Wheeler's diary of 1895—way before the term "missing link" became a popular catchphrase courtesy of paleoanthropologists—after the first ascent of the mountain on a sunny October 7 in 1895. Possibly the name refers to this secondary triangulation station as being the missing link in the triangulation survey with Greenslope (Green Mountain) and Hoffmann. That's my theory, anyway.

21A from Nash Meadow

Short-day hike
Unofficial trail, then route
Distance 4.6 km
Height gain 466 m (1530 ft.)
Height loss 30 m (100 ft.)

Easiest and shortest from Hwy. 546 with all the height gain occurring at the beginning. I like this route a lot: the meadows and the easy open forest. Use GPS for the final stretch across the plateau.

FROM ACCESS 1

You're going to be climbing the big grassy south-facing slope rising above Nash Meadows to a southeast ridge—244 m (800 ft.) of climbing cold turkey. There are two obvious ways up: from the EAST side of the texas gate or from the interpretive sign about livestock grazing, farther to the east. (This more easterly route features research plots and signs screaming "AT-TENTION!") Either way, pick a route up faces and ribs.

#21A The southeast ridge above Nash Meadows.

On gaining the southeast ridge, turn left and on trail walk above the open face into the trees. Pass a very large cairn, then continue on trail along the very slightly undulating ridge in open forest. Reach a small top at 661149.

Care is needed on the next stretch where the trail descends the right side of the ridge on the diagonal to the head of a small valley, then climbs toward a NE–SW cutline. The trail peters out just before reaching the cutline at a tree with two red metal tags reading "Chevron permit."

Cross the cutline and head north, climbing through forest, aiming for 660156 just left of a small top. Navigation becomes more difficult as you head NNW across the eastern plateau, aiming for the summit at 653160. Cross alternating bands of trees and meadow. You know when you're almost there because the ground rises to the escarpment edge.

After admiring the view of Front Range peaks from the top of the grassy western escarpment, reverse your route back to 660156. If looping with B, aim southeast, then northeast to the end of a cutline at 664165.

21B from Missinglink trail

Day hike
Unofficial trails, then route
Distance 6.5 km from hwy.
Height gain 475 m (1560 ft.) from hwy.

This longest route has excellent trails until you reach the final plateau. A GPS receiver really helps if you are returning the same way and absolutely must find the end of the cutline cum access road.

FROM ACCESS 2
West fork Canyon Creek 1 km
Follow Missinglink trail for 1.6 km to the Y-junction in a meadow just after the second creek crossing.

Keep left on a track that follows the right bank of the west fork through trees. Cross a side creek into meadows. At some trees, take the higher trail through grass

Above: #21B The cutline access road just below the east ridge.

Opposite: #21C Climbing to top no. 3 on the escarpment.

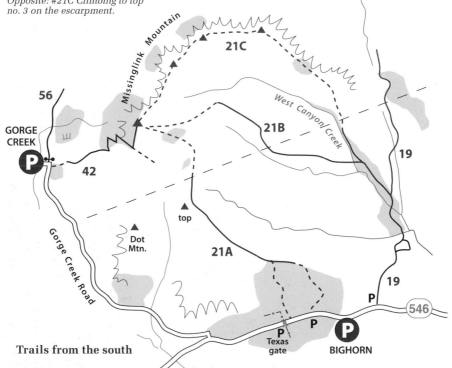

Trails from the south

and shortly intersect a wide E–W cutline. Here turn left and cross the creek.

Cutline cum access road section 2.5 km
Follow the cutline up a long hill that steepens near the top. Then, reverting to grassy cutline access road, it traverses hillside on the left side of an east ridge. Where a snippet of cutline climbs steeply ahead, keep left on the access road and cross a NE–SW cutline. After the road turns right it climbs steeply at times to the ridge crest.

Turn left and in matchstick pine forest follow the wide cutline to near its end at 664165. Pull out the GPS.

To summit 1.4 km
From just before the end of the cutline cum access road, a flagged trail turns off to the left and starts you off up the upper east ridge Flagging disappears, and eventually the trail, as you reach the eastern plateau. Head WSW through very open forest toward the summit at 653160. You know when you're almost there because the ground rises to the escarpment edge.

OPTIONAL RETURN

21C Northern escarpment

Route & game trails
Distance 5.3 km
Extra height gain 91 m (300 ft.)

Certified (some might say certifiable) bushwhackers can follow the undulating edges around to the north and east and make a 14.4 km loop with B.

From the summit head northeast down forest to col no. 1. Pick up a game trail and on grass climb to top no. 2, which has an interesting west ridge ending in a cliff. An easy treed descent to col no. 2 is followed by more on-edge meadow to top no. 3. Here you turn east, passing a spring with scattered moose bones, then gradually descending to col no. 3. Climb steeply to top no. 4, which barely rises out of the trees.

Turn southeast into matchstick pines, continually on the lookout for trees far enough apart for the human body to pass between without getting skewered. This section ends with a steepish drop to right of a rockband. Another band a little farther down diagonals right across the ridge. Find a way through, or detour down right and back up left. A grassy section ends in big pine forest at col no. 5.

Looking at the map, making for the convenient NE–SW cutline that crosses the ridge low down and connects with Missinglink seems a no-brainer. In reality the chain of knolls in between are time gobblers. Better to traverse the south slope of the first knoll a short way, then on game trail descend down right into the west fork of Canyon Creek. A trail takes you back to B's wide E–W cutline.

22 JUNCTION LOOKOUT fire road—map 2

Long-day hike, bike 'n' hike, backpack
Official trail with signposts & red markers, creek crossing
Distance 12.8 km from north access trailhead, 9.3 km from Sheep trail east
Height gain 750 m (2460 ft.)
Height loss 24 m (80 ft.)
High point 2240 m (7350 ft.)
Map 82 J/10 Mount Rae

North access Via #9 Sheep trail east. The usual one-day bash starts from Indian Oils trailhead on Hwy. 546 and follows Sheep trail eastwards to the junction at 660100 above Dyson Creek. NOTE This section of Hwy. 546 is closed Dec 1–May 15.

Top: The final approach to the lookout through meadows. Photo Jack Tannett

Bottom: The present lookout building under storm clouds. Photo Jack Tannett

South access Via #5 Junction Lookout from Coal Creek at the lookout.
Also accessible from the northwestern terminus of #23 Green Mountain trail.

Standing on a high grassy ridge below the northeast wall of Junction Mountain, Junction Lookout is an obvious attraction, though not quite as popular as Moose Mountain on account of the length of its access trail which makes it a one day marathon. It must be said that the fire road—maintained by Alberta Transportation—makes for a boring walk, compensated by grizzly tracks, upland meadows and views. Biking entails much uphill pushing, the anticipated descent a "bumpy thriller."

TRAIL NAME NOTE On the signposts and in brochures, this trail is called Junction Mountain trail, a name many scramblers find misleading.

HISTORY NOTE The 2004 lookout building is the fourth at this location, the first one being built in September of 1929 when snow lay thick on the ground and pack horses plodded up a trail as yet unstumped.

FROM NORTH ACCESS
To Green Mountain trail 600 m
At the junction 660100 on Sheep trail, stay straight ahead on the fire road and descend to Dyson Creek meadow, the site of Bighorn Lumber Company's camp in the 1940s. (Note Benjamin Teskey's grassed-over logging road joining the fire road in a vee as you enter the meadow.)

This is a lovely, sunny spot with a view of Green Mountain's craggy west face, the usual ascent route seen in profile. Just downstream is little Dyson Falls where *Collomia* grows in the spray. According to Laureen Harper, her grandmother, Phyllis Teskey, stored food in the recess behind the falls to keep it cool.

Wade the creek above the falls. It can be rock-hopped later in the season. In spate, it may be impassable. Climb to the junction with Green Mountain trail. Keep right around the bend.

Junction Lookout 8.7 km
For the next 2 km the fire road wanders along in a southwesterly direction, paralleling Dyson Creek, with overgrown logging roads peeling off to left and right. After rounding a forested ridge, look for the glimmer of a small pond through a belt of trees on the left. Just after the pond, a stub of logging road heads left into a meadow née cutblock This is OPTION B.

Dyson Falls.

Coming up is the hard work of the day: a long flog up a north ridge, the gradient easing as you wind in and out of all the headwaters of North Coal Creek on steep, heavily forested east slopes. The spruce forest is hauntingly beautiful with a mossy understorey and running water in all the tributaries. At one point you touch a shaley gap—momentary view of mountains to the west—then it's back to the forest grind. Eventually the fire road turns southwest (first view of the lookout) and arrives at Col 656046. Ahead are meadows!

Climb to the broad ridge swung northeast from Junction Mountain and follow it southeasterly up the final stretch of road, which is flagged on the east side by a line of wind-battered spruce. Look back for a fabulous view of Bluerock Mountain's southeast ridge. Note two cairns and a horse rail on the right side of the trail marking route #5's departure down the south flank to Coal Creek.

It takes more than 100 m of remaining road to make you forgo the lookout and the chance of saying hello. Since the last edition there has been a proliferation of satellite buildings you can shelter behind while taking in the views. The view west is blocked by the long northeast wall of Junction Mountain. But looking southwest beyond the wall, you can spot Sullivan Pass and the mountains of the Highwood, including Mt. Burke.

OPTIONS

22A Hill 651038

Route
Distance 1.6 km return from fire road
Height gain 113 m (370 ft.)
High point 2292 m (7520 ft.)

From the saddle at 658040, just before the final straight to the lookout, you are lured up the grassy hill to the west by its easy-angled open slope.

From the summit the main view is of the last stretch of trail to the lookout. Though now even closer in to the east wall of Junction, you can look north along it to Peak 619048.

22B North Coal Creek

Route, unofficial trails
Distance 2.2 km to meadows, 5.2 km to Green Mountain trail
Height gain 15 m (50 ft.) to meadows
Height loss 46 m (150 ft.) to meadows
High point 1682 m (5520 ft.)

If you can't hack the long haul to the lookout, try this easy alternative to the meadows of North Coal Creek. Experienced cutline hikers have the option of making a loop with Green Mountain trail via the north end of Phone Line.

To North Coal Creek meadows 2.2 km
As mentioned, follow the stub of logging road into an old-fashioned cutblock deserving of the name "meadow." Head

right to its upper end where the watershed between Dyson and North Coal creeks is incredibly low. At the demarcation with trees find a dirt road that descends gradually through pine forest (some step-over deadfall) and through a drift fence (no gate) into the gorgeous meadows of upper North Coal Creek. From the valley trail the meadows extend right to the top of the ridge to the north. Before returning, it's worthwhile climbing up there for the view west.

GOING FARTHER
To Green Mountain trail 3 km
Wish in vain for a nice little game trail along the banktop above North Coal Creek. Your route is a roller-coaster NE–SW cutline cum access road. Add on 98 m (320 ft.) height gain, 171 m (560 ft.) height loss.

Continue along the trail in the valley bottom to the cutline that heads left up the hillside into the trees. After a particularly onerous ascent and descent (no cutoff trail that I could see), the cutline descends a long hill to a side valley. Just before, the access road turns down right and describes a semicircle across the creek back to the cutline. Turn right and cross a side slope—a long uphill, then downhill with a drift fence in the middle—to flat ground.

Phone Line joins in from the right at a red marker. A short distance on, follow Phone Line where it turns left off the cutline onto a trail that descends and crosses a side creek to the 3-way "junction" (sign removed) with Green Mountain trail (left) and Mount McNabb trail (right) at 694091. Above the junction towers Spaulding Point on Green Mountain.

Turn left to return to Junction Lookout fire road above Dyson Creek.

Opposite top: #22A View from Hill 651038 of the fire road to the lookout.

Middle: #22 The fire road just below the lookout, looking north toward little Peak 619048 and the mountains of the upper Sheep. Hill 651038 at left.

Bottom: #22B The meadows of North Coal Creek.

23 GREEN MOUNTAIN TRAIL — map 2

Day hike, backpack
Equestrian
Official trail with signposts & red markers, creek crossing
Distance 3.6 km
Height gain W–E 58 m (190 ft.)
Height loss W–E 110 m (360 ft.)
High point 1625 m (5330 ft.)
Map 82 J/10 Mount Rae

West access Via #22 Junction Lookout fire road at 664102.
East access The "junction" of #8 Mount McNabb and #6 Phone Line at 694091.

A mostly forest trail that crosses a low pass between Dyson Creek and North Coal Creek. Although an easy and important connector between Junction Lookout fire road and the Mount McNabb/Phone Line network, most hikers use it to access Green Mountain, a popular one-day trip from Indian Oils trailhead.

NOTE Bear prints are often seen in muddy and snowy conditions, but never the shy grizzly. Just be aware.

FROM WEST TO EAST

To Green Mountain access 1.3 km
At the junction keep left onto Green Mountain Trail (logging road). Not far along, it descends to cross a side creek, then climbs steadily to its high point. En route, secondary logging roads (most narrowed to trail) peel off to left and right. Just stay on the main logging road, which is always obvious.

The descent to North Coal Creek is a long-drawn-out affair. Straight off, the road descends, flattens, then climbs a little and it's here at the top of the hill at 675100 that the best route to Green Mountain takes off left at some flagging. A little way in, to the right, is a mossy-walled outhouse — as usual, the sole remnant of a logging camp. The usual scattering of rusty cans on both sides of the trail alerts you to its presence.

Green Mountain trail not far from the "junction" with Phone Line and Mount McNabb trails.

To Mount McNabb trail 2.3 km
The logging road passes over the watershed (that meadow to right) into forest hung with the pale green lichen *Usnea*. A larger meadow with side creek is crossed, then it's back into trees. The next side creek crossing, with a bit trail climbing up the far bank at 688093, is the earliest place where hikers can head up to Spaulding Point. See OPTION A Green Mountain.

Enter a strip of meadow rising up the left slope and in 200 m come to the 3-way "junction" (sign removed) at 694091, with Phone Line trail (right) and Mount McNabb trail (straight on), the latter destined to become an extension of this trail.

Disappointingly, there have been absolutely no views of Green Mountain from anywhere along the trail. No views, period. So walk down the meadow on Phone Line and look back. Rising above the trees is Spaulding Point, the southernmost tip of the mountain.

OPTION

23A Green Mountain

Route, game trails
Distance 1.2 km, 13.2 km return from
Indian Oils trailhead, Spaulding Point
loop 17.1 km return from trailhead
Height gain from trail 219 m (720 ft.)
High point 1844 m (6050 ft.)

This hill appears to be a dark green mound from Hwy. 546, but concealed behind that facade of lodgepole pines lies grassy slopes and fascinating sandstone escarpments facing south and west.

Green Mountain is a popular climb despite there being no trail to the top. The usual route is a moderately steep pull up a southwest ridge direct to the summit, most people descending more or less the same way. Lately, though, a loop incorporating Spaulding Point, the southernmost tip of Green Mountain, has become popular. This lengthens the hike trailhead to trailhead by almost 4 km.

NAMING & HISTORY NOTE Originally the mountain was named "Greenslope" by A.O. Wheeler during the Irrigation Survey, and was likely first climbed in 1895, certainly on August 15, 1896, on "a rainy cloudy day."

The route leaves Green Mountain trail at 675100 at flagging. Head up a bit of a draw to the right of a small open ridge. On intersecting a narrow cutline, turn right and follow the cutline up a steepish hill onto the broad southwest ridge. When the cutline gives out, continue upwards to a levelling. Once again the ground steepens and you plough through last aspens onto a steep grassy slope above. Aim just to the right of the upcoming cliff (the castle).

Arrive at the head of a secret valley between the castle, the cormorant and the escarpment. The castle is easy from this direction, its pinnacle a fun scramble.

Tackle the escarpment above via the ridge to the right of the castle. You pass the Mushrooms, then weave between Limber pines clinging to the rocks. Stop awhile to enjoy a superb panorama of familiar mountains, then continue through a few trees, wending right to a sheltered glade occupied by three survey markers and a cairn.

Return the same way. It doesn't matter if you miss the top of the cutline. Just head downhill and sooner or later you are going to end up on Green Mountain trail. Alternatively, try the Spaulding Point loop back to Green Mountain trail.

#23A The pinnacle from the castle. The ridge at right is the ascent route to the summit.

#23A Green Mountain. View from near the summit of the castle and the far-off peaks of the Highwood and Misty ranges, including Shunga-le-she, Mist Mountain and Gibraltar.

Mushrooms on the upper ridge, looking toward Spaulding Point and Mount Dyson.

GOING FARTHER

Spaulding Point loop 1.9 km to #23

This loop takes in the south end of Green Mountain, known as Spaulding Point, and a return along Green Mountain trail.

From the summit cairn descend in a southeasterly direction along the strip of meadow at the top edge of the escarpment. Where the meadow gives out, move left into the pines and cross a couple of narrow cutlines. After the ground levels it pays to return to the escarpment and follow it around above a cliff to the point itself. A new view has opened up to the northeast of North Coal Creek meadows and Mount McNabb.

The cormorant. Photo Allan & Angélique Mandel

Descend to a large prominent cairn on a lower ledge, the last resting place of Phil Spaulding, a published anthropologist and long-time member of the Rocky Mountain Ramblers.

Scramble down the cliff via a weakness to the right of the cairn. Continue down steep grass to a flattening. Then either head right on a bit of a game trail, aiming for Green Mountain trail at 688093 at a side creek crossing, or follow a trail along the aspen ridge in front of you. When it gives out, descend pines to Green Mountain trail, which is reached 300 m west of the 3-way "junction" at 694091.

The big cairn on Spaulding Point.

24 MOUNT HOFFMANN — maps 2 & 3

The summit area of Mount Hoffmann.
The view north to Bluerock Mtn.

Day hike
Unofficial trail & route
Distance 2.4 km from Sheep trail east,
4 km from trailhead,
Height gain 478 m (1570 ft.) from
trailhead, 372 m (1220 ft.) from Sheep
trail east
High point 2018 m (6620 ft.)
Map 82 J/10 Mount Rae

Access Hwy. 546 (Sheep River Trail) at Indian Oils trailhead. Via #9 Sheep trail east.

Christian Hoffmann's mountain (two n's, please) is a good day trip from Indian Oils trailhead. The going is occasionally steep but easy to follow. Well, almost. A 400-m-long hiatus requires that you be a good routefinder or have a GPS.

NAMING NOTE Contrary to expectations, this "boring, tree-covered" hill is an excellent viewpoint and was in fact used extensively as a camera station during the Irrigation Survey of the mid-1890s. It was first climbed in 1895 and another seven times in 1896 by various members of A.O. Wheeler's party. Hoffmann, by the way,

was a chemist and mineralogist with the Geological Survey of Canada and a close friend of Wheeler's.

Logging road section 1.4 km
From Indian Oils trailhead follow Sheep trail (fire road) heading east. Leave the road at 642099, at the point above where it dips to cross Hoffmann Creek, and turn right onto a logging road.

The 1940s logging road winds fairly effortlessly uphill to a meadow above Hoffmann Creek—site of a logging camp strewn with the usual bedsprings, oven parts and rusted cans. This point can also be reached via trail from the salt lick at the second right-hand bend in the road.

At this point the road, temporarily reduced to trail, turns right and climbs gently up the west fork to the col at 634094 between Mount Hoffmann and two lower hills described under OPTION A.

At the col you turn left uphill, pushing through some alder to a junction with a dead-end road. Go left. A little farther on, the logging road flattens and dead-ends.

Trail to summit 1 km

A trail leaves the right end of the road and climbs steeply in pine forest for about 60 vertical m. It then makes a rising traverse left, finally emerging on the broad, flattish north ridge where it ends at 634088.

On the same line, pick a way through trees with snags and deadfall to the meadow on the other (west) side of the ridge at about 634086. On the return, navigating between these two points to the start of the trail is tricky. I recommend using the tracking device on your GPS.

At the meadow turn left and follow the forest edge to the shaley summit of Hoffmann with its distinctive inukshuk. It was dismantled in 2006 by cairn haters, but may be up again by now, courtesy of X.

The view west and north is stupendous, taking in everything from Junction Mountain through Gibraltar to Bluerock Mountain and beyond. Down below is Bluerock Campground and a heaving sea of foothills rolling up against the Front Ranges.

Going a bit farther 1.1 km

An even better viewpoint exists at the next top to the WSW at 625077.

A fairly gradual descent of 122 m (400 ft.) with shale, step-over rockbands

and open trees lands you at a col. From here climb 91 m (300 ft.) to a big meadow facing west with a cairn on top.

Going even farther along the WSW ridge would be tempting if there weren't so much deadfall. FUTURE NOTE The Sheep River management plan shows a trail climbing over this ridge from the Sheep River to Dyson Creek, thus opening up three loops. In the meantime return the same way.

OPTION

24A "The Humps"

Distance 400 m
Height gain 52 m (170 ft.)
High point 1832 m (6010 ft.)

The sandstone crags of the twin hills at 636095 are fun to play around on.

Hike to the col at 634094. To gain the lower hill, push through a few trees to the rockband and find easy ways up.

The bigger hill is more easily reached from open slopes above the trail before you reach the col. With luck you'll hit a trail taking you through the rockband to the forested topknot. A cairn on the edge overlooks Indian Oils parking lot.

Top: #24A One of the many faces on the rockband of the lower hump. This one is Frankenstein.

Left: #24 The logging road (here reduced to trail) between the logging camp and the col.

25 INDIAN OILS TRAIL — map 3

Half-day, day hike
Official trail with signposts & red markers, creek crossings
Distance 8.8 km via access 1
Height gain S–N 411 m (1350 ft.)
Height loss S–N 296 m (970 ft.)
High point 1875 m (6150 ft.)
Map 82 J/10 Mount Rae

Access Hwy. 546 (Sheep River Trail). NOTE This section of hwy. is closed Dec 1–May 15.
1. Official start at Indian Oils parking lot.
2. Pullout 300 m west of Indian Oils.
3. Sheep Falls day-use area.
4. Parking area on east side of the highway, 800 m west of Indian Oils access road.
Also accessible from #9 Sheep trail east at the bridge over the Sheep River at Tiger Jaws Fall, #9 Sheep trail east from west of Sheep Falls, #43 Gorge Creek trail at 601141, the western terminus of #47 South Gorge Creek.

An undulating trail that crosses the group of low hills between the Sheep River and Gorge Creek to Gorge Creek trail at 601141. You'll notice it's carefully routed to include a fine viewpoint at the first pass, which makes a good half-day objective. Unless you're making a loop or point to point with other trails, don't bother cross-

The view from the first pass of Junction Mountain (left), Junction Creek and Shunga-la-she.

ing the second pass. Instead, take in one of the three side trips.

ACCESS NOTE Officially, the true start to this trail for hikers is access 1. While of historical interest, it's the longest approach, and you may prefer starting from access 2 or 3.

If parked at access 2, why not take in Sheep Falls trail as well? Interestingly, the bench near the overlook is in memory of Bob Iceton, the son of Bill Iceton who decades ago blasted the road around Windy Point to Bighorn Ranger Station.

HISTORY & NAMING NOTE The intriguing trail name comes from an early well drilled near the parking lot. In 1919 a fire, credited to Pat Burns's road-building crew, swept down the valley to the forest boundary, in passing burning out Indian Oils, which luckily was not operating at the time. Later reports indicate another well on the site was drilled to a depth of 1,130 ft. in 1929. Around the same time, various coal companies were taking an interest in the area, starting with Indian Oils (1929–31) and ending in 1945–51 with Payne's strip mine. The coal spoil can still be seen on the slopes above start 1.

SOUTH TO NORTH
There are four starts:

Accesses 1 and 2 to 4-way, 810 m
The trail leaves the far end of Indian Oils parking lot at the signboard and in a short distance arrives at a T-junction with the equestrian trail from Tiger Jaws Falls. Turn right.

The trail crosses the highway at access 2, a small pullout 300 m west of Indian Oils parking lot access road and begins a gradual climb along a mine access road to Payne's strip mine site where coal spoil is thinly disguised by new tree growth. Up-slope on a bench is the Indian Oils well site.

Descend, then cross a small side creek draining underground from the seasonal pond (see SIDE TRIP B) just prior to your arrival at a signed 4-way junction on the north bank of a bigger side creek. Turn right. (The trail ahead that crosses the creek is access 3 from Sheep Falls parking lot. The trail to left is the unofficial shortcut from access 4.)

Access 3 to 4-way, 520 m
From the end of the parking lot walk out to the highway and turn left. On the far side of the road pick up the trail that has come in from the Sheep River. Follow it below the campground ridge to the side creek. Cross and climb to a 4-way junction. Turn left on Indian Oils trail.

Access 4 to 4-way 180 m
Walk west for a few metres to the side creek. Follow an unofficial trail along the right (east) bank to the 4-way junction. Go straight.

To first pass 2.2 km
From the 4-way junction the trail rises gradually along the right bank of the unnamed creek for 1.5 km, then after a few zigs climbs very much more steeply onto the grassy ridge to the northeast at 612104. This first pass (bench, horse rail) is the high point of the trail and a satisfy-ing viewpoint for the mountains about Junction Creek and the unnamed ridges southeast of Mount Burns. Directly west, at the head of the unnamed creek, rises the rocky knob visited by #26A. This is where SIDE TRIP A turns off to the right (south).

(FUTURE NOTE Within the next few years, a trail will branch off the pass and head west across the hills to join Bluerock Creek trail high on its southeast ridge.)

To South Gorge Creek trail 2.7 km
From the pass the trail descends in waves down the northeast slope into the dim light of mature spruce forest. At a low point a cairn indicates the side trail to the meadow-with-seasonal-pond. (See SIDE TRIP B.)

Climb alongside a wee creek into sunnier country with meadows. (In case you're wondering, a cairn on the left side at the top of the hill indicates the route to a rocky knob sticking out of the forest.)

After a flat stretch, start the long, gradual descent to the next official junction. En route you pass between two small hills. The one on the right is Hill 617118. (See SIDE TRIP C.) At about 613123 South Gorge Creek trail comes in from the right.

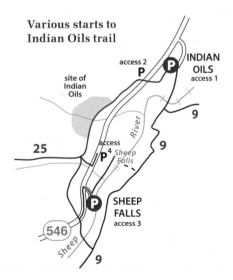

Various starts to Indian Oils trail

The west side of the second pass.
Bluerock Mountain in the background.

#25A The route follows the escarpment edge.

To Gorge Creek trail 3.1 km,
The trail climbs a little to a gap in the hills to the west—second pass—and crosses it. Just past the full-width viewpoint of Bluerock Mountain, the trail twists steeply down the shaley west flank to the Gorge Creek drainage. Beyond a drift fence cross a tributary that flows through gap no. 1 into Gorge Creek. As you'll see there are actually three such gaps separated by three conical hills covered in pines.

The trail heads left along a small ridge, then crosses a westerly fork of the same creek that arises from a large boggy meadow. It then cuts behind the first hill.

Cross a narrow cutline. The next descending cutline to right is a shortcut. Alternatively, keep left on official trail and at an unsigned T-junction turn sharp right. (Trail ahead is the shortcut to Bluerock Creek Trail. See SHORTCUT D.)

After the cutline comes in from the right, the trail passes through gap no. 2, keeping high above its creek. Eventually you cross the tributary, and a few metres later wade Gorge Creek to north bank meadows, where you intersect Gorge Creek trail at a signpost at 601141. (Often the wading can be avoided by heading upstream around the bend to where a fallen tree spans half the creek width.)

SIDE TRIPS

25A Escarpment

Unofficial trails, route
Distance 400 m from pass

This is a flat, easy walk to a southwest-facing escarpment. Bushwhackers can continue down the southeast ridge to Indian Oils trail at the 4-way junction.

Start from first pass. Head right (southeast) along a broad southeast ridge in the pines where you'll find a faint trail that continues on above an escarpment on the right (southwest) side of the ridge. Follow the edge curving left to the high point with cairn. The view has opened up a little more, and now includes Green Mountain, Mount Hoffmann and Bluerock Mountain.

Optional return 1.2 km

Descend the southeast ridge all the way. This entails heading farther east to where the crags peter out, then descending the steep grass slope below the high point. All is then straightforward through open forest until low down where another rockband cuts across the ridge. On a faint trail, again head left to the end of the band and step down steeply. The angle eases and you intercept Indian Oils trail just west of the 4-way junction.

25B Seasonal pond

Distance 200 m return
Height loss/gain 46 m (150 ft.)

A short side trip to a large meadow.

At the low point 615207 in the spruce, a cairn on the right (east) side indicates a 100-m-long trail heading straight to a large grassy basin where a grizzly killed a cow in 1980. You may be lucky enough to be there when the pond is full, concentric rings of vegetation showing the fluctuating water levels over the years. From the open ridge rimming the meadow to the east, you can see View Hill and the intriguing rocky knob poking up in the middle of the forest.

25C Hill 617118

Distance 360 m return
Height gain 60 m (200 ft.)
High Point 1875 m (6150 ft.)

A short, easy climb to the hilltop at 617118.

At 615115, where the trail passes between two hills, turn off right on a narrow trail that leads in a minute or two to the foot of a grassy slope. Climb the slope and at the top continue up the trail that leads through a few pines to the grassy summit nubbin—a very pleasant spot for whiling away the rest of the afternoon doing absolutely nothing. Peruse the view, perhaps, that encompasses Mount Burns, Bluerock Mtn, Mount Rose, Mount Ware and Surveyor's Ridge, Junction Mountain, Mount Hoffmann and Junction Lookout.

#25B The seasonal pond in the meadow.

#25C On top of Hill 617118. The view northwest to Bluerock Mountain, Mount Rose and Threepoint Mountain.

#25D Crossing the meadow in the west fork of Gorge Creek. In the background is Mount Ware. Ascent route follows the right skyline. #55 descends the open slope left of the summit.

SHORTCUT

25D Indian Oils to Bluerock–Gorge shortcut

Unofficial trail, route
Distance 1.9 km
Height gain E–W 67 m (220 ft.)
Height loss E–W 15 m (50 ft.)

This E–W route heads *behind* the three gaps and conical hills into the meadows of Gorge Creek's west fork where it connects with #28B, the Bluerock–Gorge shortcut. Think about using it if headed for Bluerock Creek trail going south. Not only does it avoid four crossings of Gorge Creek, it saves 2. 5 km in distance. "Great" you think. "I'll take it."

However, be aware the ground is a little sloppy near the start and some easy route-finding is needed.

EAST TO WEST

Leave Indian Oils where it turns sharp right into the second gap at 597133. Go straight on a pretty good trail.

Fairly soon the trail loses definition crossing a squelchy meadow. On the far side of the meadow you cross the second gap creek into a much larger meadow of bunchgrass. Where goes the trail? After the creek crossing, head rightward into the trees bordering the right side of the meadow, and there pick up the trail that continues westwards near the forest edge below the second hill.

Follow the slightly rising trail into the pine forest. At a junction go left. (Trail ahead leads into wet meadows behind hill no. 3, and while you can connect with the meadow of the west fork, why get your feet wet if they aren't already?)

The trail and its many variations stay in the trees, following the edge of the wet meadow around to the left. At 584138 it spits you out onto the dry meadow of the west fork. Ahead rises shapely Mount Ware with Little Ware to its right. This is a good place from which to view the various routes described on page 158.

Cross the meadow (no trail) in a NNW direction, in a belt of trees crossing the tiny west fork and then a dry ditch. Intersect #28B along the south edge of a big meadow at 583141.

Turn left for Bluerock Creek trail 1.3 km distant, or right for Gorge Creek trail at 1.2 km. Now read #28B Bluerock–Gorge shortcut.

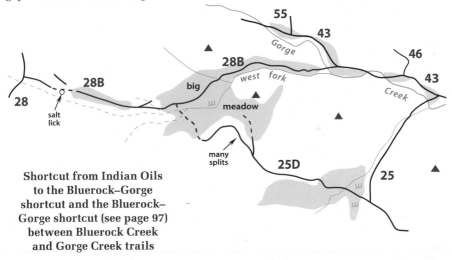

Shortcut from Indian Oils to the Bluerock–Gorge shortcut and the Bluerock–Gorge shortcut (see page 97) between Bluerock Creek and Gorge Creek trails

26 RIDGE 608091 from Bluerock Campground — map 3

Half-day hike
Unofficial trails
Distance 2.3 km return
Height gain 216 m (710 ft.)
High Point 1817 m (5960 ft.)
Map 82 J/10 Mount Rae

Access Hwy. 546 (Sheep River Trail) at Bluerock Campground. Keep left at the first junction, then park in a parking area on the right side adjoining a meadow. NOTE This section of Hwy. 546 is closed Dec 1–May 15.

The ridge with the big cliff above Bluerock Campground is an irresistible come-on for campers looking for something more exciting than the interpretive trail. Just don't try and scramble up the cliffs; some one got badly hurt here in 2009. All sensible people trog up the slope farther east, taking one of multiple trails leading upwards onto the east ridge.

Cross the meadow to the campground road on the other side. Find the trail starting behind site #18 in the forest. Shortly, it crosses a dry creekbed onto a rib to the right of a gully, This rib is followed all the way to the main east ridge: Through trees initially, then up steeper-angled grass, finishing on shale with bits of rock poking through it. Reach the forested east ridge where you intersect a good trail. Note your entry point carefully, otherwise you are sure to descend on another look alike piece of shale. Not that it matters; all developing trails lead down to the campground.

The ridge from the campground. Ascent routes follow the easier slopes at centre right.

Turn left and follow the trail up the ridge to the summit, a mini-rockband above a shale slope located at the apex of the east and northwest ridges. (The cairn atop the band is presently strewn.)

This is not the main viewpoint. For that, head downslope for about 20 vertical m to the bench above the big cliff. The prime view is to the west, looking through the narrows of the Sheep River Valley to Gibraltar and Mist Mountain.

The summit cairn, looking south to Shunga-la-she.

From here a trail heads right along the bench and joins the trail along the northwest ridge. Turn right to return to the summit area.

GOING FARTHER

26A The Knob

Day hike
Route
Distance one way from 608091, 2.1 km
Height gain add 198 m (650 ft.)
Height loss 30 m (100 ft.)
High point 1996 m (6550 ft.)

Because there is no trail, only experienced navigators should aim for the rocky knob at 593099. Poking up between forest ridges, it acts like a magnet when seen from afar.

The trail continues along the flat northwest ridge a way, then after intersecting the trail from the bench, gets bogged down in deadfall. Keep on to the col at 603093, where it's a good idea to mark a waypoint on your GPS for the return. Trust me.

From here it's easier to contour up left through open forest to gain ridge 597098. No need to go right to the summit. Just below is a band of orange shale that leads down to the next col below the knob—a far easier walk than picking your way among the rocks of the ridge crest.

Walk up the shale skirt of the knob to two rocky tops giving a step or two of easy scrambling. The view is expansive, taking in new views to the north and east—albeit low rounded hills covered in pines. The impressive view is south to the Junction Mountain massif. In front and looking lost among the bigger peaks is peak 619048, showing the north ridge route from the Sheep River.

Another place to play around on before turning around is the little rock ridge bordering a line of orange cliffs to the north. Going even farther over sprawling hill 588107 to connect with Bluerock Creek and Indian Oils trails is an interesting navigational exercise.

The Knob from the north, looking toward Junction Mountain. Photo Alf Skrastins

27 BLUEROCK CREEK Interpretive trail—map 3

One hour plus
Official trail
Distance 1.9 km return from hwy.
Height gain 91 m (300 ft.) from hwy.
High Point 168 m (5500 ft.)
Map 82 J/10 Mount Rae

Access Hwy. 546 (Sheep River Trail) at two places:
1. Just east of Bluerock Creek bridge, pull off the north side of the road onto the grass.
2. Bluerock Campground. From the far end turnaround point near site #30.
NOTE This section of Hwy. 546 is closed Dec 1–May 15.

A short easy loop along the northeast bank of Bluerock Creek canyon.

HISTORY NOTE The trail reaches an area first logged by John Lineham's crew at the beginning of the 20th century. A major fire in 1910 put an end to it and it wasn't until the 1940s that the loggers moved back in, specifically Napp Lefavre, not to salvage poles and posts from fire kill, but to cut a large swath of green timber that extends much farther west than the trail. Trees of less than 10 inches in diameter were left to grow into the big trees around you.

From start 1 climb steps up the right bank of Bluerock Creek to start 2 at the end of the campground road. Below you unseen the creek moves jerkily, pouring through chutes, then idling in potholes—well worth a closer look from start 1 before starting out up the steps.

From start 2 the trail and variations climb to an unsigned junction above the canyon. Go right on the upper leg.

Switchback uphill, then traverse a steep slope of shale, scree and scrub. Just past #3 interpretive sign, the trail descends through the logged area to the loop's low point (#4) with bench. From the sunny meadow is a view of mountain tops and a meadow down below that was the site of Lefavre's logging camp.

The return (lower) leg is the more scenic as it runs along the top of the canyon on a shaley slope. On reaching the junction with the upper leg, keep straight and return the way you came up.

GOING FARTHER
Up Bluerock Creek 1.1 km return
From the bench at #4, an unofficial trail descends the hill into the meadow where you can search the grass for rusty cans.

The trail carries on along the right bank of Bluerock Creek, eventually winding down to the river opposite some black crags and there ends within view of a steep shale bank.

The lower leg of the trail above the canyon.

28 BLUEROCK CREEK—maps 3 & 5

Kiska Mnoga iyarhe from the trail's high point.

Day hike
Equestrian
Official trail with signposts, red markers & cairns, creek crossing likely
Distance 11.2 km
Height gain 625 m (2050 ft.)
Height loss 472 m (1550 ft.)
High point 2134 m (7000 ft.)
Map 82 J/10 Mount Rae

Access Hwy. 546 (Sheep River Trail). NOTE This section of Hwy. 546 is closed Dec 1– May 15.
1. Shorter equestrian start Just west of Bluerock Creek bridge turn right and drive to the equestrian day parking lot.
2. Official, longer, hiker start Junction Creek day-use area. Use the upper loop parking lot.
Also accessible from #43 Gorge Creek trail at 576152, #28B Bluerock–Gorge shortcut at 594143, #9 Sheep trail east at the terminus and at the equestrian trail into Bluerock Creek equestrian campground.

This rather strenuous trail runs from the Sheep River at Bluerock and Junction creeks to the middle reach of Gorge Creek. Few hikers make it to Gorge Creek, let alone do a whopping loop with Gorge Creek trail, Indian Oils trail plus the highway.) Most aim for the trail's high point—the stunning alpine meadows on the southeast ridge of Bluerock Mountain. About half the hikers still don't make it this far. So for all you frustrated people longing for a view, I present the meadow at 580105 which is written up under #28A.

Very fit scramblers use this trail to access the southeast ridge of Bluerock Mountain (see #29).

TRAIL NOTE Know that the bridge over Bluerock Creek, continually pushed aside by spring floods, may soon be removed permanently.

ACCESS NOTE For law-abiding hikers starting from access 2, this already long trail is even longer. Consequently, many hikers use access 1 and hope not to get a ticking off by an unsympathetic campground operator. Your choice.

Presently, campers at Bluerock must get in their cars and drive to the trailheads. Unless, of course, you are willing to add on even more kilometres to an already long trail by walking down the steps of the interpretive trail to the highway, and walking along the highway and then the access trail to the equestrian trailhead.

FUTURE TRAIL NOTE A third-best option as shown in the Sheep River management plan calls for a hiker-only trail along the northeast bank that connects Bluerock Creek interpretive trail to Bluerock Creek trail above the big hill. Good things about this route: no mud, no extraneous descent, no crossing of Bluerock Creek, a gradual climb. While a preliminary line has been worked out, the problem is where do day hikers park? Right now there is space for only a few cars at the bottom of the interpretive trail.

HISTORY NOTE Logging roads in the area come courtesy of Napp Lefavre. Umpteen years ago we found a dump of china cups and plates just off the trail, but they seem to have disappeared in the interim.

There are two official starts.

1. Equestrian access 160 m

If starting from the parking lot, follow the trail by the side of the horse ramp onto an old logging road (also called Sheep horse trail at this point) and turn left.

If you've been turfed out of the parking lot and have parked back on the highway, rather than walk up the access road, there is an equestrian trail available (add 290 m). Connecting Sheep trail with Bluerock equestrian campground, it crosses the highway a little to the east of the access road. Plod straight up the bank, ignoring the old highway circling around to the right and crossing the trail higher up. After a straight, you cross the equestrian campground access road (campground to right, day parking lot to left). Then cross the access road to the corral where Bluerock Creek trail officially starts. Soon after, the trail comes in from the day parking lot on the left.

The next section of logging road climbs gently, curving left then right to the unsigned junction with access 2 on your left. Keep straight on the road.

2. Hiker access 630 m

From the far end of the upper loop road, a trail leaves behind the biffy and heads east to a junction. To right is the Junction Creek interpretive trail. You keep left, winding about pine forest, up over a low ridge and across a small creek, finally climbing to a T-junction with Bluerock Creek trail about 500 m from the Bluerock Creek equestrian trailhead. At last check, this junction was not signed.

To Whiskey Lake turnoff 480 m

The logging road dips to cross the effluence from Whiskey Lake, then passes one good trail and two grassy tracks on the right leading to Napp Lefavre's sawmill

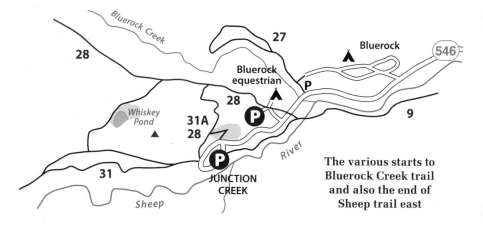

The various starts to
Bluerock Creek trail
and also the end of
Sheep trail east

site on the banks of Bluerock Creek. Come to the signposted junction where #31A Sheep horse trail turns left. Go straight.

To Bluerock Creek crossing 2.3 km
What follows is an uninteresting section on logging road that climbs fairly gradually through gloomy spruce forest into the confines of Bluerock Creek Valley.

After crossing a small meadow (sawmill site) with picnic table available for collapse on the return trip, the road narrows to trail width and at the top of a hill turns sharp right and downhill. (The logging road ahead becomes hopelessly overgrown and ends soon anyway, with game trails splintering off down to the creek.)

The zigzagging descent to Bluerock Creek is a wallow after rain. Reaching the creek you wash the mud off your boots and grumble about losing 100 m of altitude and having to backtrack at the same time, both no-no's in the school of advanced trail building. Likely you'll have to paddle to the northeast bank.

Approaching the shale traverse at the top of the big hill. Top ahead is 580105, the alternative objective #28A. Route 2 climbs the ridge directly ahead.

The big hill 1.2 km
Up next is a long, relentless climb, starting with a zigzagging ascent up the left flank of a side valley. The trail then turns left and climbs a ridge. The hard work ends at the shale traverse below a little summit that is ALTERNATIVE OBJECTIVE A. The cairn at the start of the traverse signifies the emergence of a future trail from the interpretive trail. This is where many hikers running out of time call it a day.

To high point 2.8 km
Back in trees, head slightly downhill through mud to a side creek with occasional water. The faint trail to right is A's route 1.

The short, steep rise following gains you the main south ridge of Bluerock Mountain, which is broad and pine-covered. For a while the going is flat and pleasant. Then you're into a set of even steeper zigs up a flowery glade. Push through a few pines at the top and emerge into meadows below *Kiska Mnoga iyarhe* (meaning Ram Mountain) — the gable end of Bluerock Mountain's south ridge, and the payoff for kilometres of exasperating trail.

This is a beautiful place with meadows that fall away into Bluerock Creek, the rarely visited upper valley revealing some of its secrets from this vantage point. The trail's high point is marked by a horse rail and bench.

To Bluerock–Gorge shortcut 2.7 km

Too short in the alpine, the trail swings over to the east side of the ridge and zigs down in a dark forest of spruce and fir. Reach a side creek and follow it down a way. The trail then sets a northerly course across the skirts of Bluerock's east face, crossing dry, stony creekbeds and bits of meadow. Apart from one glimpse of Mount Ware, views are non-existent. Nevertheless, the going is quite pleasant and fast. Disregard a side trail to right and carry on to the unsigned T-junction at 572141. This is where SHORTCUT B to Gorge Creek, which is also the shortcut to Indian Oils trail, takes off to the right.

Bluerock Creek trail on the descent to Gorge Creek. Ahead is the western outlier of Mount Ware.

To Gorge Creek 1.1 km

Keep left (red marker). After a slight rise it's nearly all downhill through pine forest, grassy avenues on the final descent allowing views of Mount Ware's western outlier. Reach the T-junction with Gorge Creek trail at 576152.

ALTERNATIVE OBJECTIVE

28A Top 580105

Route
Distance 400 m via 2.
Height gain 107 m (350 ft.)
High point 2027 m (6650 ft.)

For people unable to reach the alpine meadows, the perfect alternative is this little hilltop with its pocket meadow tilted southwest toward the afternoon sun.

Follow Bluerock Creek trail to the start of the shale traverse. There are two ascent routes that can be used to make a loop.

1. Easy. Continue on Bluerock Creek trail to the muddy side creek. Here a trail starts off up the right bank in the trees, eventually emerging into the lower end of the meadow. Walk up to the cairn at the edge of the little eastern escarpment.

2. Harder. Climb straight up the ridge on shale at the tree edge. At the rockband go right in trees or scramble up the right side. Make your way back left to a shale bench below the upper step. Climb shale to a grassy gangway at the right end of the rocks, then walk easy ridge to the cairn.

Look north along the meadow to Bluerock Mountain and the headwaters of Bluerock Creek from where a wall of unnamed summits extends south to the Sheep River Valley. Across the valley rise Shunga-la-she and Junction Mountain. Close by, but separated by hours of bushwhacking, is the curious rocky knob 593099, which is best reached via #26A.

#28A The summit meadow limber pine. Looking northwest up Bluerock Creek to Bluerock Mtn.

SHORTCUT

28B Bluerock–Gorge shortcut

Unofficial trail, creek crossing
Distance 2.5 km
Height loss W–E 146 m (480 ft.)

The trail along the west fork of Gorge Creek is quite well used, as it cuts off a corner for anyone travelling east on Gorge Creek trail or connecting with Indian Oils trail. In fact, the eastern half was once the main Gorge Creek trail that ended at a range rider's cabin in the big meadow. See the sketch map on page 89.

At unsigned T-junction 572141 turn right (east), following a narrow trail to the left of a dry, stony creekbed. Around a salt lick the trail is vague. Stay on the same line. (If walking the trail in the opposite direction do NOT follow a cattle trail up a wooded hill.) Walk through a long meadow, then a small round meadow with a lone pine. In trees keep straight (don't cross a dike) and enter the big meadow with a view of Mount Ware. Bit trails to the right around 583141 indicate the turnoff place for Indian Oils shortcut. Read #25D.

#28B Heading E–W toward Bluerock Mtn.

After a side creek crossing, the trail runs alongside the west fork and below a low ridge to the main Gorge Creek Valley. Paddle Gorge Creek to an intersection with Gorge Creek trail at 594143.

97

29 BLUEROCK MOUNTAIN via southeast ridge — maps 3 & 5

Long-day scramble
**Distance 3.4 km from Bluerock Creek
trail, 10.8 km from trailhead**
**Height gain 716 m (2350 ft.) from
Bluerock Creek trail, 1326 m (4350 ft.)
from trailhead**
High point 2789 m (9150 ft.)
Map 82 J/10 Mount Rae

Access Via #28 Bluerock Creek trail at the high point.

The long southeast ridge of Bluerock is the skyline ridge of the mountain's most prominent characteristic: the furrowed eastern escarpment.

In the third edition I stated firmly that "this ridge is not for the walker–scrambler." Not so, said Julie Muller of Millarville; there is a reasonable way up the formidable-looking second step, and she sent photos to prove it. Nevertheless, it's a challenging ridgewalk offering "a good balance of fun, excitement and suffering," to quote scrambler Sonny Bou. While there is little exposure, expect one section of hands-on scrambling up the second step. And because of its length, you do need to move fast and keep an eye on the time.

Logistics are a problem. Climbing this ridge on top of Bluerock Creek trail dictates a dawn start from the trailhead (that's the suffering part). Consider walking in the evening before and bivvying at the high point of the trail. Either way, lots of water needs to be carried up from Bluerock Creek.

Optional returns are A via upper Bluerock Creek, or #45 via the north slope,

*Bluerock Mountain from Mount Hoffmann,
showing the southeast ridge rising from
left to right over three tops to the summit.*

for which you WILL need to camp or bivvy at some point.

First step, Kiska Mnoga iyarhe

From below, Kiska Mnoga iyarhe looks a bit daunting. (See the photo on page 93.) Up close, it's not half as steep as it looks and the scree is firm.

Head up a grassy runnel onto orange scree. Go right of the first small crag, then climb diagonally up right to a line of broken outcrops. Break through by going right, to the edge of a small gully and up the left edge of it. The final slope is a mix of scree and broken attached rock rimmed by a rockband that offers a few metres of easy scrambling. On topping out, you discover the other side is a gentle scree slope.

Second step

The second step — a huge prow of rock — looks totally impossible. However, there is a chink in the armour, and that's a gully in the corner where the great cliff turns southwest.

Wander toward the prow on the broad scree ridge that gradually steepens. Climb the first cone of scree, then traverse left on a trail below the cliff. Crossing the outcrop partway along requires a few careful steps, as does getting to the gully in the corner.

The gully is narrow, its scree bed punctuated by rock steps. First up is the crux, a slightly awkward overhang requiring brute strength or a shove up if you're 5 ft 4 or smaller. Alternatively, climb the delicate wall to the right. This is followed by two much easier steps to the gully top. Note the cairn on the left side. Turn right and grovel up the usual scree and slab to regain the ridge at another cairn.

Third step, the south top

The ridge is straightforward over two small rises to the foot of the third step that is 152 m (500 ft.) high. A faint trail leads up the initial hump. Then, below a craggy mass, you traverse left along a scree ledge to a cave. Just beyond the cave the ledge gives out, leaving you to toil upwards via a slab and tiring scree runnels. High up, it's easier to wend right a bit before finishing with a scree traverse heading left.

Below the second step. Starting the traverse to the bottom of the gully (red arrow) at left.

Looking toward the third step. Note the cave. Behind rises the summit of Bluerock.

To the summit

Walk down to a col. The fourth step is straightforward scree. At the top, the ridge narrows and turns right—keep left of a rock fin—to the summit cairn.

Naturally, from such a prominent peak Mount Assiniboine and the Royal Group can be seen off in the distance above a welter of lower peaks. Just as interesting is the view east—Bluerock looms over everything—and so you look down upon countless foothills traversed by a large portion of the trails described in this book.

OPTIONAL RETURN

29A Upper Bluerock Creek

Getting off the mountain is fast and easy. The rest, not so much!

Backtrack to the col between the top and the south summit. Turn right and descend a gentle slope of stones, gravel and dryas into a north fork of Bluerock Creek (water). Stay on the left-hand slope and cut off the corner where the creek turns south. On reaching a side ridge above a gully-like side creek, descend the ridge to meadow with dead standing trees and grizzly digs. Cross the main fork that rises below Mount Burns just uphill of the confluence with the side creek (rock step below), then descend to the main creekbed, which at this point is flat with willow bushes.

Looking back along the summit ridge to the fin. In the background is the south summit.

It may be that you can follow the creekbed all the way out without too many nasty surprises. I have never tried, so I can only describe the return to Bluerock Creek trail. Cross to the left bank, climb up it to a sloping terrace and turn right following a faint game trail that can be traced across forest and scree ribbons. A deeper dip to cross the side creek between the prow and Kiska Mnoga iyarhe requires you find the trail. Shortly after, start heading uphill and right near the bottom of scree slopes to gain the meadows near the high point. Another option is to keep on traversing and intersect the trail much lower down. Have fun. The terrain is far more complex than it appears on the map.

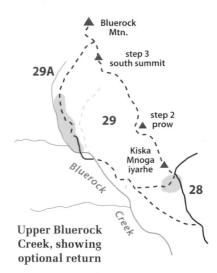

Upper Bluerock Creek, showing optional return

30 JUNCTION CREEK — map 3

*The upper main valley under the Dogtooths. The
trail heads into the side valley at right.*

Day, long-day hikes, bike 'n' hike,
backpack
Unofficial trails & routes, major river
crossing, creek crossings
Map 82 J/10 Mount Rae

Access Hwy. 546 (Sheep River Trail) at Junction Creek day-use area. Use one of the lower parking lots. NOTE This section of Hwy. 546 is closed Dec 1–May 15.
Also accessible from Picklejar Lakes (Volume 5).

Junction Creek flows noisily through a dark, spruce- and fir-filled valley with numerous side valleys branching off to east and west. It's unusual in that it's completely enclosed by peaks of the Highwood Range that bar easy escape to the outside. Numerous waterfalls and swim holes make it the perfect destination on hot summer days.

The main valley is served by a logging road and good trail shared with hunters and equestrians; side valley trails are very rough and best avoided by inexperienced hikers. And while trips can be done in one day, I recommend camping at Junction Lake or Waterfall Valley junctions and taking time to explore the options.

NOTE Going anywhere is dependent on being able to wade the Sheep River right at the start! Try from midsummer on.

HISTORY NOTE In the late 1880s the lower valley was logged by John Lineham's lumber company, the logs floated down Junction Creek by means of tumbling dams, one of which you'll spot from the logging road. The first person to venture farther into the valley was A.O. Wheeler on September 3, 1896. (As was usual, he got back to camp at dark.) Perhaps the most notable visitor since these times has been R.M. Patterson, who rode to the valley head in September 1944, two years before he left the Rockies for good.

30A Main valley trail

Unofficial trail, creek crossings
Distance 11.5 km
Height gain 549 m (1800 ft.)
High point 2124 m (6970 ft.)

This is the main thoroughfare from which all other trails branch off. The forest trail is more interesting than you might think,

The beautiful three-tier waterfall near the camping area. Photo Allan & Angélique Mandel

particularly where it nears the river and crosses lively tributaries with many rapids and waterfalls to delight in, including the greatest swim hole this side of the Pacific Ocean. Bikeable to the sawmill site when dry.

To Junction Lake junction 4 km
From the middle of the lower parking lots a trail makes a beeline past the interpretive sign for the Sheep River. Wade across.

On the south bank follow the logging road, a stretch of historic corduroy requiring concentration from bikers. Don't bother with the odd detour made by equestrians, except where it sidesteps the odd deadfall. At one point you draw close to Junction Creek and view the remains of a tumbling dam built to ease the passage of logs over rapids between the sawmill and the Sheep where logs were further jockeyed along the river to the mill in Okotoks.

Enter the sawmill site at 3.5 km. As you stand there, slowly sinking up to the ankles in sawdust, look up right to the cliff. In 1918, R.B. Spackmann noted a cave "about 12 m in diameter and about 13 m up from the talus." In fact, there are several intriguing holes on the lower slopes of Shunga-la-she.

A trail continues into the trees. Close to Junction Lake turnoff go straight. (Side trail to left leads to a three-log-high enclosure, the flat ground alongside a popular camping spot. This is the turnoff for East Fork Tarn and Peak 619048. See E and F.)

Come to the first tributary to the west at 604044. Go straight and cross the lively creek between waterfalls. (A trail to right along the near north bank is B to Junction Lake.) Interestingly, both east and west side creeks join Junction Creek diametrically opposite each other.

To Waterfall Valley junction 2.9 km
The next section of trail follows a high bank, then drops to crunchy gravel bars. Again you climb high and on the following traverse run into quickmud where springs tend to puddle below high dirt banks.

Shortly after this, the trail turns right up the second side creek to the west, en route passing camping sites.

At a T-junction at 2.5 km, detour upstream to a lovely three-tier waterfall which must surely be a sight at runoff if one can only figure out a way to cross the Sheep River. The trail beyond the viewpoint IS NOT the route up Waterfall Valley.

Return to the T-junction and turn right. Cross the waterfall creek above a waterfall, then climb sharply to a junction with cairn. Keep straight. (Trail to right is C to Waterfall Valley.)

To Junction Mountain cirque 1.6 km
Descend to Junction Creek at the swim hole—a magnificent piece of river architecture that starts higher up where a small fall pours into a deep circular jacuzzi. Separating that pool from the swim hole downstream is a wide, flat underwater shelf, ideal for lying around on while wearing a full body neoprene wetsuit. There's even a lower ledge for deeper sitting.

Having fun in the swim hole.
Photo Clayton Ditzler

If going farther, wade Junction Creek below the swim hole and climb steadily up the east slope out of earshot of the river. The trail drops to cross the creek issuing out of the second side valley to the east (usually dry), then climbs its south bank to a high point and T-junction. Turn right. (Trail ahead is D to Junction Mountain's east cirque.)

Valley head 3 km
Drop back down to Junction Creek where a side trail crosses the river to a hunter's camping spot. The main trail stays on the east bank a little longer, then crosses above the third side creek to the west.

Above the trees rises a spectacular cliff which is replaced by an equally spectacular cliff as you press on south across the dry creekbed of the fourth side creek to the west. The excitement mounts as you catch a glimpse of the Dogtooth Mountains between the trees. The valley is curving around to the southeast, but not the trail. Unexpectedly, it turns right and climbs to the lip of a cirque at 614976, a flat meadow locked below an impenetrable headwall at the foot of the Dogtooths. Across the valley is Pyriform Mountain, whose orange scree slopes appear from this direction to offer a straightforward slog to the summit ridge.

Junction Lake on a July long weekend.
Photo Alf Skrastins

30B Junction Lake

Unofficial trail & route
Distance from A 4.9 km
Height gain 503 m (1650 ft.) from A
High point 2210 m (7250 ft.)

While the lake at the head of this long valley is not always full—it's an underground seeper—it's the journey that's so enjoyable: the lush green meadows and the lively stream.

Turn right up the first big side stream flowing out of the west at 604044.

By late August, Junction Lake diminishes to two tarns. Photo Alf Skrastins

A well-used trail runs along the north bank above a little canyon whose creekbed offers interesting problematical steps for those with time to play around in it. Sooner or later, though, you descend to creek level above the canyon and, following the right bank mainly, climb past a procession of small waterfalls.

Slow progress ends at the point where the creek turns southwest, level with a cirque to right at 586038. Here, a deeper rift not apparent from the topo map forces the trail up to the bench on the north side of the valley. Once you've gained the height, it's fast, easy walking for many kilometres through spruce forest and lush green meadows.

The gradient steepens as you near the lake and the terrain becomes more barren; less trees, lots of grass still, but also scree. Before the creekbed steepens, cross to the left bank at the obvious place and follow bit trails to the grassy basin enclosing the lake.

Early in the hiking season water spills over the lip of the basin and tumbles down the rocky creekbed in a waterfall. Unfortunately, the lake is not always full to the brim, and after the snowbanks have melted, underground seepage reduces the lake to two shallow tarns rimmed with mud and stones.

But whatever state the lake is in, you can't deny its dramatic situation in a basin ringed by high nameless mountains. The peak to the south with the precipitous north face is the highest in the Highwood Range—higher even than Mount Head—and officially nameless. When climbed by 11,000ers guru Don Forest in 1996, he wrote a note calling it Mount Peggy after his wife and slipped it into the film canister register in the cairn. He never told his family about it, nor, strangely, did he make a note of climbing this "horribly loose" peak in his calendar book. The note was discovered by Allan Schierman the same year, but only came to light years after Don's biography, including his climbing lists, was published in 2003.

30C Waterfall Valley

Unofficial trails, route
Distance to lakes from A 4.6 km
Height gain 606 m (1890 ft.) from A
Height loss to lakes 226 m (740 ft.)
High point 2405 m (7890 ft.) at col

This valley leads to the one break in the mountains enclosing Junction Creek. This is not the same as saying the route over to Picklejar Lakes is a doddle. This is a rugged hike with steep scree on the south side of the col. The name comes from the three-tier waterfall that identifies the valley from Junction Creek trail.

NOTE This is NOT the trail climbing up the right bank of the waterfall.

To Col 579992, 4.2 km
At the cairn on the main valley trail at 6.9 km, turn right onto a narrower trail that is blazed both sides. To get above the big waterfall step, the trail makes a few preliminary windings, then zigs up the steepest slope you'll encounter on the whole ascent. This is followed by a gently rising traverse through forest and across a stony avalanche gully to the banktop above the creek.

The trail is faint as it rounds the base of a grassy ridge in trees and descends slightly into the creekbed. Rather than follow the bed (possibly dry at this point), climb back up the left bank and on trail traverse scree to a side creek. Cross and continue on trail through meadows beneath a spectacular rock buttress. Cross another tributary, then climb a grassy ramp to the left of waterfalls into a basin.

Cross the basin (meadow, larch, spruce), aiming for the "obvious scree col" ahead. But after slogging up scree, nowadays made easier by a diagonal right to left trail, all you find yourself in is another basin, this one lacking the loveliness of the lower one, just minimal grass and shale.

Below a rock glacier sweeping down from Peak 571002, steer for the lowest gap

Top: The valley midsection. The route follows the obvious ramp to the left of the creek into the first basin. Photo Alf Skrastins

Bottom: In the upper basin, headed for the col. Photo Alf Skrastins

in the rim, at 579992 to the left of the rocky knob. Down below is a beautiful sight: two of the Picklejar Lakes glittering in the afternoon sun. If not going on, climb higher up the rim wall for even better views of all the lakes.

To Picklejar Lakes 410 m
Descend a worn yellow scree runnel for about 100 vertical m (330 vertical ft.). The going is steep but straightforward, with no hidden crags. Lower down, cross mounds of scree, heading for the nearby north shore of fourth lake from where you can cut across to Third Lake (the big blue one). You'll find a trail running along its north shore that will take you out past the other two lakes to Hwy. 40. (See Volume 5.)

Top left: #30C Third and fourth Picklejar Lakes from the col above the descent gully. Photo Alf Skrastins

Top right: #30C Descending the gully to Picklejar Lakes. Photo Alf Skrastins

30D East Cirque

Unofficial trail, route
Distance from junction 2.8 km
Height gain 274 m (900 ft.)
High point 2225 m (7300 ft.)

A trail gets you started into the cirque southwest of Junction Mountain. Carry water up from Junction Creek.

At the junction go straight on a trail that continues climbing up the south bank of the side creek, ultimately petering out in clearings below the mountain wall. Come up here for the view of the Dogtooth Mountains at the head of the valley, their strata revealed more boldly by sun.

Changing direction, head northeast across the two heads of the creek into the cirque. The timberline spruce are particularly beautiful, but the cirque is arid; just strips of dryas. You were expecting flower meadows? At its head, Junction Mountain is an unappealing mess of steep scree half smothering slabs and cliff bands. Andrew Nugara toots it as an optional descent route off the summit for experienced scramblers.

#30D East cirque, looking toward Junction Mountain.

30E East Fork Tarn

The grassy bench. Tarn is located in the hidden valley to right. The hiker–scrambler route up Junction Mtn. (centre) follows the scree ridge to the shoulder at centre, traverses left on an unseen bench, then climbs steep scree to the col from where it's an easy plod to the summit.

Route
Distance to tarn 4.3 km
Height gain 506 m (1660 ft.) from A
High point 2198 m (7210 ft.)

This is the only side valley with no trail. The tarn under Junction Mountain at 627031 tends to be seasonal, so go mainly for the scenery or to access Peak 619048 or Junction Mountain from the north. Water flows intermittently but is always available at 630031.

From the log structure just before Junction Lake turnoff head down to Junction Creek and wade downstream of the forks. Upstream is a cataract.

Turn left into the east fork valley. Initially follow the south bank dryas flat past a camping area, then cross to the north bank where the going is easy through trees and across a side slope to avoid a mini-canyon. Eventually, you're forced into the stony creekbed for a long stint of rockhopping. En route note the exciting entrance to the side valley at right.

Easy progress ends at the second side gully to left at 621043. Its right-hand bank is the start/finish of the direct route up Peak 619048.

Here the main creekbed turns right, squeezed in with bigger boulders and overhanging bush. Initially use trees on the right side. Then scree. The bed widens between high side slopes preceding the undercut rockband blocking the way ahead. Climb the grassy left-hand slope onto a forested bench, turn right and regain the creekbed above the impasse.

Continue easily to just before a right-hand bend, where it's an easy climb up right on open slopes to a bench. Follow it south through trees to the grass beyond. Ahead is a barren landscape of scree slopes culminating in Junction Mountain.

Before hitting scree, cross to the left bank at the descending rib and continue south on grass. At 630031 recross the creek at a game crossing with water, and head up-slope (west) to a rounded ridge overlooking a hidden valley with tarn. The upper tarn as shown on the topo map is mud and damp grass.

GOING HIGHER

30F Peak 619048

Scramble route
Distance 19.7 km return to trailhead via Junction Creek, 16.5+ km via north ridge
Height gain 274 m (900 ft.) from 630031, 405 m (1330 ft.) from 621043
High point 2280 m (7480 ft.)

For experienced scramblers, Peak 619048 is merely the prelude to the exceedingly long north ridge route up Junction Mountain (rated difficult by Andrew "More Scrambles" Nugara). For hikers who can hack steep scree and easy scrambling it is a worthwhile objective in its own right. And not necessarily via its north ridge that involves much bushwhacking.

I prefer to ascend the peak from the east fork, combining a visit to the tarn with a ridge walk, an ascent of the peak and a fast return to the creekbed. If you want to miss out the tarn, ascend by the descent route.

FROM CREEK CROSSING 630031
South ridge to the summit 3.1 km
Having refilled the water bottle, head back north along the grassy bench above the creek, there picking up a trail that climbs gradually across scree at last trees and around a corner into a scoop. Climb the scoop to the north ridge of Junction, with the option of traversing left near the top to miss out one bump. Walk south over three more bumps, where necessary taking to the forested east slope to avoid ridgecrest rocks. (At 629045 you can descend a side ridge into Dyson Creek Valley, should you find a reason to do so.)

While Peak 619048 remains an uneasy sight ahead—those rockbands!—the view behind you of Junction's north ridge and the east fork is stunning. You'll be taking lots of pics. Farther to the left you can spot Junction Lookout.

Arrive at the col below your peak. As mentioned, the ridge above has two rockbands precluding direct access unless you're a climber. Miss them both out by traversing the east face on a sketchy game trail in shale and scree. Above you is a horizontal rockband. At a breakdown, head up and scramble through it onto a steep scree slope leading to the summit ridge. Turn left to gain the high point at a very small cairn.

Peak 619048 from the easy approach ridge.

Descent 1.8 km

Head north along the summit ridge a short way to where you can descend the first scree ridge to the right. Low down pick up the traversing game trail and follow it back right back to the col.

The slope down to the east fork is only moderately steep. Initially head diagonally left on a game trail. Then descend a treed spur, hopefully on the left side of a gully that can be followed all the way down. Aim for 621043.

OPTIONAL DESCENT

The North Ridge ~4.8 km or ~5.4 km

Following the North Ridge to the Sheep River seems an attractive option but can have an unhappy ending.

Follow the stony summit ridge north—one down-step in the middle—and off the end. Arriving above the rockband, scramble down right in the trees where the band is more broken, then bypass two rocky knobs by descending grass to their right. Deke around the bottom of the second one back onto the ridge and follow it down to a col in the trees.

Walk up a gentle slope to a grassy bump. Turn left and follow a meadow strip down and up onto hill 613066, which is a fabulous viewpoint for Peak 619048 and the overhanging profile of Gibraltar.

Descend the northwest-trending ridge—careful route-finding needed—to the saddle at 609071 below a large area of shale. The final drop to the Sheep River can be a doozy in the deadfall department. You may miss the worst of it or you may not and night will fall and your headlamp won't work and you must wade the Sheep in complete blackness. I DO KNOW that the ridge to the east of the side creek is relatively free of the stuff.

On flat ground hit a bisecting game trail. You can either follow it leftwards and when it starts heading south cut across to Junction Creek near the confluence. Or you can cut across country to reach Sheep trail at the river crossing opposite Bluerock Creek. Then return via Sheep trail.

Top: The summit ridge looking north.

Bottom: The north ridge of the peak from Hill 613066, showing the rockband and the two rocky knobs that are bypassed on the left side.

31 SHEEP TRAIL WEST—maps 3 & 4

Long-day hike, backpack, bike 'n' hike
Official trail with signposts & red markers, river crossings
Total distance 21.6 km
High point 2118 m (6950 ft.)
Map 82 J/10 Mount Rae

Highway access Hwy. 546 (Sheep River Trail) at terminus of highway at Junction Creek day-use area. NOTE This section of Hwy. 546 is closed Dec 1–May 15.
Western access Big Elbow trail at 428154 (Volume 2).
Also accessible via #39 Rickert's Pass and Burns Lake from Arethusa Cirque (Volume 5).

This is a long-distance trail that had its beginning at Sandy McNabb Recreation Area on the eastern fringe of the foothills. This western section follows the Sheep River Valley from Junction Creek day-use area through some spectacular Front Range scenery over the Elbow–Sheep watershed to Big Elbow trail in the Elbow River valley. Near the end on you can choose

Near the high point, looking south to the north peak of the Rae Creek Hills. Photo Alf Skrastins

from a number of finishes depending on where you are going next. See OPTIONAL ENDING C and #33, which describes the watershed trails with a sketch map. Only one crossing of the Sheep River is bridged. The rest you wade.

This trail is also the basis for a whole raft of interesting trips: see #32 through to #41. Scramblers use it to access the east peak of Mount Burns, Gibraltar Mountain and Cougar Mountain via its west ridge.

CAMPING NOTE Part of the route runs through private land owned by the Burns Foundation. Sadly, after generations of happy co-existence with recreationists, the foundation is suddenly making noises. For now, no camping is allowed on their property and Denning's Cabin is locked.

HISTORY NOTE The basis for the trail is a coal mine access road still maintained by Alberta Transportation to Burns Mine (now closed), then a fire road that we used to drive. Read SIDE TRIP B and #39.

Junction Creek to Burns Mine
Distance 9.6 km
Height gain 168 m (550 ft.)
Height loss 46 m (150 ft.)
High point 1798 m (5,900 ft.)

Highway access at Junction Creek.
Also accessible from Mist Creek (Volume 5) via #39 Rickert's Pass, and via #31A Sheep horse trail from #28 Bluerock Creek trail.

The section on undulating mine access road features three river crossings, one of which is bridged. The scenery is magnificent, dominated by Gibraltar, whose powerful presence is useful to measure your progress by. En route, trails spin off to Cliff Creek, Gibraltar Pass and Rickert's Pass.

To the Burns bridge 3.4 km
The ongoing route (gated mine road) starts from the end of the upper loop road and is really a continuation of Hwy. 546.

Climb a stony hill and keep left. (The right-hand track is OPTION LOOP A.) From the high bench is a view of Peak 619048 and Junction Creek Valley. A little farther on Sheep horse trail comes in from the right via Whiskey Pond. Almost straightaway a horse trail alternative takes off from the left side of the road at red markers and is well worth taking. Not only does it cut out an extraneous hill, it is also downhill and gives you a chance to see what the river is up to. Such is the lure of noisy rapids.

Back on the fire road, you enter the narrows between Shunga-la-she on the left and an unnamed ridge on the right that displays a small arch not far above treeline at 578078. Up ahead are increasingly dramatic views of Gibraltar, called "Sheer Cliff" by George Dawson and party when first seen from the west in 1884. In 1896 and on it was traditionally known as "Big Rock," (courtesy of A.O. Wheeler), so predating by 100 years the name of Alberta's most popular brewery that was named after the Okotoks rock.

Arrive at the bridge over the Sheep River, this third version a tame affair you can bike across. The original bridge called Brown's Bridge, nearer the water, was superseded by a bridge built by the Pat Burns Coal Company, which, before K Country nailed down a few more planks, was auditioned for an Indiana Jones movie. Even after improvements there were crash barriers and posts warning of "Danger" at each end of the bridge.

To Cliff Creek trail 1 km
A steep uphill introduces the undulating stretch along the sunless south bank. The second side creek you cross is Cliff Creek, a boisterous stream that has to be waded. A few metres on, the Cliff Creek trail takes off from the left bank. (See #41.)

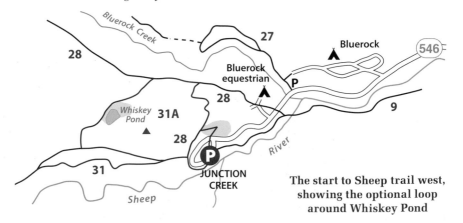

The start to Sheep trail west, showing the optional loop around Whiskey Pond

OPTION LOOP

Whiskey Lake backdropped by Shunga-la-she.

31A Whiskey Lake loop

Half-day hike
Official, unofficial trails
Distance loop 3.7 km
Height gain/loss 61 m (200 ft.)

Hikers would be crazy to use Sheep horse trail as an alternative start to the regular Sheep trail west; it starts from Bluerock equestrian campground, for one thing. However, it can be combined with Junction Creek interpretive trail and Bluerock Creek trail to make a half-day loop from Junction Creek day-use area around Whiskey Lake. See the sketch map on the previous page.

Junction Creek interpretive trail.

Start from the lower loop road. From the middle lot head out on trail toward the Sheep River. In a minute turn left at an interpretive sign re log drives. Keep left and cross both the lower and upper loop roads. Climb a grassy bank, at the top turning left to a slew of interpretive signs about lumber boss John Lineham, who had numerous mountains, ridges and creeks named after him.

At a T-junction turn right onto Bluerock Creek hiker's trail and wander along to an intersection with a logging road which is Bluerock Creek trail AND Sheep horse trail. Turn left. At the next T-junction turn left on Sheep horse trail. (Logging road ahead is Bluerock Creek trail.)

After a stint through spruce forest you arrive at Whiskey Lake, as named by Lineham. Its grassy surround is a very pleasant spot from which to view the peak Shunga-la-she, a beautiful-sounding name meaning "the mountain white man shit on," according to Rob Z, who used to man the Bighorn ranger station eons ago.

Continue straight on the trail that descends to a T-junction and turns left. (Trail to right joins Sheep trail west heading west.) You eventually joins Sheep trail above the last hill down to the upper parking lot. Beyond the gate turn right onto a trail that follows the perimeter of the road around to your starting point.

Gibraltar from above the Burns Bridge.

To Burns Mine 5.3 km

The south bank section ends with ford no. 1 of the Sheep River under the looming presence of Gibraltar.

Climb a long stony hill onto the north bank bench. This is the perfect place from which to view the overhanging north face of the mountain, in the afternoon glowing yellow from reflected sunlight off the bright rocks of the ridge opposite. In 1971 this was the scene of an incredible nine-day climb by Jim White and Billy Davidson—the first-ever extended aid climb in the Canadian Rockies. To its right is the more conventionally built Gibraltar Mountain, as marked on the topo map. In 1918 four mine workers climbed to the top the easy way and were peering over the drop when the youngest lad—a nephew of Okotoks postmaster George Patterson—slipped and fell down the face. It's sobering to realize his body is still up there somewhere.

But back to the road. After a detour to avoid a collapsed bridge over a side creek—single log remaining for tightrope walkers—the going becomes easy. The valley floor is widening and the mountains falling back, letting in the sun. Ahead are new views of Mount Rae and Storm Ridge.

Enter private land at the warning sign. Recross the Sheep River (ford no. 2) and a stony channel and after one flat kilometre arrive in a large meadow with T-junction and signpost. Straight ahead is Sheep Trail. To left is Mist Creek trail to Rickert's Pass and Gibraltar Pass. Looking back, you're treated to a magnificent new view of Gibraltar showing the northeast face in overhanging profile.

Forget about camping down near the river. For the last 3 km you have been travelling through private land, 67 per cent of it owned by the Burns family, the rest held in trust for five charities by the Royal Trust Company. Where you are now is the site of the Burns Coal Mine townsite—the cultural highlight of the trail. For a self-guided tour of the mine sites see SIDE TRIP B on the next page.

Gibraltar from the Burns Coal Mine townsite.
Photo Alf Skrastins

SIDE TRIP

31B Burns Coal Mine

History buffs will have a field day exploring what's left of the mine.

HISTORY NOTE First of all read #39 for background information on Julius Rickert. In 1909 Pat Burns bought the mining and surface rights from Rickert, set about obtaining land grants and established the P. Burns Coal Mine Company. Today's Hwy. 546 is actually built on the railbed for the Calgary & Southwestern railway, which came to naught when the postwar slump closed the mines in 1923. The mines were reopened briefly from 1945–51 by promoter Mervin Brown of Allied Industries, who sent a few truckloads of coal over Brown's bridge to Okotoks.

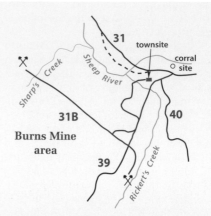

Just beyond the trail junction are two stockpiles of coal. The old corral to the right of the junction, which I photographed for 40 years showing its slow disintegration, is now completely gone.

Head left up Mist Creek Trail. Cross Rickert's Creek and straightaway start climbing. At the intersection with the tramway turn left and reach the mine site near Rickert's Creek: rail lines disappearing into rubble, piles of plywood, the usual slag.

Return to the intersection and keep straight to another mine near Sharp's Creek where you'll find an exciting amount of junk to sift through, including frame buildings in ruins, drill bits and hundreds of pipes made in Okotoks. It invites the question: at what point does abandoned junk become historic relics?

Return to the last junction and turn left, winding down the tramway into the townsite, which was located on a sloping meadow above Sheep trail. Only one foundation is left of a compound that consisted of a bunkhouse, cookhouse, hospital, storage cabins, bathhouse and barns. In 1960 when the Forest Service razed the remaining buildings, they made a pathetic discovery: still lying in the corner of a room in the hospital was a trunk containing all the belongings of the ill-fated Patterson lad.

Frame buildings near Sharp Creek.

Burns Mine to Big Elbow trail

Distance 12 km
Height gain 335 m (1100 ft.)
Height loss 131 m (430 ft.)
High point 2118 m (6950 ft.)
Map 82 J/10 Mount Rae

Accessible from Mist Creek (Volume 5), #34 the Elbow–Sheep cutoff and from Big Elbow trail west of Tombstone backcountry campground (Volume 2).

Aside from 10 river crossings, the going is pleasant and easy on fire road. The valley is broad and flat, a mix of meadow, spruce forest and willow, the only real hill occurring at the end as you climb over the watershed to Big Elbow trail. Horse trails on one side or the other offer alternative routes, but for the hiker few are worth taking. The exception is the pack trail finish described separately under C. En route are many outfitter wilderness camps and informal camping places, usually at fords.

Fording Burns Creek. Photo Alf Skrastins

Many interesting trails lead off this section: #38 Burns Lake, #36 Outfitters trail with a connection to #37 the Rae Creek Hills, #32 Cougar Shoulder, #35 Lake Rae trails with connections to the welter of trails on the Elbow–Sheep watershed that includes the original pack trail finish.

To Denning's Cabin 2.3 km

The fire road, initially duplicate trails in the meadow, heads off between the two stockpiles of coal, crosses tiny Rickert's Creek, then, reverting to recognizable road, crosses the Sheep River at ford no. 3. The road winds along to Sheep ford no. 4. Then follows a long stretch on the left bank to ford no. 5. After the ford, a horse trail leaving the left side cuts off a substantial corner and for once is worth taking. This is followed by a long straight through spruce avenue to ford no. 6.

Just after this crossing, a grassy track on the left side leads to the front door of Harry Denning's Cabin, also known as the Sheep River Cabin (495098). Located in a big meadow opposite Mount Burns, it is

Denning's Cabin below Mount Burns.

no longer available for overnights. Only associates of the Burns Foundation who arrive there by quad have the key. I'm guessing the friendly sign of yore "You are welcome to use this cabin. Leave things as you have found them with a little food and dry firewood" is gone from the door. You can't even camp in the field around it.

The structure was built as a range rider's cabin in 1947 and used until 1971 when cattle were trailed out of the valley for the last time. Much of it was salvaged from the Burns Mine: windows, rough lumber, galvanized iron for the roof, planks for the floor. Its amenities included a wood stove, table, two benches, three bunk beds with sagging springs, one covered by plywood. I'm happy to report it was kept in good shape as per the sign, though I wouldn't have said no to more plywood on the beds and new curtains! Recently, someone constructed a brand new biffy with a blue tarp roof and yellow toilet seat.

To Burns Creek trails 1.1 km
Continue up spruce avenue, at its end turning left and wading Burns Creek, which is as deep as the Sheep River. On the near bank the south bank trail to Burns Lake turns left up Burns Creek Valley. (See #38.)

After a long stretch (horse trail alternative to right) you cross the Sheep River twice in quick succession (fords no. 7 and 8). Not far beyond at 489106 opposite a high stump, a shortcut trail leaves the left side of the fire road bound for Burns Creek cutline cum access road. Around the corner, at a dead tree, the access road to Burns Creek connects with the cutline. Here ends private land.

To pack trail finish 3.4 km
This section accesses the southeast accesses to Outfitters trail and the south access to Cougar Shoulder.

Shortly, cross the Sheep River at ford no. 9. Then follows a long straight on the northeast bank between the grassy green Rae Creek Hills on the left and the grey screes of the Burns massif on the right. Side trails start appearing on the left side leading to a hunters camp, to a weather station, and to Anchor D's wilderness camp across the river. This is the southernmost access to Outfitters trail at 478120.

After an uphill, the main wagon trail to Anchor D's camp turns off to the left at 476123 and is another access to Outfitters trail. Only a few metres on, Cougar Shoulder trail turns off to the right at 474124.

Ford the Sheep at crossing no. 10, back into forest. After an uphill, pass a wallow and game trails to left, then note a couple of game trails to right. The next trail to right at a blazed tree is the historic pack trail to the Elbow River, which can be used as an alternative finish if you're making for Tombstone backcountry campground and Big Elbow trail heading east. See OPTIONAL ENDING C.

To Big Elbow trail 5.2 km

This section accesses the northwest access to Outfitters trail, two trails to Lake Rae, the Elbow–Sheep cutoff and numerous trails in the Elbow–Sheep watershed.

Just upstream of the forks, cross Rae Creek, which is really Sheep River crossing no. 11. Strangely, the left-hand fork of the Sheep River which carries 90 per cent of the water is named Rae Creek, now the true head of the Sheep River that has its birthplace below the great east face of Mount Rae. I say "now" because at one time the true head was the Rae Glacier until the Elbow River, cutting back, captured the headwaters.

Here, the river and the road go their separate ways, the fire road angling up onto the meadows of the Elbow–Sheep watershed. When Dr. George crossed it in 1884 the whole watershed had been devastated by fire. It wasn't much different in the 1920s or in the early 1970s, even when we drove the road, but now, 40 years on, it sports an attractive checkerboard look of meadows and spruce.

Nearing the high point you cross a horse trail connecting to Outfitters trail. At the road's high point, at 445138, four trails meet. Immediately left, heading down a gully, is the northwest access to Outfitters trail. Second left is the trail to Lake Rae and the overlook. To your right the track climbing the hillside is one of the Elbow–Sheep watershed trails.

The fire road is obvious as it trends downhill. Just before a right-hand bend an older version of the fire road turns off to the right. (From it you access Sheep Lakes and the Fish & Wildlife cabin.) After the old road comes back in, an equestrian trail turns off to the right. Cross Lake Rae Creek via culvert. Immediately following, the main Lake Rae trail via Lake Rae Creek turns off to the left at a cairn.

There's a long straight, then the road bends left. At the bend at 432148 the Elbow–Sheep cutoff turns off to the left. Around the next left-hand bend is a straight leading to a meeting of fire roads at 428154. Straight and left is Big Elbow trail. Go straight for Tombstone backcountry campground, left for Elbow Lake and Hwy. 40.

See the sketch map on page 125.

The fire road on the Elbow–Sheep watershed, looking north to ridges east of Tombstone Pass.

Sheep Lakes. Photo Alf Skrastins

OPTIONAL ENDING

31C Pack trail finish

Unofficial trail, river & creek crossings
Distance 4.6 km
Height gain 165 m (540 ft.)
Height loss 131 m (430 ft.)
High point 2088 m (6850 ft.)

The original pack trail used in the late 1800s crosses the Elbow–Sheep watershed just east of Sheep Lakes and joins Big Elbow (horse) trail just east of Tombstone backcountry campground. For anyone going to the campground or turning east down Big Elbow trail, this delightful trail is the recommended shortcut. However, it entails crossing both the Sheep AND the Elbow rivers. See sketch map on page 125.

To Cougar Shoulder north access 2.6 km
Leave the fire road at about 469105. The blazed trail makes a beeline for Rae Creek (Sheep River) and crosses it to an outfitter's camp on the far bank. Continue through a buttercup meadow into the valley of the north fork (that arises from Sheep Lakes) and cross its tiny creek. The trail continues upstream along the right bank, then climbs to a bench where it levels off. Keep left, passing camping spots en route to a side creek crossing. During the next stretch of meadow Cougar Shoulder north access turns off to the right at ~450146.

To Sheep Lakes access 350 m
Continue through meadow, where we once met a griz, to a Y-junction. Rising up ahead are the mountains of the Elbow. Keep straight. (Trail to left descends to the north end of north Sheep Lake, from where you can pick up another trail returning you to the pack trail.)

NOTE Should you step off the trail to the right at the aforementioned Y-junction and follow the strip of meadow northwesterly you would end up at a third lake, the loveliest of all the lakes on the watershed.)

To Big Elbow equestrian trail 1.6 km
After the Y-junction the trail climbs to its high point, then descends to a junction. Keep straight. (Trail to left leads past the Fish & Wildlife cabin to meadows at the north end of North Sheep Lake.)

After a long forest flat, the trail traverses a grassy bank above a tributary of Lake Rae Creek (not marked on the topo map), then zigs downhill. A longer traverse above deeply incised Lake Rae Creek ends with a short steep downhill to the junction with Big Elbow (horse) trail in the valley bottom.

Turn left for Tombstone backcountry campground (crossings of both Lake Rae Creek and the Elbow River). Turn right for Little Elbow Recreation Area (one fording of the Elbow River).

32 COUGAR SHOULDER — map 4

Backpack, day hike from campground
Unofficial trail
Distance 5.4 km
Height gain N–S 268 m (880 ft.)
Height loss N–S 411 m (1350 ft.)
High point 2332 m (7650 ft.)
Map 82 J/10 Mount Rae

Access #31 Sheep trail west at two places:
1. North via #31C pack trail optional ending at ~450146.
2. South at 474124, just south of the 10th river crossing.

A trail made by outfitters leaves the Elbow–Sheep watershed, climbs onto the prominent grassy triangle below the west ridge of Cougar Mtn., then rejoins Sheep trail some way down the Sheep River Valley. This is a very enjoyable trail to hike: it is moderately graded, is liberally supplied with meadows giving fantastic views and you have the option of climbing higher.

Most obviously the northern half can be accessed from Tombstone backcountry campground as a there and back trip to the trail's high point. Hikers can continue up the west ridge to the flatiron and experienced scramblers can scramble all the way to the summit of Cougar Mountain. If based at Denning's Cabin or camped near Anchor D Camp, you have two options: making a loop with either Sheep trail or Outfitters trail.

NORTH TO SOUTH

To Cougar Shoulder 2.1 km

After leaving the pack trail you parallel it for 200 m heading southeastwards, then turn left across an open ridge and plunge into a willowy tributary of the north fork. The trail—a little vague from horses walking every which way—heads right, down the valley a short way, then cuts across the floor to 454148, where you can be sure to pick it up.

From the waypoint a good trail corkscrews and zigs up the hillside through woods and a meadow. At a second, larger meadow it makes a long traverse right to the col at 463152. The surprise here is the view of Outlaw and Banded Peak straight ahead!

The trail continues, winding up right (southeast) on stony ground with burnt black trees. As you climb, Cougar Mountain comes into sight, its entire west ridge displayed in profile.

View from the shoulder of Cougar Mountain, showing the flatiron (scree top at centre) climbed by #32A.

Descending the meadows from the shoulder, looking toward the Rae Creek Hills in the middle ground and the east peak of Mount Rae.

The trail fades as you reach your objective—a large flat bench of short-cropped grass and clumps of spruce below the flatiron. The view to the west is panoramic, taking in all the southern Opals (Tombstone predominant), the entire Misty Range and the Rae Creek Hills. Hogging the limelight as usual is the spectacular east peak of Mount Rae.

To Sheep trail 3.3 km
Continue on the same line across the bench. On the far side the trail picks up and descends beautiful meadow alongside a small creek bubbling away on your right. Ahead is a new view looking down the Sheep River Valley to Gibraltar Pass.

Re-enter forest. Soon the trail is corkscrewing downhill. Cross the small side creek and traverse a flowery meadow. A much longer, twisty descent through fir and spruce forest ends in another lush meadow just metres away from a fire road that is Sheep trail. The junction lies at 474124 just north of the outfitter's camp.

GOING HIGHER

32A Flatiron 476151

Distance 820 m
Height gain 274 m (900 ft.)
High point 2606 m (8550 ft.)

To the west rises a flatiron, a triangular-shaped ridge shaped by erosion that is common all over the Front Ranges. They lure by their easy west slopes, then leave you stranded. This one isn't much different. Go for the view.

Climb grass up the left-hand ridge to a bench at the halfway point. The upper half is steeper and the game here is to join up as many grassy strips as you can between scree runnels. Arriving at the top—a small comfy pad of grass with cairn, you discover another feature of flatirons, the steep drop to a neck connecting with the main body of the mountain. So this is the end for hikers. Enjoy the Google Earth view of the Elbow–Sheep watershed.

Scramblers can continue up the moderately graded west ridge to the summit of Cougar Mountain.

#32A View from the summit of the flatiron of the west ridge of Cougar Mtn.

#31C and 33 The third lake on the Elbow–Sheep watershed. Cougar Mountain in the background at left, showing the flatiron (#32A) and the west shoulder traversed by #32.

33 ELBOW–SHEEP WATERSHED TRAILS—map 4

Backpack, half-day trips from Tombstone backcountry campground, river & creek crossings
Unofficial trails
Height gain main trail N–S 171 m (560 ft.)
Height loss main trail N–S 37 m (120 ft.)
High point 2128 m (6980 ft.)
Map 82 J/10 Mount Rae

Access #31 Sheep trail west at five places.
Also accessible from #31C pack trail finish, and from Tombstone backcountry campground on Big Elbow trail (Volume 2).

The watershed between the Elbow and Sheep rivers is an attractive mix of forest, meadows and small lakes, backdropped by the high peaks of Tombstone, Rae and Cougar. Criss-crossing it is a mesh of new equestrian trails, old roads (tracks) and older pack trails that connect with Sheep trail west and Big Elbow trail.

Looking toward the north peak of the Rae Creek Hills (left) and the east summit of Mount Rae.

They have three uses: 1. for side trips onto the watershed to view Sheep Lakes; 2. as connectors from Tombstone backcountry campground to other trails; and 3. as alternative routes between Tombstone and Sheep trail west. Trails at the north end are hilly with steep sections where they descend to the Elbow River.

This description highlights the main N–S trail between Tombstone backcountry campground and Sheep trail west at the high point.

FROM TOMBSTONE BACKCOUNTRY CAMPGROUND
To Sheep Lakes 1.6 km
The trail leaves Big Elbow (horse) trail adjacent to the campground and heads downhill to cross the Elbow River.

Climb a willowy meadow onto a treed ridge. Descend to a tributary of Lake Rae Creek. Cross and climb to an open ridgetop. Descend to Lake Rae Creek. Cross and zig up a steep grassy bank. The gradient

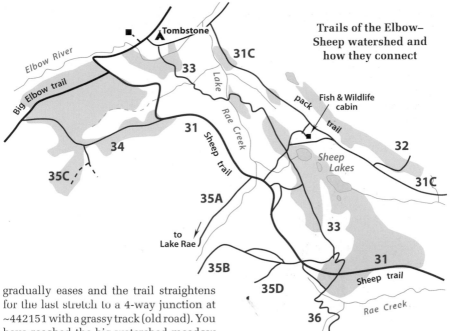

**Trails of the Elbow–
Sheep watershed and
how they connect**

gradually eases and the trail straightens
for the last stretch to a 4-way junction at
~442151 with a grassy track (old road). You
have reached the big watershed meadow
on which lie the Sheep Lakes.

To visit north Sheep Lake (outlet to
the Elbow), continue ahead. Separating it
from the slightly larger south Sheep Lake
(outlet to the Sheep) are two small pools.
Both lakes are shallow reflecting lakes
with a surround of bog, so getting close is
like walking on a water bed.

To high point of Sheep trail west 2.7 km
Back to the 4-way junction. The track to
left leads to the Fish & Wildlife cabin and
the pack trail finish. The trail to its right is
a shortcut and is the route to take if headed
for the third lake and Cougar Shoulder.

Turn right on the track or use the trail
that parallels it to the left. Almost straight
off, a trail heading right descends to Sheep
trail west, en route crossing the outlet from
north Sheep Lake. It reaches the fire road
just south of Rae Creek, thus giving access
to the usual Lake Rae trail.

The track crosses the outlet from north
Sheep Lake on planks and comes to a
4-way junction at ~445145 (counting in
the parallel trail that comes in from left).

The track to right descends to a 3-way
junction with the original fire road. Go either left or right to reach Sheep trail west.

Continue ahead on grassy track, enjoying great views ahead of the Rae Creek
Hills and the east summit of Mount Rae.
Enter open forest where the track down-
grades to trail and splits temporarily. Reverting to track, it winds slightly uphill to
a junction at 449138. Here the track turns
right, climbs to a meadow, then drops
to the high point of Sheep trail west at
445138. From here you can access Lake
Rae via #35B, Lake Rae Overlook and the
gully start to Outfitters trail.

To Sheep trail west at 448136, 300 m
Back at junction 449138, the trail ahead
leads past a large rock, then turns right
and up to the same meadow crossed by the
track. Turn left and follow the edge of trees,
gradually curving right and down to Sheep
trail west. The trail crosses the fire road
and continues downhill and right to join
Outfitters trail on the east bank of the gully.

34 ELBOW–SHEEP CUTOFF — map 4

Day hike, backpack
Unofficial trail
Distance 1.6 km
Height gain W–E 30 m (100 ft.)
Height loss W–E 15 m (50 ft.)
High point 2027 m (6650 ft.)
Map 82 J/10 Mount Rae

West access Via Big Elbow trail at 420147 (Volume 2).
East access Via #31 Sheep trail west at 432148.

This well-used trail connects Sheep trail west to Big Elbow trail and is a worthwhile shortcut if headed for Hwy. 40. Mostly, though, it's used by hikers coming in the opposite direction from Hwy. 40 to Lake Rae. So that is the way I describe it — a slightly undulating route nearly all through meadows.

Heading east through the gap. In the background is Cougar Mountain.

ELBOW TO SHEEP

To junction with #35C, 610 m
A narrow trail leaves the south side of Big Elbow trail at a cairn and heads east through trees initially, then through a grassy gap between Mount Rae and a low hill on the left. Cougar Mountain comes into view ahead. Farther on, look back through the vee to Tombstone Mountain and Piper Creek Valley to its left.

Reach a Y-junction at 424148. Keep left. (Right is route #35C to Lake Rae.)

To Sheep trail 950 m
The trail passes through a draw, then climbs into meadows with a small scattering of spruce. Meander along (the trend is now downhill) and pass an historic rain gauge shortly before reaching Sheep trail west at an inside bend at 432148.

35 LAKE RAE—map 4

Backpack, long-day hike from Hwy. 40
Unofficial trails & routes
High point 2179 m (7150 ft.) at lake
Map 82 J/10 Mount Rae

Lake Rae is a little green gem tucked under the northern outliers of Mount Rae.

It is accessed by three trails, two from Sheep trail west and one from the Elbow–Sheep cutoff. Most obviously, it makes an excellent short-day option from nearby Tombstone backcountry campground. Of course, you can also camp in the trees near the lakeshore. If you don't want to lug in camping gear, a one-day hike from Highway 40 is popular via Elbow Lake (Volume 1), Big Elbow trail (Volume 2) and #34 Elbow–Sheep cutoff. But at 12.6 km return, this option leaves little time for exploring.

See the sketch map on page 125.

Lake Rae below the eastern cliffs of Mount Rae's northern outliers. Photo Alf Skrastins

35A via Lake Rae Creek

Unofficial trail
Distance 1.4 km
Height gain 122 m (400 ft.)

Access #31 Sheep trail west, on the northwest bank of Lake Rae Creek.

The usual easy way in.

The trail follows the northwest bank of the creek issuing from Lake Rae. It's a comfortable walk through alternating meadows and forest to the lake shore. The camping area is to the right.

The scene is exquisite, the lake and its surround of larch meadows cradled between the arms of two ridges with the precipitous east wall of Mount Rae as the backdrop. Make a circuit of the lake or climb the overlook to left.

35B from Sheep trail's high point

Unofficial trail
Distance 1.4 km
Height gain 61 m (200 ft.)
Access #31 Sheep trail west at the high point at 445138.

A pleasant way in that also accesses the north leg of Lake Rae Overlook.

From Sheep trail's high point a trail heads west into the forest. At a really big split a short way in keep left. Shortly after, at 444138, the north leg of OPTION D. Lake Rae Overlook, takes off left up the hill. You will likely miss the junction.

Below #35B, nearing Lake Rae.

The main trail contours below the north slope of the overlook to a side creek crossing. (Just before, the two heads of the right-hand split join in from the right.) The trail then makes for the southeast bank of Lake Rae Creek and follows it along to the lake. En route a small muddy section can be avoided by a detour to the left. To reach the camping area, cross the outlet on logs.

35C from Elbow–Sheep cutoff

Unofficial trail & route
Distance 1.8 km, 6.3 km from Hwy. 40
Height gain 183 m (600 ft.)
Height loss 30 m (100 ft.)
High point 2210 m (7250 ft.)
Access Via #34 Elbow–Sheep cutoff.

If approaching from Hwy. 40, take this shortcut from the Elbow–Sheep cutoff. Part trail, part route and marked with yellow flagging, it should be used only by experienced hikers who enjoy crossing a great tract of open hillside pitted with grizzly diggings. Since the last edition the route has been simplified.

Leave Elbow–Sheep cutoff at the end of the open valley—at 424148—where the trail splits and there are stumps in the angle between. Turn right onto a narrower trail.

After a short distance, keep an eye out for flagging up the slope to your right. (The trail ahead leads to terrain you don't want to get into.) So turn right off the trail and follow flagging tied to the tree up a gentle hillside of grass to the left of a small gully. Come to a cairn.

At the cairn turn left onto a trail. Occasionally faint but flagged, it traverses increasingly steeper hillside, crossing a couple of gullies and at one place passing behind a large, prominent boulder. A steeper, stonier climb gains you the grassy gable end of the ridge bordering the lake to the north. A cairn and dead trees mark the trail's high point.

Top: #35C Looking back across the hillside from the trail's high point to Tombstone Mountain. The trail runs just above the big boulder.

Bottom: Lake Rae Overlook from the north shore. The route traverses from right to left.

The trail continues intermittently down other-side meadows, dropping about 30 m (100 ft.). Lake Rae comes into view and the big grassy ridge behind it, which is Lake Rae Overlook.

At the water's edge join the round-the-lake trail. Turn left for the camping area at the outlet.

OPTION

35D Lake Rae Overlook

Unofficial trail & route
Distance 3.1 km
Height gain 244 m (800 ft.)
Height loss 305 m (1000 ft.)
High point 2423 m (7950 ft.)
Lake access Start from the outlet.
North access Via B at 444138.

In the mists of time we used to park the car at the high point of the Sheep fire road,

#37D The summit of the overlook, looking down to Lake Rae.

clamber up the south arm of the lake to its high point at 438127, descend steep shale to the lake and return to the fire road more or less on the line of #35B. Nowadays, a rough-hewn trail made by adventurous outfitters does the job. However, this is still not a route for everyone. The trail is discontinuous and sometimes steep. At such places look for scuffed ground made by horses' hooves.

LAKE TO NORTH ACCESS
To summit 1.5 km

From the camping area at Lake Rae cross the outlet and turn right along the east shore on trail. Easily ignore steep game trails heading up your objective, the hill to your left; there is an easier way. When the trail gives out, keep walking up the grassy valley beyond the lake, following the left bank of the little creek. Only when you reach a prominent boulder in the creekbed do you strike uphill, using grass to either side of a stony runnel. When level with a bench on the left side, go left along it and up to intersect a traversing trail.

Turn right and follow the trail on its ascending traverse across grassy slopes. Just before reaching the neck connecting the hill to the main body of the mountain, you come upon a rock, a tree and a small gully where the trail splinters. My choice is to ascend the left side of the gully, but please yourself. On reaching the summit ridge simply head left to the high point with cairn.

This is an amazing viewpoint for sorting out the complexities of the Elbow–Sheep watershed and its lakes. On Cougar Mountain you can pick out the route taken by the trail to Cougar Shoulder. Look south to the Rae Creek Hills and the fabulous east peak of Mount Rae. Possibly the best view is to the north: down to Lake Rae and across a line of cliffs to Tombstone Mountain and Cat's Ears.

Looking up at the overlook from the descent trail below the col. The route leaves the summit ridge at far left and step-traverses left to right across the open slopes.

Descent to Sheep trail 1.6 km

Return along the summit ridge a short way. In front of a prominent rock, your trail descends the stony left (east) slope. A steep left-hand bend leads into a downward-stepping traverse across stones and tree ribbons to a point just below a col. Rather than go over the top of the lower summit, the trail sidles down its east slope in much the same sort of way, only this time you're slip-sliding down grass.

Entering trees, traverse left, corkscrew down the fall line, then make a longer traverse left. A bit of shale starts you off on the final, twisty descent through spruce and larch forest where you take every downhill option with intersecting game trails. Low down, the forest opens up and the trail fades seconds away from reaching B. Manoeuvre around a few bushes onto the trail at 444138. (This lack of a trail at the end can be tricky for anyone going in the opposite direction. When you find it, keep right at a Y-junction.)

Turn left to return to the lake, right to reach Sheep trail west.

36 OUTFITTERS TRAIL — map 4

Backpack
Unofficial trail, creek crossings
Distance 4.5 km
Height gain NW–SE 64 m (210 ft.)
Height loss NW–SE 259 m (850 ft.)
High point 2103 m (6900 ft.)
Map 82 J/10 Mount Rae

Access #31 Sheep trail west in four places.
Northwest access At the high point of the trail at a 4-way junction at 445138. Also at 448136 a little to the south. See the map on page 125.
Southeast access At ~476123 at the Anchor D camp wagon trail junction. Also at 478120 downstream where a trail turns off across the Sheep River. See the map on this page.

Outfitters runs parallel to Sheep trail west, but takes a more strenuous line across the lower slopes of the Rae Creek Hills to the west. It's mainly a forest trail with moderate hills and occasional good viewpoints in little meadows.

This new trail provides hikers (and the outfitter who made the trail) bush-free access onto the Rae Creek Hills. No longer do you need to push your way up from Rae Creek. It can also be used as a more strenuous alternative to upper Sheep trail west or as part of a loop with Cougar Shoulder.

NORTHWEST TO SOUTHEAST

To Rae Creek Hills junction 1.4 km
At the 4-way junction at 445138 head southeast down the left bank of a gully. Halfway down is a T-junction with another trail come in from Sheep trail west at 448136. Turn right.

Cross the gully and wind down to Rae Creek. Cross, and climb a steep muddy bank. On level ground the trail heads right above the banktop, then left into a meadow. From here it's a straightforward climb through trees onto a billowy side ridge — the trail's high point at 454131. The small meadow with larches is a really nice viewpoint for Lake Rae Overlook, the watershed and Cougar Shoulder below Cougar Mountain. Just be alert for the local griz going walkabout.

This is where the trail to Rae Creek Hills turns off to the right.

To Sheep Trail 3 km and 3.1 km
Outfitters continues in an ESE direction across a bit of a bowl to a split on a bit of a ridge. Take either way down the left slope of a creek: the left-hand forest trail continues along the ridge a way and then twists down the fall line; the right-hand trail descends more gradually above the grassy bank of the creek. After the trails unite, you cross a muddy side creek.

Continue above the grassy bank of the creek. One steep drop takes you down to the Sheep River Valley. Shortly, cross the side creek, whose waters are now augmented by a much bigger creek coming off the cirque below the Rae Creek Hills. Ignore a side trail to left. Continue into Anchor D campsite.

There are two exits onto Sheep trail west. Either follow the wagon trail back left across the Sheep River to ~476123. Or cross the meadow beyond the camp and pick up a trail that crosses a side creek and then the Sheep River to join Sheep trail west at 478120.

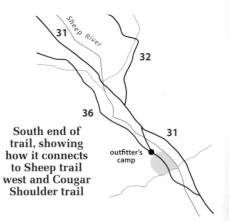

South end of trail, showing how it connects to Sheep trail west and Cougar Shoulder trail

#36 Outfitters trail above the side creek, with various ridges of Mount Rae poking up ahead.

#37 The Skyline trail, on the traverse below the north peak. The trail passes below the shadowy crag, then ascends to the north–south col.

37 RAE CREEK HILLS — map 4

Looking to north top from the north–south col.

Backpack, long-day hike from camps
Unofficial trail, route
Distance via tops to Burns Lake 8.3 km
Height gain 948 m (3110 ft.),
Skyline trail 564 m (1850 ft.)
Height loss 811 m (2660 ft.),
Skyline trail 457 m (1500 ft.)
High point 2688 m (8810 ft.),
Skyline trail 2627 m (8620 ft.)
Map 82 J/10 Mount Rae

North access Via #36 Outfitters trail at the high point at 454131.
South access Via #38 Burns Creek at 473085 or at Burns Lake.

The remote and very beautiful Rae Creek Hills lie between Burns Creek, Rae Creek, Mt. Rae and the Sheep River Valley. These are hills fit for walkers: the ridges not too narrow, the footing mostly grass with a little rock and scree near summits.

Doing the Rae Creek Hills usually requires a three-day weekend from any trailhead. You can backpack over to Burns Lake, or make exceedingly long day loops (headlamps required packing) from Tombstone backcountry campground on the other side of the Elbow–Sheep watershed, or from Denning's Cabin near Burns Creek and from camp sites in between. For instance, if looping from Denning's Cabin, the height gain of nearly 1219 m (4000 ft.) is guaranteed to leave you benighted with several creek crossings to go should you be daft enough to hike the loop in late October like we did. But it must be said the larches and the rich colours of the grass are incredibly beautiful at this time of year. Overall, though, as a responsible guidebook writer I would have to recommend a dawn start on a midsummer day.

Loops can be shortened by dropping down the north ridge of the highest top to Outfitters trail, or by descending the ridge above Burns Creek to the northwest. Another option is there and back forays onto the hills from a camp at Burns Lake or at waterfall camp.

TRAIL NOTE Since the last edition a horse trail — Anchor D's fabulous Skyline trail, "showing dudes from overseas the best the Rockies has to offer"—crosses the hills from north to south and can be utilized in whole or in part. This is not a hiking trail, so expect the odd missing section where horses have spread out across the grass. It also takes the easiest line, so missing out all the tops. Hikers worth their salt must visit all the summits.

FROM NORTH ACCESS
To north–south col, 2.8 km via Skyline trail, 2.5 km over north top

From the high point of Outfitters trail turn right if coming from Rae Creek, left if approaching from the south. The trail heads SSW and is faint for the first few metres. On entering trees it climbs steeply up a rib through larches and meadows. At the top of the second meadow the trail swings up right below a small crag, then, heading west, traverses scree and grass just above a prominent rockband on the north end of the north top. See the photo on page 111. There are two ways on to the col.

1. Traverse on Skyline trail
Round the north end of north peak onto the west slope and head south. The wonderful traverse above treeline ends at the top of a side ridge. Climb diagonally up right to gain the north–south col. Through the gap appears the west face of east top.

2. Over north top 453117
Climb 366 vertical m (1200 ft.) up the grassy north ridge. The going is relentlessly steep, so breath stops are permissible, ostensibly to admire the spectacular east summit of Mount Rae. Three-quarters of the way up is an easing, after which the ridge crest narrows and steepens for the last lap to the large summit cairn at 2606 m (8550 ft.) elevation.

Losing 152 m (500 ft.) in elevation, walk down the wide, gently angled south ridge to the north–south col.

To south top 461098 730 m
At the col the trail reasserts itself, but does not head for the next summit. So either toil 213 vertical m (700 ft.) up the ridge, or on trail traverse the steep west face to a saddle between the top and its lower west summit, and THEN climb to the summit up 30 vertical m (100 ft.) of rocks and scree. This top is a little higher at 2667 m (8750 ft.).

The summit of south top, dwarfed by the east peak of Mt. Rae. Photo Alf Skrastins

135

This summit is marked by a metal post. From its vantage point you look straight down the flat valley floor of upper Rae Creek, the grass a suspiciously bright green colour littered with herds of grazing hippos. A new view has opened up to the south of Burns Creek, Storm Ridge and the mountains Storm and Mist.

If you want to miss out the detour to the east top, skip the next section.

To east top 465105 2.1 km return

Descend two easy steps of the northeast ridge to the southeast col. Start up east peak, its broad ridge crossed by little rockbands, all of which except the first and highest can be taken direct. Higher up, the ridge narrows to scree with splintery outcrops—a suitably impressive approach to the highest summit of the day at 2688 m (8810 ft.). Not far below the summit on the north side we found woolly fleabane and its sidekick the alpine poppy growing among the rocks.

Purists can also pick off a lower summit farther to the east at 470105.

Return to the saddle south of south top.

Getting off

From the saddle the trail aims for the lower top, but before getting there traverses grass and scree on the left side to a southeast ridge. Descend to a low point at 461094. (NOTE If making for the Sheep River, it's tempting to continue along the grassy ridge in an ENE direction and drop off onto Burns Creek trail, aiming for 483096 at the meeting of starts.)

Leave the ridge here and drop down the steep right (south) slope on grass to a side valley below the Rae Creek col. In mid-slope, zigs make the going much easier. Head downstream above a gully. After the trail peters out in grass, look for where it crosses the gully and shortly a second gully. The trail is very clear at this point. On lightly treed grass slopes the trail again disappears.

1. To Burns Lake 3 km

If you climb higher you'll find the upper trail which traverses a scree slope. Most often, though, people use the lower trail. Just traverse and pick up the trail in a meadow where it is climbing uphill to-

The ridge leading to the highest east top in the background. From the summit you can descend its occasionally steep and grassy north ridge into forest above Outfitters trail.

View from near the saddle of the lower south top behind the hiker. From here the route traverses the left slope to the southeast ridge at left and drops over the other side.

ward the first fan of scree. Cross a second scree fan not far above the vegetation and another meadow, finishing with a steady uphill climb on shale onto the little grass and shale ridge bounding Burns Lake to the east. You top out just below the craggy steepening. Here the trail turns left and follows the ridge down south. Turn first right if aiming on camping by the lake.

If headed for campsites below the waterfall, continue along the ridge.

2. Shortcut to Burns Creek 3.8 km

This is a very fast direct route to Burns Creek Valley, made by outfitters, which misses out all the interesting stuff. Use if heading out to the Sheep River.

In the meadow where you pick up the lower trail before scree, descend to the bottom right-hand corner as you look out. An obvious trail starts here and twists downhill through trees at a very moderate grade. At junctions keep left, low down traversing left to reach Burns Creek trail at 473085. (See also #38A.)

According to Dewey a right turn at the lowest junction leads to Burns Creek trail nearer the falls.

The lower trail traversing to the ridge (middle foreground) above Burns Lake. Photo Alf Skrastins

137

38 BURNS WATERFALL and LAKE—map 4

Backpack, day hike from Denning's Cabin.
Unofficial trail, creek crossing via south bank start
Distance 4.4 km to falls, 5.3 km to lake
Height gain 213 m (700 ft.) to falls, 411 m (1350 ft.) to lake
High point at falls 2042 m (6700 ft.), at lake 2240 m (7350 ft.)
Map 82 J/10 Mount Rae

View from the ridge above Burns Lake to Storm Mountain. Photo Alf Skrastins

Access Via #31 Sheep trail west at two places.
1. Trail from south Turn left (west) off Sheep trail on the south bank of Burns Creek.
2. Cutline from north The cutline access road at ~489106. A dead tree marks a trail leading onto the access road.
Also accessible from #37 Rae Creek Hills and from Arethusa Cirque (Volume 5).

A long forest approach up Burns Creek Valley on cutline and assorted trails leads to Burns Creek waterfall, candidate for the highest non-continuous fall in K Country. Lovers of high alpine lakes should carry on uphill into the cirques tucked under the south face of Mount Rae, but be aware a penance must first be exacted in the

shape of a stiff 244-vertical-m climb up the headwall. Take comfort that an even more exacting route into the cirques exists from Hwy. 40.

NEW TRAILS NOTE Since the third edition a new start has come into favour for anyone approaching Burns Creek from the south (which is most people). I highly recommend it. Not only does it reduce the distance by a kilometre, it cuts out two river crossings and the worst excesses of the cutline route.

You can camp at the bottom of the waterfall. But if camping at Burns Lake consider using Outfitters trail, #38A.

HISTORY NOTE Burns Creek will forever be associated with High River's Don King and the Blayney Brothers, Len, York and Alan, (plus assorted friends) in their herculean efforts to make the first ascent of Mount Rae in the 1940s. Back then, there was no convenient Hwy. 40 and the nearest approach was by car up the Sheep River fire road—an adventure in itself!

This valley was also special to another old timer. When he died his ashes were placed in a can of his favourite brand of coffee and stashed away in a secret location, never to be found.

Two starts:

1. South bank start 1.1 km
Just before crossing Burns Creek on Sheep trail west, turn left on a trail. In a few minutes wade Burns Creek to the northwest bank. After this the trail ambles pleasantly through mature forest close to the creek. You cross a side creek off the Rae Creek Hills, then make a gradual climb to intersect the NE–SW cutline at 483096 (small cairn). Turn left.

2. NE–SW cutline 1.2 km
From Sheep trail west follow the cutline access road up a steep, stony hill. At the top turn southwest onto the cutline proper. After a brief respite you climb a three-tier hill. To avoid a boggy meadow detour to the right on cutline access road. Over the years, more and more bypass trails have developed to the right of the now muddy access road.

Back on the cutline, you endure one of those awful cutline dips, after which the cutline descends and jogs right to cross a side creek from the Rae Creek Hills. Shortly after getting back on line, look for a small cairn on the left side indicating the south bank start.

To waterfall via cutline, 3.3 km
As the cutline nears Burns Creek, stay on it, disregarding a horse trail foray across the river (unless of course you want to access the steep open slopes of Storm Ridge; game trails lead uphill near the return crossing). Shortly after the horse trail comes back in from the left, another takes off on the right. Take this one. It avoids two crossings of Burns Creek.

A long, uneventful straight follows, slightly undulating. Use the access road three times to avoid boggy cutline. A horse trail taking off up-meadow on the right side at 473085 at 1.6 km is route A to the Rae Creek Hills and Burns Lake.

Cross the side creek emanating from the Rae Creek col. After another wee side creek crossing, the cutline and access road part ways:

1. Cutline
The cutline ahead descends slightly past camping areas to the north fork (the creek flowing out of Burns Lake) that is reached just above the forks. Here a trail leads right, then splits. The right-hand trail climbs the headwall to join the route from the cutline access road at the viewpoint. The left-hand trail leads to the foot of the 150-m-high Burns Creek waterfall; not a single leap like Takakkaw but a series of high steps connected by ladders of white water.

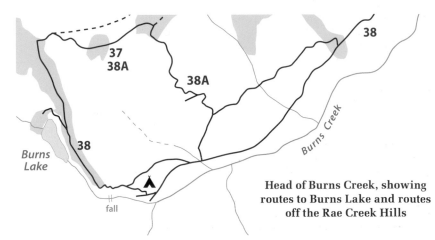

Head of Burns Creek, showing routes to Burns Lake and routes off the Rae Creek Hills

Burns Creek waterfall from the higher viewpoint.

2. Cutline access road

The road to right, soon narrowing to trail, is the shortcut to the headwall trail—joining in at the lower viewpoint for the waterfall.

The headwall to Burns Lake 900 m

The hard work of the day: climbing 244 m (800 ft.) up by the waterfall in one fell swoop. If you're toting a heavy pack, it makes more sense, says Alf, to take ALTERNATIVE ROUTE A to Burns Lake, and then explore the waterfall's many viewpoints unencumbered the next morning.

Take the cutline route to the north fork. Here a trail heads right, then splits. Turn right (left leads to the bottom of the waterfall) and start climbing. The ground levels above cliffs, then steepens to the lower viewpoint for the waterfall, where the alternative route joins in from the right.

From the lower viewpoint continue up a steep, twisting trail to a higher viewpoint and on up onto the flat grassy ridge bounding Burns Lake to the east. (The lake is pie-shaped, wedged between a steep boulder field and a rock wall, which makes shoreline walking difficult.)

Ahead rises the east summit of Mount Rae. Two rivulets rush feverishly down grassy slopes from cirques on either side of its south ridge but sink underground long before reaching the lake. To the right you can spot trails crossing the scree slope en route to the Rae Creek Hills. In the opposite direction across the lake is a view of Storm Mountain revealing its eastern precipice. Below its patch of névé lies a tarn, this one seasonal.

The trail continues along the ridge crest. Keep left, gradually descending the left side of it through a few trees into the large flat meadow at the head of the lake. (The trail ahead along the ridge leads to the Rae Creek Hills and the east cirque.)

A camping area is located in trees before the meadow. This is where Don and the Blayney brothers cleared the ground in preparation for a cabin that was never built. Most people just camp on the grass.

Burns Lake from the ridge, looking toward King's Cirque, King's Ridge
and the bench holding Blayney Tarn. Photo Alf Skrastins

ALTERNATIVE ROUTE TO THE LAKE

38A via the horse trail

Unofficial trail
Distance to Burns Lake 4 km
Height gain 244 m (800 ft.)

If you want to camp at Burns Lake and dread flogging up the headwall, this outfitter's trail is for you.

It starts from the valley trail at 473085 in a meadow. It traverses up left, crosses the side creek from Rae Creek col, then descends a little. At the following junction, turn right (north) up the fall line. Keep right and shortly start a twisty but moderately graded climb through trees into a meadow at treeline. Turn up left.

Near the top of the grass join a traversing trail heading left that crosses two fans of scree and a meadow before climbing up onto the little ridge bounding the lake to the east. Turn left down the ridge, then next right to reach the lake shore.

GOING FARTHER

38B "Blayney" Tarn

Route
Distance 1 km from lake
Height gain 168 m (550 ft.)

Pick your way up the left side of the cirque between waterfalls to beautiful Blayney Tarn — another good camping spot a stone's throw away from the one-day route over from Hwy. 40. That's the gully leading to the col southeast of Mount Arethusa (see Volume 5 for details).

38C King's Cirque

Route
Distance 1.9 km from Blayney tarn

From Blayney Tarn it's a flat, easy walk into the claustrophobic valley between Mount Arethusa and King's Ridge on the left and a totty rock ridge on the right with unclimbed summits. Ahead rises Mount Rae and its lower summit, known as "the pinnacle." Don't bother looking around the end moraines; there's no blue tarn hidden within its folds.

Incredibly, the nasty slope rising to King's Ridge was the ascent route taken by Don and co. in their numerous attempts to climb Mount Rae. In 1949 they struggled almost to the lower summit in a "furious blizzard" and hurriedly placed a bronze memorial plaque to fellow climber Cuzzy Cousins among its rocks. In '51 the plaque had vanished, perhaps fallen into a crack or taken down the south face by an avalanche. It was Don's wish, just before he passed over the Great Divide in 2007, that it be found and properly installed. So, scramblers, should anyone be willing to take on the challenge, let me know and I'll give you the specifics.

Finally, on their 11th try in 1953, Don and Len succeeded *from the Highwood Pass side* (today's normal route) in a five-day epic of travel and learned that Gordon Langille and E.H.J. Smythe had beaten them to it a year earlier. That's not the end of the story. While on a recce prior to their ascent, Langille and Lawrence Grassi spotted a cairn already on top! So who made the first ascent of Mount Rae remains a mystery.

38D The east cirque

Unofficial trail, route
Distance 2+ km from lake
Height gain 198+ m (650+ ft.)

Follow the ridge to the east of Burns Lake. After the trail to Rae Creek Hills turns off to the right, continue on into the cirque—all meadow—its creek deeply incised with waterfalls below a line of wavy cliffs. If you want, you can struggle up scree to the little top at 449096 for a vertiginous view into Rae Creek Valley.

#38B Blayney Tarn, looking up King's Cirque to Mount Rae. Photo Alf Skrastins

#39 View from Rickert's Pass trail across the cirque to the northernmost end of Mist Ridge. Photo Alf Skrastins

143

39 RICKERT'S PASS to MIST CREEK — map 4

Nearing the pass.

Backpack, half-day from Sheep trail west
Official trail
Distance 2.6 km
Height gain 549 m (1800 ft.)
High point 2332 m (7650 ft.)
Map 82 J/10 Mount Rae

Access #31 Sheep trail west at the junction with Mist Creek trail at Burns Mine.
Also accessible from Mist Creek to Rickert's Pass and from Mist Ridge (Volume 5).

A steep, sustained climb to the pass at 520062 between Mist and Storm ridges. Bill Sumners, who was caretaker at the Burns Mine in the 1920s reckoned he could run up in 45 minutes. (He was in his early 70s at the time.) Admittedly, it's a bit hard if you're carrying a bike. Amazing to me, this pass is part of a popular long-distance bike loop called "Around the Misty Range."

HISTORY & NAMING NOTE The pass was first crossed by geologist George Dawson in 1884 after a foray in Mist Creek Valley. He described the descent as "practical though steep and rough." En route he found good-quality anthracite coal and in longhand wrote that a "more complete examination might lead to the discovery of workable deposits."

Julius Rickert, sporting a trademark handlebar moustache, was a self-styled mining engineer from the eastern U.S. but let it be understood he was of French nationality: the Comte de Brabant no less. Later it was discovered that the title belonged to the crown prince of Belgium, after Pat Burns's lawyer Paddy Nolan found a 1932 photo of the real count in *L'Illustration* magazine of Paris, but that's another story. Anyway, Rickert, with ex-cop Arthur Brown, was sent in 1896 to prospect for coal up the Sheep River and, having no doubt read Dawson's account, headed straight up Rickert's Creek. Now turn to #31B SIDE TRIP BURNS MINE for the continuing saga.

At the signpost head left up Mist Creek trail. Cross Rickert's Creek and straightaway start climbing. Ignore the intersecting tramway. (See the sketch map on page 116.)

The marked trail continues ever more steeply onto a heap of coal spoil, then on into fir forest with blazes dating back to the beginning of the 20th century. A long, steep straight leads into zigs that take you out of the old forest onto the grassy slopes of a cirque. Note the black-streaked hillsides, which on close inspection reveal hundreds of miniature coal heaps below ground-squirrel homes. More zigs and one last straight gain you the rocky defile between two grassy ridges.

Backpackers continue on the trail into Mist Creek Valley and out to Hwy. 40. Day hikers can turn left at the pass onto a side trail for a spot of ridge wandering.

40 GIBRALTAR PASS — map 4

Backpack, half-day from Sheep trail west
Unofficial trail
Distance 2.4 km
Height gain 442 m (1450 ft.)
High point 2210 m (7250 ft.)
Map 82 J/10 Mount Rae

Access #31 Sheep trail west at the junction with Mist Creek trail at Burns Mine.

The pass at 520062 between Mist Ridge and Gibraltar Mountain is reached by a good, occasionally steep trail improved by outfitters. Apart from leading to the beautiful meadow country at the head of Cliff Creek, it also serves as access to Gibraltar Mountain, a moderate scramble.

Start off on #39 Rickert's Pass trail.

In only a few metres, turn left onto a trail that follows the left bank of Rickert's Creek. Shortly it veers left (a muddy, rooty section), then, turning uphill, gets into a routine: up alongside a tributary of a creek falling from the north side of Mist Ridge, across the tributary's head to another tributary, up alongside that tributary and so on. This happens innumerable times, each uphill getting steeper until you cut behind a promontory of large spruce. You are now in the larch zone and it's an enjoyable traverse across the three heads of another deep creek into meadow. Look back and left for a fine view of the upper Sheep River Valley.

Shortly the trail curves right, into the pass at a salt lick. The north top of Mist Ridge rises steeply on the right, Gibraltar Mountain a little less so on your left. (NOTE Gaining the first top of Gibraltar, incorrectly marked on the map as the summit, is easy.)

A pass implies you can continue on, and sure enough a game trail continues innocently down meadows into the north fork of Cliff Creek. A more feasible objective is Picklejar Pass, seen in the far distance. The problem here is joining up the surfeit of game trails. See Volume 5 for details.

Gibraltar Pass, looking south into the north fork of Cliff Creek. To right is Mist Ridge. The col in the far distance is Picklejar Pass.

#41 Cliff Creek below the southern cliffs of Gibraltar.

41 CLIFF CREEK—map 3

Day hike or bike 'n' hike from trailhead
Unofficial trails, creek crossings
Distance 1 km to end of good trail
Height gain 46 m (150 ft.)
High point ~1768 m (5800 ft.)
Map 82 J/10 Mount Rae

Access #31 Sheep trail west.

In the past we've always followed the time-consuming trail along the southeast bank The easier way in nowadays follows a good horse trail along the right (north-west) bank. The end attraction here is the vertical southeast face of Gibraltar. You thought the north face was spectacular?

The horse trail leaves the northwest bank of Cliff Creek. After a steep beginning, it rises more gradually through open forest to a high point, then descends above small crags lining the bank into the valley of Cliff Creek. Here ends the good trail.

GOING FARTHER
Downstream to waterfall
Turn left on a fainter trail. Shortly, wade the creek to the southeast bank and continue on trail below mossy, dripping crags to a 10-m-high waterfall tumbling into a rock-girt bowl.

Upstream to canyon 900+ m
On fainter trail continue upstream a way, then cross to the southeast bank. The trail continues through open forest and willows to a grassy avalanche gully in 500 m. For most people this viewpoint for Gibraltar is the end of the trip.

I don't know of anyone who's found a good way onward. The bush is dense and scratchy with deadfall. That leaves the creek. Paddling, uphill detours, delicate slab moves I can handle, but I draw the line at swimming. So just go as far as conditions warrant. The rock scenery in the canyon around the bend is stunning.

The slabs above the 10-m-high waterfall. In the background rises the east face of Gibraltar.

42 MISSINGLINK MOUNTAIN from the west — maps 2 & 5

A spring day on the summit.

Half-day hike
Unofficial trail, then route
Distance 1.8 km
Height gain 335 m (1100 ft.)
High point 1945 m (6380 ft.)
Map 82 J/10 Mount Rae

Access Gorge Creek Road at Gorge Creek parking lot. NOTE This road is closed Dec 1– May 15.
Also accessible from #21 Missinglink Mountain from the south.

The grassy western escarpment offers the shortest route to a fabulous summit viewpoint. Presently, you follow a cow trail, a cutline and a game trail with short steep sections.

See #21 for naming history.

From the parking lot walk out to the road and turn right. After crossing a wee creek by culvert, turn left into a big meadow. Walk to its far end where a good cow trail takes off into the forest to the left of a NE–SW cutline.

Straightaway, stay on the right bank of the wee creek, at the next junction turning right to intersect the cutline, which is narrow and identified by stumps. (NOTE If you keep left and cross the creek, bit trails wander up the hillside to connect with the cutline higher up.) Turn left onto the cutline and climb a steep hill. (From the top is a view of the parking lot biffy.) Descend slightly and cross the creek. Continue up the gently rising cutline through pine forest with grass underfoot to where it fades away on a grassy rib.

A game trail takes over, zigging uphill through gnarly dwarf aspens to a split. Go left onto a grassy slope, then zig back right across a treed ridge (where the other trail comes in) onto another grassy slope which extends to the top of the escarpment.

Just before trail disappears over the top into pine forest, cut left along the escarpment edge, dodging around small outcrops and finishing with a level, grassy promenade to the summit cairn.

What a place to view the Front Ranges all the way from the Highwood to the Elbow! Down below you can see all the forks of Gorge Creek snaking around forested foothills from their sources on Bluerock Mountain, Mount Rose, Surveyor's Ridge and Volcano.

43 GORGE CREEK—map 5

Day hike, backpack
Official trail with signposts & red markers, creek crossings
Distance 11.4 km
Height gain 411 m (1350 ft.)
High point 1951 m (6400 ft.)
Map 82 J/10 Mount Rae

Access Gorge Creek Trail (road) at Gorge Creek day-use area. NOTE This road is closed Dec 1–May 15.
Also accessible from the southern terminus of #49 Gorge–Ware connector, the northeastern terminus of #47 South Gorge Creek trail, the southern terminus of the #43A Gorge to Northwest fork, the northern terminus of #25 Indian Oils trail, the northern terminus of #28 Bluerock Creek trail, the western terminus of #66 Volcano Creek trail and the southern terminus of Threepoint Mountain trail (Volume 2).

A scenic and hilly trail that follows Gorge Creek Valley through alternating meadows and gorges into the Front Ranges between Mount Rose and Bluerock Mountain. At the northern terminus it connects with Threepoint Mountain and Volcano Creek trails near Threepoint backcountry background. As you can see by the large number of "also accessibles," all kinds of circuits are available. Most popular is its use as an access trail to Mount Ware. For a short stroll on a hot day I highly recommend the northwest fork cascade.

To Gorge–Ware connector 1.1 km
The trail begins beside the biffy and heads muddily downhill into a meadow above Gorge Creek. Here use the single-track trail at farthest right. After the trails unite, Ridge 636167 can be seen rising to the right. (See OPTION B.)

Descend slightly and come to another split. Go rightward up a hill. On the descent to the northwest fork crossing, you'll spot a trail plummeting down the shaley left bank. This leads to the northwest fork cascade, which can also be reached along the bank from just before the bridge. This is one of my favourite K Country waterfalls, particularly at spate when water streams down slabs in a classy, lacy effect into Gorge Creek. The dry slabs at the confluence are great for sunbathing.

Continue down the trail and cross the bridge over the northwest fork that arises from the south slopes of Surveyor's Ridge. A few metres beyond is the junction with the Gorge–Ware connector. Turn left.

The bridge over the northwest fork.

The middle section of the northwest fork cascade.

The rocky hill in the narrows just east of Indian Oils junction.

To Indian Oils trail 4.1 km

Walking on old exploration road, pass the northeastern terminus of South Gorge Creek trail a few minutes later.

After a flat stretch in the pines, the road starts to climb, following the undulating banktop of Gorge Creek. Three steep uphills are irritating when you know the road will later be descending to valley bottom. Between the first downhill and the third uphill, a cutline heading north at ~623145 is the route we took pre K Country to Volcano Creek. Nowadays it marks the start of SHORTCUT A to Gorge's northwest fork and the Gorge–Ware connector.

A long downhill (gruelling on the return) leads back to creek level, where the next point of interest is a delightful section of cascades and pools below a shaley bank. Not too much farther on, a newer version of trail turns to the right up a hill and traverses a steep bank high above the narrows. Having paddled my way through the narrows in the past, this is one hill I welcome. On your way back down to the creek, pass through the drift fence into cow country. The side trail heading up right at 603141 is the route to the lower top of Mount Ware. (See OPTIONAL RETURN #46B.)

Continue descending and from the cattle drinking place look back at the rocky hill above the narrows. Then veer right, into meadows. At a signpost at 601141, Indian Oils trail turns off to the left across the meadow toward the creek. Keep straight.

To Bluerock–Gorge shortcut 860 m

About 360 m west of the junction the Mount Ware trail turns off to the right at a cairn. (This is the second trail to the right.)

Enter another meadow with a view of Bluerock Mountain up ahead, then wade Gorge Creek twice within a very short distance. Continue under a steep bank to an unsigned junction at 594143 with the Bluerock–Gorge shortcut. (See #28B.) This occurs just upstream of the junction with the west fork of Gorge Creek. Pre K Country days we used to end our Gorge Creek forays up this tributary because

that's where the trail led, to a range rider's cabin that has long since disappeared.

To Bluerock Creek trail 2.1 km

Today's Gorge Creek trail continues up the right bank of the main valley in meadows below the rugged south slopes of Mount Ware. In 420 m, at 591145, #55 Surveyor's Ridge to Gorge Creek comes in across the grass from the right. There is no actual junction—you can spot the trail climbing the slope in the trees.

Wade Gorge Creek a third time, then after a while start a slow climb through alternating meadow and forest to the signposted junction with Bluerock Creek trail at 576152. Keep straight.

To Threepoint Mountain, Volcano Creek & Mount Rose Meadows trails 3.2 km

The valley is squeezing in again, forcing the trail to climb up and over a couple of forested side ridges. The first hill is the longest. On your way down the second hill, the side creek below a steep drop in the trail is the best place to fill up the water bottles.

Cross Gorge Creek for the fourth and final time, straightaway beginning the long climb out of the valley in anticipation of the black shale gorge up ahead. Initially the trail is steep, the shale worn to a groove between bedrock from speeding downhill bikers, forcing hikers, horses and their riders to take to the dicey side slope below the trail. The trail then improves, but it's still a laborious, twisting climb to the caution sign suggesting bikers walk their steeds down the hill. Fat chance!

The view at the trail's high point a little farther on is one of K Country's finest: the upper valley between Mount Rose and Bluerock Mountain, the splendour of the scene further enhanced by the dramatic situation of the trail as it follows the lip of the gorge toward the big bend where the valley turns sharp west.

(NOTE In case you are wondering, the cutline with good trail heading east from

the high point undulates along the north slope of Surveyor's Ridge to the foot of the meadow below the viewpoint on Surveyor's Ridge trail.)

Gorge Creek trail continues in a northerly direction, descending into forest featuring one muddy dip and a muddy section of trail leading to the 4-way junction with signpost at 565178.

The better-used right-hand trail is Volcano Creek trail to Threepoint backcountry campground in Volcano Creek. Ahead is Threepoint Mountain trail (see Volume 2). To left is the trail to Mount Rose Meadows and Bluerock Mountain from the north.

Northwest access #48 NW fork of Gorge Creek in two places.

SHORTCUT

43A To the northwest fork

Unofficial trail, creek crossing
Height loss S–N 40 m (130 ft.)
High point 1625 m (5330 ft.)

South access #43 Gorge Creek at the N–S cutline at ~623145.
Northeast access #49 Gorge–Ware connector in the big meadow.

Connector trails made by equestrians cut off the corner if you're doing a loop with Gorge Creek trail and 1. Gorge–Ware connector and Volcano South trails and 2. the northwest fork of Volcano Creek. I've also used it as an alternative to Gorge Creek trail when returning from Mount Ware. It's a shade longer but it's flatter.

FROM GORGE CREEK TRAIL
1. To Gorge–Ware connector 1.2 km
Head north on the N–S cutline for a short distance, then turn off to the right onto a trail. It heads northeast through open pine forest and after crossing a narrow

circles around to the left. After detouring around some fallen trees, you descend a steepish hill, then turn right onto the cutline access road that zigs down to a faint junction on the banktop with #48. Keep left on the access road that descends to the northwest fork and crosses it.

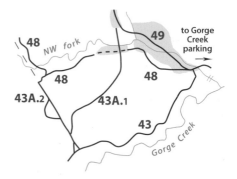

#43A shortcuts to the northwest fork of Gorge Creek

NE–SW cutline, splinters into many trails that coalesce beyond a small damp area. Not long after, the trail reaches the banktop of the northwest fork and descends into a meadow. Here you cross route #48 which is faint at this point. (NOTE Going rightward on #48 leads to Gorge–Ware connector just north of the junction with Gorge Creek trail.)

Continue ahead and rockhop the northwest fork. Then veer to the right through trees into the big meadow where you'll pick up the Gorge–Ware connector.

2. To northwest fork 760 m

Head north on the N–S cutline. Stay ahead on the cutline where 1. turns off to the right and a cutline access road semi-

OPTION

43B Ridge 636167

Half-day to short-day hike
Route
Distance to summit 2.1 km, loop 6.6 km
Height gain 247 m (810 ft.)
High point 1814 m (5950 ft.)

Access ~600 m from Gorge Creek trailhead, cross the southeast ridge at ~636151.

This is the low, undulating ridge between Gorge–Ware connector and Ware Creek trail (aka Gorge Creek Road). Despite its treed appearance, it offers views from its western escarpment.

To the first top 600 m
Simply climb the grassy southeast ridge to your right to a levelling. Before entering pines, look back for a fine view of "Dot Mountain," the southerly spur of Missinglink Mountain as named by researchers at the nearby R.B. Miller Field Station.

The first top at the south end lies in trees, so you must walk a little bit farther to a long grassy strip lining the western escarpment for the view west over the Gorge Creek headwaters to Bluerock Mountain.

To the high point 1.5 km
Now heading NNE, the route undulates over a couple of tops through easy and pleasantly open pine forest to a low point crossed by a game trail which was briefly considered for an official trail connecting Gorge–Ware connector to Ware Creek trail. A more concentrated climb (again crossed by a game trail) leads to the high point. Nearly all the way along this final stretch you can follow the open escarpment top.

Looping? 4.5 km
Continue along the ridge. All is straightforward, pines alternating with open stretches allowing views of Volcano, until you come to 640178 where the escarpment curves around to the east and ends. Trying to reach the northern terminus of Gorge–Ware connector from this point is not fun: a steep drop amid deadfall followed by a bumpy ridge with deadfall. Far better to drop off the right (east) side of the ridge to Ware Creek trail, which will return you to the trailhead easily.

View from the western escarpment of the Gorge Creek headwaters.

44 MOUNT ROSE MEADOWS — map 5

Mount Rose and its meadows from near the three skulls camping area.

Backpack
Unofficial trail & route
Distance from 4-way 3 km
Height gain from 4-way 213 m (700 ft.)
Map 82 J/10 Mount Rae

Access The 4-way junction at 565178 where #43 Gorge Creek, #66 Volcano Creek, Three-point Mountain (Volume 2) and Mount Rose Meadows trails all meet.

The objective is the Gorge–Cougar col at the head of Gorge Creek, the attraction the beautiful meadows of Mount Rose which K Country planner Don Cockerton once likened to the Swiss Alps after hearing clanging cow bells.

For anyone camped at Threepoint backcountry campground, this is the best side trip. You can also camp along the trail at three deer skulls at the start of the meadows. For scramblers this route accesses #45 Bluerock Mountain.

To campsites 1.4 km
Take the narrower trail heading west, climbing gradually through trees. A brief visit to the edge of Gorge Creek canyon elicits the comment "must be exciting for the dudes on horseback" from Tony. Then it's back into trees to cross a side creek, where narrow trails heading right appear to access an open ridgetop. After a less vertiginous stint on the banktop above grass, the trail moves away from the creek and dips to cross a side creek that has plenty of water. Climb up right, then cross another smaller creek to three skulls at the edge of the trees. Ahead are the meadows.

To Gorge–Cougar col 1.6 km
A narrower trail carries on across meadow low down on the skirts of Mount Rose. Reaching trees on the far side, it splits. Stay high near the meadow edge and gradually contour up rightward to the col between Mount Rose and Bluerock Mountain, a wide meadow sloping into the dark forests of Cougar Creek, a little-known valley that harbours a small blue tarn at its head.

Return
If returning via A, traverse the meadow to 553176. The going is easy on short grass with drifts of flowers growing on the damper facets of the hillside. Nearing trees, pick up an emerging trail that takes you out to the trail junction. Turn left.

44A Shortcuts to Threepoint Mountain trail

Distances 2 km, 2.1 km

From the three skulls camping area, trails developed by outfitters connect to Threepoint Mountain trail in two places. If backpacking north to the Elbow or Threepoint Creek, use 1. If returning to Threepoint backcountry campground or backpacking down Volcano Creek, use 2.

From the three skulls head north to the left of the forest, looking for where a good trail starts cold turkey at the forest edge. A little way on at 553176 is a junction. Keep right. (The trail to left leads higher into the meadows, so if you are reversing the route, this is the trail to take to the col.) Cross a couple of meadows to a gap between two grassy hills.

The trail heads downhill through trees. At a puzzling 3-way split keep left into a small meadow. After the other two trails join in, you walk alongside a small creek in a longitudinal meadow. Immediately after crossing the creek come to a Y-junction at 559183.

1. To Volcano–Rock watershed 560 m

Keep left, following the right bank of the creek in a northwesterly direction. Recross the creek in a boggy area, then shortly leave it and head even more northerly on a muddy trail. At the first junction you come to, descend right and cross a narrows of boggy meadow to Threepoint Mountain trail, reached at 561188 just south of the Volcano–Rock watershed. (In reverse, the shortcut trail is very evident.)

2. To Volcano Creek 620 m

Go right and continue through the meadow. In trees the trail splinters and winds about, then descends to cross the fledgling Volcano Creek in a meadow. Follow the creek downstream, at the end swinging left to cross the wee north fork

prior to reaching Threepoint Mountain trail at the top of the bank just north AND south of the signpost at 564183. NOTE If travelling south on Threepoint Mountain trail to Gorge Creek trail, this good trail is often mistaken for Threepoint Mountain trail, despite the fact it heads west and not south. When the missing section of Threepoint Mountain is restored with red markers, all will be made clear.

Trail just west of the Y-junction, Mount Rose ahead.

45 BLUEROCK MOUNTAIN from the north — map 5

Backpack scramble
Route
Distance one way 2.7 km from col
Height gain 640 m (2100 ft.) from col
High point 2789 m (9150 ft.)
Map 82 J/10 Mount Rae

Access Via #44 Mount Rose Meadows at the Gorge–Cougar col.

An easier and simpler way up than the south ridge route. However, it does require an overnight, either at the three skulls on the Mount Rose Meadows trail, or better still, at the meadow above the rockband.

From the topo map it appears you can approach the mountain by walking straight up the creek from the meadows. Not so. There's a waterfall, and the cliff encircling it requires a stiff scramble with a heavy pack. It's far better to start from the Gorge–Cougar gap at 541168, from where numerous game trails traverse south through trees into upper Gorge Creek above the cliff. A meadow is the perfect campsite.

The fact that our short evening stroll before turning in evolved into an ascent of Bluerock explains why I have no photos of the climb, because quite apart from leaving the camera in the tent, the sun was setting.

Bluerock Mountain, showing the campsite, the scree step and the upper slopes below the northwest ridge. Photo Alf Skrastins

Walk up the valley, turning the waterfall step on left-side scree via a sheep trail. Continue easily toward the notch at 550154—an amazing fossil bed of horn corals and brachiopods. Then grovel up the north face on good, stable rubble, aiming for a breach in the rockband that lets you onto the northwest ridge. Turn left and in less than 10 minutes reach the summit.

Looking back down the northwest ridge from the summit toward mounts Three-point and Rose, and Gorge–Cougar col.

157

46 MOUNT WARE — map 5

Day scramble
Unofficial trail & route
Distance one way 2.1 km, 7.6 km from Gorge Creek trailhead
Height gain 448 m (1470 ft.) from Gorge Creek
High point 2127 m (6980 ft.)
Map 82 J/10 Mount Rae

Access Via #43 Gorge Creek trail ~360 m west of Indian Oils junction at 599142. A cairn marks the spot. This is not the first trail heading up right, but the second, steeper, more obvious one.

This shapely little mountain overlooking Gorge Creek at 592155 has characteristics of a higher peak: steepness of ascent, crags and an airy summit ridge. Expect a wee bit of easy scrambling and possible route-finding difficulties down in the forest. (If returning the same way, take a GPS to help you retrace your steps.) It has one drawback. It's very attractive to sheep, so naturally it's one of the tick summits of the world. Just don't go in spring.

#46A On the summit ridge, looking to Bluerock Mountain, Mount Rose and Threepoint Mountain.

Most people climb this in one day from Gorge Creek trailhead and return the same way. For an even better trip, I urge you to try one or both of the two options. Alternatively, make a 16.1 km loop with #55 down to Gorge Creek. You can make a slightly longer 16.5 km loop by taking #55 to Surveyor's Ridge and returning via #54 Surveyor's Ridge, #53 Volcano South and #49 Gorge–Ware connector trails.

NAMING & HISTORY NOTE Ware Head, as named by A.O. Wheeler, or John Ware's Head, as others called it, was first climbed on August 18 and 19, 1897, by Wheeler and his assistant Hector, who used it as a secondary triangulation station during the Irrigation Survey of the foothills.

From the cairn a good trail heads up the hillside. Keep right and climb more steeply by the side of a gully into pine forest. The gradient eases as you come to a 3-way split. Take the obvious left-hand trail.

The trail wends left through gradually rising forest for quite a way before fading. This is where a GPS comes in useful on the return. Continue on the same line, following flagging, and intersect a good up-down trail at a small cairn. Turn right. (The trail to left appears to leave the Gorge Creek Valley west of the two creek crossings.)

The trail twists rather steeply up the left side of an intermittent gully, then becomes faint in long, lush grass under open pine forest. Follow flagging and cut branches, keeping an eye out for where the trail traverses left onto the open southeast spur, reached just above treeline.

Turn right and climb the spur on grass and shale over several rises and above a ring of crags to the left to the foot of "the head." This final slope is steeper and higher than it looks, a messy mix of shale, dryas and broken rocks. Just below the top, aim to the right of crags, where there are signs of people going for a slither on the descent.

Surrounded by drop-offs, this little summit has a feeling of height remarkable for such a low hill, and a tremendous view of Bluerock Mountain, Mount Rose and Threepoint Mountain off to the west. To the south you overlook the forest and meadows traversed by Bluerock and Indian Oils trails. To the east rises Little Ware (see OPTIONAL RETURN B). To the north you can trace the route to Surveyor's Ridge should you be heading that way.

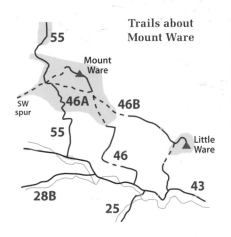

Mount Ware from the ascent route. The summit is at far right.

OPTIONAL ADD-ON

46A The Traverse

Scramble
Unofficial trails & route
Distance add 1.2 km
Height loss 116 m (380 ft.)

A little loop on the end that takes in the delectable summit ridge and the southwest spur. This is also the prerequisite for longer loops using #55.

To Southwest spur
Walk along the summit rock ridge to its west end above a cliff. At a weakness on the right (north) side, scrabble down to the right on scree, then head back left under the cliff. Keep left until you hit a twisty trail taking you down shale and rubble onto the broad, grassy southwest ridge. Follow the ridge to the saddle, where you intersect route #55. There's no trail at this point; it starts a little way down on both sides.

While this is already a fine viewpoint for Mount Ware, walk up the southwest spur beyond the saddle. Now the whole south face of the mountain is disclosed and you can pick out your return traverse across the south face, a well as route #55 winding down a shaley slope to Gorge Creek.

Back to ascent route
Return to the saddle and turn right. A little way down the south slope, pick up #55 heading east, soon dropping into a flat, grassy basin where the trail turns south. Leave it at the basin and continue eastwards, climbing slightly on grass to a perpendicular patch of shale with cairns. Find a faint trail marked with the odd cairn that traverses the grassy south face of Ware to the top of the southeast rib that was your ascent route. At the midpoint, you cross the fledgling south face gully just above a spring that appears to run all year round.

Now turn right and return the same way you came up or tack on B.

#46A Mount Ware from the southwest spur. The route descends the left skyline to the saddle at left, then traverses the right slope at last trees.

Little Ware from Mount Ware's ascent route, showing the route taken by #46B.

46B via "Little Ware"

Route & unofficial trails
Distance to Gorge Creek 3.2 km
Additional height gain 76 m (250 ft.)
High point 1939 m (6360 ft.)

Why not take in the little summit book-ending the southeast ridge of Mount Ware? If time is short, make this top your day's objective from Gorge Creek trail by reversing the descent trail. Height gain is 268 m (880 ft.).

Summit of Little Ware, looking toward unnamed peaks south of Mt. Burns.

To Little Ware 2.1 km

From the summit of Mount Ware descend the normal route to the top of the southeast rib, then head down the slope to its left, the going easy on meadow among a few pines to the broad, flattish southeast ridge. In a meadow with a reddish-coloured rock veer to the right of it where you will pick up a trail. Follow it left through open pines to a shallow pond. A trail continues from the other side in much the same sort of way to open slopes below the nubbin.

Still on a trail, head diagonally up left on shale below a small crag, then circle around to the right on easy-angled grass to the summit—a cairn perched on the edge of southwest-facing cliffs. Enjoy fine views of Mount Ware, Bluerock Mountain and a slew of peaks south of the Sheep River Valley.

To Gorge Creek trail 1.1 km

Return to the bottom of the nubbin.

Head south, descending steepening grass into a draw at first trees where a trail starts. In forest the gradient eases right off, the trail wandering off to the left, then returning down a hill to the left bank of the draw (now deepened to creek) that is followed out to Gorge Creek trail. At a split near the bottom, keep left and join Gorge Creek trail just west of the drift fence gate at 603141.

Turn left to return to the trailhead.

47 SOUTH GORGE CREEK TRAIL — maps 5 & 3

Day hike
Official trail, with signposts & red markers, creek crossing
Distance 5.3 km
Height gain NE–SW 213 m (700 ft.)
High point 1783 m (5850 ft.)
Map 82 J/10 Mount Rae

Northeast access Via #43 Gorge Creek trail, 200 m west of the north fork crossing.
Southwest access Via #25 Indian Oils trail at 613123 just east of the second pass.

This not very scenic trail enables the day tripper to access Indian Oils trail from Gorge Creek trail and make a 14.9 km loop. Pine forest, a few meadows and cows just about sums it up. TRAIL NOTE Since the third edition, there is no bridge over Gorge Creek.

FROM NORTHEAST ACCESS

Straight off, the trail winds down to Gorge Creek. Wade across and climb the bank to a gate in a drift fence. Zigzag up the remainder of the bank, then head through pine forest between two forested hills to a big, lush meadow. Edge around two sides of it to a T-junction with a NW–SE cutline.

Turn left and follow the cutline for only a short way before detouring left across a swampy meadow. Logs delineating the trail keep in water as deep as the Mariana Trench. This is one place where you walk OUTSIDE the trail. After a stint through trees, you cross the meadow creek on a bridge back to the cutline. Turn left.

The cutline descends slightly to a valley whose creek — NOT named South Gorge Creek — flows into Gorge Creek near Hwy. 546. A red marker indicates the turn right onto a trail heading west.

This is the best part, where the trail makes a gradual ascent along the north bank of the creek into rather more open country with aspens and patches of meadow. At the valley head you cross the creek on a bridge and a few minutes later arrive at the T-junction with Indian Oils trail at 613123.

Turn right if aiming for the middle section of Gorge Creek Valley, left for Hwy. 546.

The bridge over the meadow creek.

48 NORTHWEST FORK of GORGE CREEK — map 5

Day hikes
Unofficial trails, creek crossings
Distance to forks 2.6 km
Height gain to forks 113 m (370 ft.)
Height loss to forks 40 m (130 ft.)
High point at forks 1652 m (5420 ft.)
Map 82 J/10 Mount Rae

Access Via #49 Gorge–Ware connector 80 m north of the junction with Gorge Creek trail.
Also accessible from #43A Gorge Creek to the northwest fork, #54 Surveyor's Ridge, #53 Volcano South trail.

A less frequented valley accessed by a cutline and its access road. Pre K Country this is the route we used to take to Surveyor's Ridge before Volcano South trail became available. You still can. But rather than start from a high point on Gorge Creek trail as we used to, it's less effort to follow cow trails along the valley bottoms. The first part you share with #43A. See the sketch maps on pages 153 and 164.

Use in combination with Volcano South trail to make loops, or as access to the hill at 618163.

To creek crossing 1.2 km
At the T-junction with Gorge Creek trail, head north on Gorge–Ware for about 80 m, then turn left and cross meadow toward the trees. A good cow trail materializes and leads up a bank into pine forest. Follow it along the banktop and back down into a meadow above the confluence with the north fork.

Heads upstream (west) through meadow and trees into a longitudinal meadow where the ongoing trail is faint. In 500 m cross trail #43A. Continue along the meadow to a salt lick in the trees, then, leaving cows and calves behind, follow the trail up the bank. Head west along the banktop to a junction with a grassy cutline access road. Turn right and descend the road to the northwest fork. Cross.

To forks 1.4 km
The access road veers left, then starts a long, winding climb up a hill to get above steep shale banks. Some 390 m distant from the creek crossing, at 619155, turn left onto a worthwhile shortcut trail. (NOTE If bound for OPTION D, stay on the road.)

The trail traverses above steep banks — keep straight at a split — and joins the cutline. Easy walking brings you to a Y-junction with the cutline access road that has come zooming down a very steep hill from your right. Keep left.

Shortly, turn left on the road (the cutline continues straight) and descend to valley bottom meadows. The road heads upstream below a steep grassy bank.

At an impasse, where the creek curves against a steep shale bank, you have three choices of route:

1. Scrabble up and down the right bank.
2. Cross the creek twice at the bend to the continuation of the road.

Then continue up the road to the meadow just above the forks at 613161.

The creek above the forks.

3. Cross the creek once, then follow a trail along the left bank. Shortly, it crosses the left-hand fork above the forks to a junction. Head left for #48A, right for #48 B and C, which entails crossing the right-hand fork back to the cutline access road at the forks meadow.

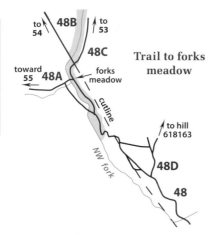

Trail to forks meadow

GOING FARTHER

48A to Ware–Surveyor's col

Unofficial trail, route, many creek crossings
Distance 3.2 km
Height gain 314 m (1030 ft.)

Although this lush, forested valley appears a good route on the topo map as a way to Ware–Surveyor's col, in reality it is not. The route is frequented by bears feeding on horsetails, so take precautions.

Use option no. 3 at the impasse, and after crossing the left-hand fork turn left.

The trail starts off well, then, just after the third creek crossing, degenerates in too many places amid high grasses and horsetails and muddy creek crossings. If determined to reach the col, stick to the valley bottom trail.

Hunter's trails on the right bank all turn north, following ridges between deeply incised side creeks onto the southeast slopes of Surveyor's Ridge.

48B to Surveyor's Ridge trail

Unofficial trail
Distance 2 km
Height gain 262 m (860 ft.)

Basically a cutline with some deadfall.

At forks meadow continue to follow the access road that climbs up right parallel to the right-hand fork and runs along the top of a mini-canyon with small waterfalls. Arriving at a NW–SE cutline, turn down left and cross the creek.

Follow the cutline up a very long hill into a meadow on a broad ridge. At the far end of the meadow is a cutline access road heading right. Ignore it unless aiming for the Gorge–Volcano watershed, and continue on cutline into the pines. Shortly, Surveyor's Ridge trail comes in from the right.

48C to Volcano South trail

Unofficial trails
Distance 1.3 km
Height gain 101 m (330 ft.)
Height loss 70 m (230 ft.)

Connects the northwest fork to #53 Volcano South trail in the north fork.

To the watershed
At forks meadow continue to follow the access road that climbs up to the right parallel to the right fork, and runs along the top of a mini-canyon with small waterfalls. Cross the NW–SE cutline.

A pleasant trail along the banktop gradually drops to valley bottom grass. Look for flagging, then a yellow shale trail climbing upwards. Join a narrow NE–SW cutline and turn right. Going is easy through dry pine forest to the watershed. Actually, you cross above the low point, and looking right you can spot the open slopes of Hill 618163.

#48C On the cutline at the watershed, Mount Ware at right.

#48D Descending Hill 618163 to the cutline, looking up #48A to Ware–Surveyor's col to the right of Mount Ware. Bluerock Mountain through the gap.

To Volcano South trail

Descend more steeply. On meeting deadfall and bushes, follow flagging around the right side of the cutline and down to 618171 on the Volcano South trail.

OPTION

48D Hill 618163

Unofficial trail, route
Distance 1.6 km from #48
Height gain 155 m (510 ft.)
Height loss 79 m (260 ft.)
High point 1832 m (6010 ft.)

The hill between the northwest and north forks is a good viewpoint, easily climbed from the cutline access road. On reaching C, make a loop with either #48 (west, left) or #53 (right, east).

To the summit 1.1 km from 619155

From waypoint 619155 on the cutline access road continue to follow the road up the hill to its high point, where it flattens and turns left. Shortly, turn first right onto a side road.

After the side road ends, head uphill through easy pine forest, approaching the summit via the south ridge. The summit opening is not the best viewpoint, so continue north.

To #48C 510 m

As you descend the grassy, shaley northwest ridge to the intersecting NE–SW cutline (route C) in the pines, a view is revealed of Mount Ware and Bluerock Mountain across to South Volcano Ridge.

You will also observe that your little hill is just the southern tip of a broad ridge extending to the Gorge–Volcano watershed and that there is nothing to stop you from plodding up there. Make for the grassy edge of the western escarpment that excites with unexpected cliffs and follow it up, at the last, bushwhacking through pines to the watershed viewpoint near route #53.

165

49 GORGE–WARE CONNECTOR — map 5

In the big meadow. Junction Mountain ahead.

Half-day, day hike in combo
Official trail with signposts, red mark-
ers, creek crossings & bridges
Distance 5.5 km
Height gain S–N 49 m (160 ft.)
Height loss S–N 110 m (360 ft.)
High point 1655 m (5430 ft.)
Map 82 J/10 Mount Rae

South access Via #43 Gorge Creek trail on
the west bank of the northwest fork crossing.
North access Via #56 Ware Creek trail 3.7 km
north of Gorge Creek trailhead at 650190.
Also accessible from the southern terminus
of #53 Volcano South trail, the eastern terminus of #52 Volcano Link.

This flat, easy connector, linking Gorge
Creek trail to Ware Creek trail, takes you
through typical foothills valleys of cow
meadows and pine forests.

TRAIL NOTE This is the Gorge Link
trail from the third edition with a little
bit of the old Link Creek trail tacked on
at the end.

SOUTH TO NORTH
To Volcano South trail 1.4 km
From the junction on the west bank
of Gorge Creek's northwest fork, head
north through meadows under the craggy
south face of Ridge 636167. Cross the
northwest fork (often a paddle), then the
much smaller north fork. Climb into a big
meadow with a view behind you of Junction Mountain. Enter trees and come to an
unbridged crossing of the north fork that
can usually be crossed without getting
your boots wet. At the top of the bank, go
straight. (Volcano South turns left.)

To Volcano Link 2.2 km
In a few metres, the South Volcano Ridge
trail turns left at some flagging. Go straight,
your trail steering northeast through
the odd meadow to a drift fence. Imperceptibly you cross the watershed into a
headwater of Ware Creek, evidenced by a
change in vegetation. At 636181 come to
a T-junction with Volcano Link trail that
turns off to the left. Continue straight.

To Ware Creek trail 1.9 km
Cross the bridge over a bigger side creek to
a T-junction. Keep right. (To left at 810 m
is the old Link Creek trail #52A.) The final
stretch through pines, then meadow, has
been improved with boardwalk and a new
bridge across the mud bath. A little farther
on you cross a fine new bridge over Ware
Creek. Climb to the old Volcano Ridge
trailhead and follow its access road out
to Ware Creek trail, a road.

50 SOUTH VOLCANO RIDGE—map 5

Day hike
Unofficial trail & route, flagging, cairns
Distance 2.5 km
Height gain 320 m (1050 ft.)
Height loss 37 m (120 ft.)
High point 1935 m (6350 ft.)
Map 82 J/10 Mount Rae

South access Via #49 Gorge–Ware connector near the junction with #53 Volcano South trail.
North access Via #52 Volcano Link just east of the pass.

The rocky summit of South Volcano Ridge is an excellent objective and can be used in combo with both Volcano Link and the Gorge–Ware connector, and with Volcano Link and Volcano South trails to make reasonable-length loops from Gorge Creek trailhead of 12.3 km and 11.1 km respectively. And of course, it's also the direct route to Volcano summit.

TRAIL NOTE After the trail peters out on shaley slopes, look for flagging, trimmed branches and cairns.

HISTORY NOTE "The Protest Trail," as some call it, was secretly made by disgruntled users in response to the 2005 closure of Gorge Creek Road and Volcano Ridge trailhead that formerly gave easy access to Volcano summit. The idea was to make a more direct approach to Volcano summit than that provided by official trails leaving Gorge Creek trailhead.

SOUTH TO NORTH
To summit 2.2 km

The trail leaves Gorge–Ware connector just north of the junction with Volcano South. The white sign with the name scribbled on it has disappeared, but red flagging can be seen ahead.

The trail climbs steadily up the south ridge in pine forest. Halfway along, the gradient eases and you alternate between short-treed steps and shaley flats above the western escarpment. The final approach is on stones with a smattering of small pines. It's here that a big cliff starts up on the left side and wraps around the north end of the ridge, creating a rocky knob with a cairn on top. For some time you have been treated to panoramic views westwards, but it's only here "on the edge" that Volcano summit is revealed to the north.

To Volcano Link trail 270 m

The trail zigs down the right (east) side of the rocky knob on steepish grass, then cuts left below the cliff and on down grey shales interspersed with mini-rockbands to a levelling. Rather than tackle more of the same to Volcano Pass proper, head down rightish at the edge of trees to intercept Volcano Link trail where it emerges into the meadows on the east side of the pass. See the photo on page 171.

South Volcano Ridge from Volcano South trail.
Route follows ridge from right to left.

#50 View from the summit of South Volcano Ridge of Volcano, showing the approach route up the meadow.

#50 A cairn marking the route along South Volcano Ridge.

#51 Larkspur on shale.

Summit cairn.

51 VOLCANO SUMMIT TRAIL—map 5

Long-day hike
Unofficial trail
Distance 2.5 km one way
Height gain 222 m (730 ft.)
High point 2128 m (6980 ft.)
Map 82 J/10 Mount Rae

Access Via #52 Volcano Link, 85 m east of Volcano Pass at 619183.

This is a big, grassy summit with a fabulous 360-degree panoramic view. For the most part you follow what is actually a cutline access road with one steep hill. Nowadays, open sections of the road have narrowed to single track in long grasses.

ACCESS NOTE For a generation, this route to Volcano's summit was an extremely popular hike from Volcano Ridge trailhead. Then, in 2005, easy access was cut off by the closure of Gorge Creek Road and the trailhead. So what to do now?

One option is to bike the closed section of road (now Ware Creek trail) from Gorge Creek trailhead to the old trailhead. With 13.6 km of hiking plus 7.4 km of biking, this adds up to 21 km in all, with a long uphill ride-and-push right at the end of the day. If you don't fancy biking, the shortest official approach is from Gorge Creek trailhead via Gorge Creek, Gorge–Ware connector, South Volcano Ridge and Volcano Link trails at 17.6 km return. An easterly approach via Gorge Creek, Gorge–Ware connector and Volcano Link is actually longer at 19 km return. Using the protest trail along South Volcano Ridge brings it down to a more manageable 15.4 km return the same way.

NAMING NOTE The odd name "Volcano" without the word "Ridge" dates back to 1896 when a secondary triangulation station was established on the summit by the Irrigation Survey led by A.O. Wheeler. (Interestingly, they started from "the muskeg pass" between Gorge and Ware creeks near today's Gorge Creek trailhead. They also climbed it on August 20, 21 and 22, 1897, in hopes of better conditions, but it was not to be. Every day, Wheeler complained of smoke coming in on west and southwest winds making "views very poor." Likely this constant smokiness led to its name. That it was named for its volcanic formation, as is suggested in the current place name book, would have geologists holding their sides with laughter. One can imagine Wheeler and associates having a good chuckle beyond the Great Divide over our efforts to come up with plausible explanations.

At the meeting of old Link Creek trail and new Volcano Link trail on the east side of Volcano Pass, head right down old Link Creek trail for 40 m to a junction. Turn up left on a track with flagging. Alternatively, from the junction, shortcut through trees.

The track heads north, climbing onto a grassy lightly pined ridge from the right side, and in half a kilometre leaving on the left side at some flagging. Some 50 vertical metres below you to the west is a large meadow as flat and green as a slightly tilted billiard table — a soggy south source of Volcano Creek.

After a treed section comes the big climb up the grassy south slope. Near the top, the trail heads left and through an avenue in the trees onto the west side of the ridge where I once found *Townsendia* blooming on the last grey day of October. Here the "cutline access road" heads north through flowery meadows toward the NE–SW cutline it serves. Just before the junction, leave the trail and climb up to the right on grass, following the grassy ridge to the summit cairn.

For a while the view has been growing in magnificence in one direction or the other, but it's only on reaching the top that you're rewarded with a full 360-degree panorama taking in Calgary to the east and the whole spectrum of Front Range peaks to the west. To the north and 4.5 km away as the crow flies along the connecting ridge is Allsmoke Mountain. Down below to the southeast the slope falls away in scree and rubble. In years past we used to pick a way down this stuff to the old Link Creek trail, so cutting out a dogleg.

Returning the same way you came up is easiest.

Plodding up the grassy south slope.

West-facing meadows below the summit.

52 VOLCANO LINK—map 5

The cairn at Volcano Pass, looking south to the summit of South Volcano Ridge.

Day hike, backpack
Official trail with signposts & red markers
Distance 3.5 km
Total height gain E–W 320 m (1050 ft.)
Total height loss E–W 15 m (50 ft.)
High point 1905 m (6250 ft.)
Map 82 J/10 Mount Rae

East access Via #49 Gorge–Ware connector at 636181.
West access Via #50 Volcano South trail at 618171.
Also accessible from the northern terminus of #50 South Volcano Ridge.

A fairly strenuous trail that runs between the Gorge–Ware connector and Volcano South trail via Volcano Pass (the low point between Volcano Summit and South Volcano Ridge). From near its high point, #51 takes off for the summit of Volcano.

TRAIL NOTE Since the third edition, most of the long-distance Link Creek trail that ran between Ware Creek trailhead and South Volcano trailhead has been decommissioned. Only one official remnant is left, but because it no longer follows

Link Creek, it has been renamed, the word "Link" meaning "connector" in this case.

It has also in part been rerouted. No longer do we have to endure that horribly steep cutline. In its stead, a new trail built in 2010 winds up a ridge farther to the south. Designed by Don Cockerton, K Country's first planner, who designed all of K Country's official trails back when, it is so much the antithesis of the hated cutline it is known by some as "Cockerton's Corkscrew." (This was Don's last official task before retirement, something he'd been yearning to do for some time.)

FROM EAST ACCESS
To Volcano Pass 2.6 km

From the Gorge–Ware connector turn west onto a wide trail at 636181.

Gently curving, the trail follows the left bank of a small side creek for some way, then crosses it on bridge to the right bank. Shortly it swings up to the right onto the ridge to the north and turns left. An almost flat trail soon morphs into zigzags of all lengths up a moderately steep slope with occasional viewpoints. After approaching

The trail zigging up the eastern slope.

The shale slope at the top of the zigs.

the creek to the left, the trail veers right and climbs to a shale opening below a rocky bluff.

From here on, the trail is merely curvy (but still uphill) as it heads right, below the forested east slope of South Volcano Ridge. At one point there's a view of Volcano, then it's back into trees for the final stretch into meadows covering the east flank of Volcano Pass. Cross grass, climbing a little to a junction with old Link Creek trail at 619183.

Turn left on the line of a NE–SW cutline (old Link Creek trail). In another 100 m reach the pass at a small cairn. From shaley meadows look west to Bluerock Mountain. Nearer at hand the eye is irresistibly drawn to the rocky nubbin that is the high point of South Volcano Ridge.

To Volcano South trail 900 m
The route continues in the same line on the cutline, following the rolling watershed between a Gorge Creek tributary on the left and a headwater of Volcano Creek that oozes from the big soggy meadow on the right. A final rise brings you to a T-junction with Volcano South (left and right) in the trees at 610180.

OPTIONAL DESCENT

52A Old Link Creek trail

Unofficial trail
Distance 2.7 km

Though decommissioned, de-signed and disliked as an ascent route, this NE–SW cutline cum access road is quite palatable going down. In fact the initial meadow section is very enjoyable. Then comes the plunge to a valley bottom, the tedium broken at the halfway point by an excellent viewpoint for Volcano's stony east face.

Cross a creek at the valley head and plod a straight cutline through dark forest to the Gorge–Ware connector, which is reached at 642185. Turn left for Ware Creek trail, right for Gorge Creek trailhead.

#53 Volcano South trail. The view from the Gorge–Volcano watershed of Volcano.

53 VOLCANO SOUTH TRAIL — map 5

Day hike, backpack
Official trail, signposts & red markers
Distance 5.1 km
Height gain S–N 329 m (1080 ft.)
Height loss S–N 131 m (430 ft.)
High point 1935 m (6350 ft.)
Map 82 J/10 Mount Rae

South access Via #49 Gorge–Ware connector.
North access #66 Volcano Creek.
Also accessible from the western terminus of #52 Volcano Link, and eastern terminus of #54 Surveyor's Ridge trail. See also #48 Northwest fork of Gorge Creek.

This trail connects trails in the Gorge Creek area to those of Threepoint Creek. It's not a beauty as trails go. It's a monotonous and sometimes steep plod through pine forest on what is mostly a cutline or its access road. Its only glory is the view from the watershed at 609178.

Usually it's travelled in combination to make loops, or used to get somewhere more interesting like Volcano summit or Surveyor's Ridge. If starting from the south end, the watershed is a suitable objective for a spring conditioning hike that will leave you gasping.

NAMING NOTE People found the old name "Volcano Ridge" misleading: it did not go to or over Volcano Ridge. Its new 2010 name reflects its start south of Volcano Ridge and not the fact it travels to the west of the ridge. Also note the north end has been taken over by Volcano Creek trail.

SOUTH TO NORTH
To Volcano Link trail 2.7 km
The trail branches off Gorge–Ware connector at 627161 in the north fork of Gorge Creek.

Initially it ascends very gradually up the narrow, forested valley bottom of the north fork, where work is underway to deal with muddy sections. Cross both forks of the tiny creek on bridges. After the second bridge, flagging on the left at 618171 indicates the route to the northwest fork of Gorge Creek. (See #48C.)

Up next is the never-ending climb to the junction with #52, a dusty treadmill of orange shale and loose stones that keeps on going and going. Unlike the Energizer Bunny, you'll be fading by the time you stagger up the hill's last hurrah—the steepest section of the whole trail—especially if you're toting a heavy backpack. But just ahead, promising a sit-down, is the sign-posted T-junction at 610180 and a handy bank.

Keep left. (To right is the cutline portion of #52 Volcano Link trail.)

To Surveyor's Ridge trail 260 m
Continue much more easily uphill onto the Gorge–Volcano watershed, which at this point is a large meadow dotted with windblown pines. The big grassy hill to the northeast is Volcano. A short side trail to left leads to a fine viewpoint above a western escarpment for Front Range mountains, Mount Ware and Bluerock Mountain preeminent among them. The semi-open hill you can see to the northwest is Surveyor's Ridge.

As the track starts down the north slope keep right at Y-junction 608178. (Track to left is #54 to Surveyor's Ridge.)

To Volcano Creek 2.1 km
Wind down and right into the head of Volcano Creek's south fork, turning left near the bottom onto a N–S cutline. Follow this cutline along the west bank. Apart from one stretch of meadow, you are in pine forest that lets in no views. Shortly after passing a steep cutline up left, you contour down left through a drift fence into the main fork of Volcano Creek flowing from the east slopes of Mount Rose. Cross the creek on rocks. On the far bank is a signpost at the T-junction with Volcano Creek trail at 602197.

54 SURVEYOR'S RIDGE—map 5

A stormy day on the summit.
At far left is Little Mount Ware.

Long-day hike
Unofficial trails, route
Distance to high point 3.6 km
Height gain 283 m (930 ft.)
Height loss 27 m (90 ft.)
High point 2158 m (7080 ft.)
Map 82 J/10 Mount Rae

Access Via #53 Volcano South trail at the watershed.

If you've started early enough from Gorge Creek trailhead, and the big uphill on #53 is under your belt by mid-morning, consider extending the hike to a far superior viewpoint: the big grassy ridge at 592179. It can be combined with #46 Mount Ware or with #55 Surveyor's Ridge to Gorge Creek to make even longer days.

At the unmarked Y-junction 608178, turn left on a cutline access road that descends, then flattens out, headed in a southwesterly direction. Before it reaches a meadow, transfer to a good trail on the right side that shortcuts across to a NW–SE cutline. Turn right.

Follow the cutline uphill among lodgepoles to a 4-way intersection of cutlines. Turn left. The new cutline ends above a grassy west-facing slope disclosing a superlative view to the west of Bluerock Mountain and Mount Rose. Here turn left (south) on a trail.

Initially there are occasional views of pointy Surveyor's Ridge up ahead. Then, closeted in pines, the trail climbs very gradually to another west-facing meadow immediately below the steep summit bloc. While people on horseback skirt around to the right, hikers climb through a few trees onto the steep grassy slope and weave around little outcrops to gain the top directly.

It comes as a huge surprise to find this remote foothill summit decked out with a survey post, a survey pin and a large cairn that used to be twice as high. The 360-degree panorama is amazing; such a diverse landscape of foothills, valleys and Front Range peaks.

Return the same way or see the next entry, #55 Surveyor's Ridge to Gorge Creek.

#54 Starting the trail section to Surveyor's Ridge, seen in the background.

#55 On Surveyor's Ridge, looking NE toward the summit.

#55 View from Surveyor's Ridgetop 583169, showing the trail down the southeast spur and Mount Ware.

55 SURVEYOR'S RIDGE TO GORGE CREEK—map 5

Long-day hike
Unofficial trail, route
Distance 3.8 km
Height gain N–S 113 m (370 ft.)
Height loss N–S 564 m (1850 ft.)
High point 2158 m (7080 ft.)
Map 82 J/10 Mount Rae

North access #54 Summit of Surveyor's Ridge.
South access #43 Gorge Creek trail at 591145 in a meadow.
Also accessible from #46 Mount Ware.

A wonderfully scenic trail made by outfitters follows open ridges between Surveyor's Ridge and Gorge Creek. When combined with #43 Gorge Creek, #49 Gorge–Ware connector, #53 Volcano South trail and #54 Surveyor's Ridge, it makes a 19.3 km loop.

NORTH TO SOUTH

To southwest ridge of Mt. Ware 2.3 km
Head southwest along the undulating summit ridge, soon picking up a trail that guides you around mini-rockbands, over a couple of tops and ultimately through stony, open pine forest to top 583169. View the continuing ridge to the west and the next section of your route—the southeast spur.

Crossing the Ware–Surveyor's col.
Mount Rose rises above the ridges.

The trail descends the southeast spur at the edge of trees, winding through patches of scree and shale into a large meadow. From here it veers to the right side of a rocky knob and descends shaley steps to Ware–Surveyor's col.

Cross the col and climb up to the right through a few trees onto the grassy northwest ridge of Mount Ware. Turn left. Initially there is no trail, but it picks up near the moose bones, later swinging up right, onto the mountain's southwest ridge, where it peters out at the saddle. All along this stretch are remarkable views of Ware's pointy west end.

To Gorge Creek 1.5 km
On the Gorge Creek side look for the trail heading east, soon dropping into a grassy basin. There it turns south and zigs down a soft, shaley slope into pine forest. Where it traverses left and crosses a side creek, look up for a unique view of Mount Ware. Then resume downhilling to the east of the creek, the gradient gradually easing.

Nearing valley bottom, the trail turns left, then right and drops steeply down a bank into a meadow. Cross the grass to Gorge Creek trail at 591145 and turn left. If reversing the route, you can spot the trail climbing the bank.

#55 *On the northwest ridge of Mount Ware, about to head rightward onto the southwest ridge. Shows the route off the west end of the mountain.*

56 WARE CREEK TRAIL—maps 5 & 6

Day hikes, bike 'n' hike
Official trail with signposts & red markers, creek crossings
Total distance 13.1 km
Total height gain SW–NE 125 m (410 ft.)
Total height loss SW–NE 366 m (1200 ft.)
High point 1649 m (5410 ft.)
Map 82 J/10 Mount Rae

Highway access
Southwest access Gorge Creek Road at Gorge Creek trailhead. NOTE This road is closed Dec 1–May 14.
Northeast access Hwy. 549 (McLean Creek Trail). Follow Ware Creek Road to its end at Ware Creek trailhead. NOTE This road is closed Dec 1–May 14.
East access The southern terminus of #62 9999 trail, the northern terminus of #14 Death Valley at Ware Creek.
Also accessible from the eastern terminus of #49 Gorge–Ware connector, the northern terminus of #19 Missinglink trail.

Ware Creek trail follows the valleys of Ware Creek and its tributaries between the Gorge Creek and Ware Creek trailhead parking lots. It then continues eastward to the junction of 9999 and Death Valley trails. The first section is the old Gorge Creek Road, which is boring to walk. Biking is better, even though some of us will be hiking the bike up the hills. But biking will get you faster to more interesting trails like the Gorge–Ware connector that puts you in position to climb to the summit of Volcano.

TRAIL NOTE This trail replaces the Link Creek trail of the third edition between Ware Creek and the old Volcano Ridge trailheads. The first section up Link Creek valley has been decommissioned and was always very muddy anyway, so no loss there. (I don't describe it even as an option.) The second section is still walkable. See ALTERNATIVE ROUTE A.

HISTORY NOTE Drastic changes came about in 2005 when Gorge Creek Road was damaged by floods. The only section not repaired was a section between Ware Creek trailhead and Gleason's Meadow. Nevertheless, a much longer stretch between the Ware Creek and Gorge Creek trailheads was closed without any public discussion and gates went up at both ends. In the middle of this stretch was the Volcano Ridge trailhead that gave access to popular Volcano Ridge. Despite protestations from all road users—the road was a public road after all—the powers that were decided it would remain closed and become a multi-use trail. And this is where things stand at the moment.

CREEK NAMING NOTE Before being named after John Ware, the creek used to be named "Sinnot Creek" after Harry Sinnot, a nephew of John Quirk—a very fine teamster and chocoholic. Clearly the influence of Death Valley extends to this valley, which has also seen its share of strange disappearances. Sinnot, for instance, died mysteriously during a Christmas Eve fire, not in Ware Creek unfortunately for our story, but in a little

The road section near Ware Creek trailhead.

shack on Whiskey Row north of Turner Valley. More recently, some of you may remember Lloyd Middleton's cabin The Retreat opposite the Ware Creek trailhead parking lot. (By the way, the outhouse is still standing.) He took over a trapline from an old trapper named Smiley who was found dead in the original cabin on the site. And, more lately, in 1991 a hunter and his dog went missing in the area and have never been found.

Regarding the name Link, which became official in 1951, it is actually a corruption of "Lynx," by which this creek was known on provincial forest maps prior to this time. People can surmise all they like, but there ain't no link between the names "Link" and "Missinglink." But long before all this, in 1895, A.O. Wheeler called it Gleason Creek. Nobody knows who Gleason was, but I'm guessing he ran a few cattle on the big meadow.

SOUTHWEST TO NORTHEAST

Gorge Creek Road to Ware Creek trailhead

Distance 10.3 km
Height gain 110 m (360 ft.)
Height loss 314 m (1030 ft.)
High point 1649 m (5410 ft.)

All this section follows the old Gorge Creek Road, which is starting to grow grass along its centre line. Expect a few long hills at the south end.

To Gorge–Ware connector 3.7 km
Walk back from the parking lot to the locked gate closing off the ongoing section of the road. Make a gradual ascent above the bright green swamp on the right to a drift fence with gate.

From here it's all downhill into the Ware Creek drainage, the gradient gradually flattening to the junction with ALTERNATIVE ROUTE A to right at a red marker, and a little farther on, the more obvious junction with the Gorge–Ware connector to left at 650190.

To Missinglink trail 4.1 km
Continue on the road that undulates along the west bank of Ware Creek below Volcano Ridge. At 661206 it crosses the creek on culvert. (The grassy track heading down the left bank signed "No Motorized Vehicles" is #57, the Ware Creek connector.)

From here the road climbs over a low pass below Gleason's Meadow Hill into the Link Creek drainage at Gleason's Meadow. Also known to the Stoney as *Baha bazo tîda*, "lumpy mounds of earth clearing flats," it stretches far up the southwest fork and is likely thronged with cattle. At the left-hand bend at 677207 you look straight across the meadow into the main south fork of Link Creek. (A narrow trail cutting across the grass to a post is the joint start/end to #19 Missinglink and ALTERNATIVE ROUTE A up Link Creek.)

To Ware Creek trailhead 2.5 km
Pass below Gleason's Meadow Hill and cross its side creek (starting point for SIDE TRIP B) below the washout.

Now paralleling Link Creek, the road undulates past "the gouge," gradually ironing out flat to two gates and strands of barbed wire at the border control. Use the wire cattle gate on the right side. It's the kind that's hard to open and even harder to shut unless you're an arm wrestler.

A trail bypasses the old road into Ware Creek parking lot.

To 9999/Death Valley trails

Distance 2.8 km
Height gain 15 m (50 ft.) via 1.
Height loss 52 m (170 ft.) via 1.
High point 1402 m (4600 ft.)

This is an easy riverside walk on trail through meadows and woods that makes possible the obvious 19 km loop incorporating North Fork, Threepoint Creek and 9999 trails. It also provides access to the north end of Death Valley trail, which in turn connects with ongoing trails south and west of the Sheep River.

Ware Creek trail on north bank meadows between the crossing and 9999 trail.

TRAIL NOTE Since the third edition the east end has been realigned onto the north bank. While this is fine if you're headed for 9999 trail, if headed for Death Valley use the old trail to avoid two creek crossings.

To third meadow split 1.5 km
The trail leaves the right side of the parking lot headed for the fence, where it turns left. (A defunct section of old Link Creek trail goes through the fence.) Shortly, cross Link Creek, then a large meadow to Ware Creek. Officially, you're supposed to cross to the north bank and recross 200 m farther on, but there's little point to it when there's a nice little trail along the south bank.

BUT, if transferring onto North Fork trail, then you have to make one crossing because North Fork trail takes off from the north bank. Alternatively, from Ware Creek trailhead just walk along Ware Creek Road.

But back to Ware Creek trail. After a second meadow where the official trail comes back in, the trail undulates through pine/aspen woods (one steep uphill) to a third meadow. Here, at about 709221, is a choice of routes.

1. To 9999 trail 1.3 km
The newer trail veers left for Ware Creek and crosses it at 710223. On the north bank, turn right, then keep straight, following flat meadows to the junction with 9999 and Death Valley trails at 715224.

2. To Death Valley 1.2 km
On old trail, cross the meadow and climb increasingly muddy uphills before dropping into a bigger meadow. At a post, intercept Death Valley trail at 717221. Turn right.

ALTERNATIVE ROUTE

56A Link Creek trail

Unofficial trail
Distance 4.5 km
Height gain S–N 61 m (200 ft.)
Height loss S–N 152 m (500 ft.)
High point 1600 m (5250 ft.)

This second section of original Link Creek trail links Gorge–Ware connector to Gleason's Meadow for those who don't want to road bash. While slightly shorter, the trail has disappeared in meadow crossings. Luckily, the red markers are still in place.

SOUTH TO NORTH

The route leaves Ware Creek trail (the road) at 650189 and heads down the grassy bank to a bridge over Ware Creek's south fork.

Climb gradually up the left bank of a side creek, then more steeply away from it to intersect a cutline cum access road (track). Turn left (north) and reach the route's high point at a low pass.

Shortly the track turns right (east) and starts a long, gradual descent into the southwest fork of Link Creek. Cross two bunchgrass meadows with views to the south of Missinglink Mountain and its northern edges. Then head northeast down steeper hills. After a side creek crossing, turn left off the track onto a trail and shortly cross bunchgrass meadow no. 3. The trail continues on down to intersect the same cutline access road.

Ignoring the red marker to left, turn right and on track descend slightly into meadows alongside the southwest fork. (NOTE The official route went left along the access road, then ploughed through forest and bog into Gleason's meadow at a red marker on a tree. A recent foray showed the bog is as deep as it ever was.)

Turn left and follow the meadow downstream, shortly picking up the original route at markers on posts. A good trail takes you out through Gleason's Meadow to a post above the confluence.

Turn left on a narrower trail for Ware Creek trail. For Missinglink trail keep right down the bank and cross Link Creek.

SIDE TRIP

56B Gleason's Meadow Hill

Day hike, bike 'n' hike from northeast access
Route
Distance 1.9 km one way
Height gain 168 m (550 ft.)
High point 1692 m (5550 ft.)

A straightforward climb to the hilltop at 669217, which was named in 1896 by A.O. Wheeler when he and his survey crew set up a camera station on its burnt-over slopes, though "young growth covers it here & there."

Start from the east end of Gleason's Meadow at 679208, where a side creek washed out the road in 2005.

Follow the side creek through meadow to the confines where a varying trail starts up on the right bank and leads past a spring and on up almost to the meadow atop a lower summit.

Turn left and climb to the summit marked by two small cairns. "A flat cake of conglomerate overlying Kootenay coal measures" covers the summit area. From the western escarpment edge you can hear Ware Creek gurgling down below you in the narrows and look across to Volcano Ridge and Allsmoke Mountain. See the photo on page 184.

56A Link Creek trail. View from a meadow of Missinglink's northern escarpment.

57 WARE CREEK CONNECTOR — map 6

Half-day, day hike in combo
Unofficial trail, creek crossings
Distance 4.9 km
Height gain N–S 97 m (320 ft.)
High point 1500 m (4920 ft.)
Map 82 J/10 Mount Rae

Access Ware Creek Road at Ware Creek trailhead. NOTE This road is closed Dec 1– May 14.
Also accessible from #56 Ware Creek trail at Ware Creek crossing at 661206.

*Between the wire fences and the trees.
Volcano Ridge in the background.*

Through the deep, shadowy section of Ware Creek Valley between Allsmoke Mountain and Gleason's Meadow Ridge runs an old road. While some of it still exist as a track, much of it has reverted to trail.

It accesses both routes up Allsmoke Mountain, which can be looped using this trail as the connector. (See #58A and B.) It also makes possible a loop with Ware Creek trail from Ware Creek trailhead. See the sketch map on page 185.

NORTH TO SOUTH

To Allsmoke Mountain turnoff 2.1 km
Cross the highway bridge over Ware Creek called by the Stoney *Pezuthâ gapepeyan waptan*, meaning "tall grass creek." After the signs, turn left onto a trail heading west through a large meadow. Come to a barbed wire fence strung all across it, another fence joining in a V at the trail. Both have wire gates just a few metres apart. Continue through meadow and into the trees where the trail widens to track. Round a bend and descend a hill into a straight. Just before the side creek at 673225 is a junction of sorts. The track turning right is #58A to Allsmoke Mountain. Otherwise, slip left down the bank to Ware Creek.

To East Ridge route 1.6 km
The trail runs alongside the creek a way, then crosses it. The trail as track is initially obvious, then degenerates to snippets of trail for the short distance to the second creek crossing.

Head up a dry channel, then the right bank of it. Cross the channel. The track is again clear where it wends its way across disturbed stony ground. Where it's infilled with trees, use a trail on the right side. After a long pleasant stretch the track makes two creek crossings which can be omitted by following a trail on the right bank. Continue on good track across a meadow to the side creek at 662218. The trail to right heading up the side creek is #58B. Go straight and cross the tributary.

To Ware Creek trail 1.2 km
After a steep up-down, cross Ware Creek a third time. Where the track is in the creek-bed follow a trail along the left bank. You can also omit the next two creek crossings in this way. However, crossings 6, 7 and 8 require three creek crossings. Now on the right bank, pass through a drift fence and reach Ware Creek trail (road) at a sign "No Motorized Vehicles" at 661206.

58 ALLSMOKE MOUNTAIN (SUDIKTEBI) — map 6

Day, long-day hikes
Unofficial trails
High point 2109 m (6920 ft.)
Map 82 J/10 Mount Rae

Top: The summit, looking west.

Bottom: Allsmoke Mountain from Gleason's Meadow Ridge. Red line shows the normal route to the summit. The East ridge route heads up the side valley to the left.

Access Ware Creek Road at Ware Creek trailhead. NOTE This road is closed Dec 1–May 14.

Allsmoke Mountain presents its best side from Quirk Creek Valley, an approach complicated by the intervening Three-point Creek gorge. This leaves the eastern approach from Ware Creek. For years I resisted climbing Allsmoke Mountain from this direction, put off by its covering of dark green pines. Luckily, there is a fairly good trail up a long southeast ridge which has become the normal route up the mountain. Another trail up a short east ridge gains you Volcano Ridge between Allsmoke and Volcano Summit, so

184

enabling you to make a loop using both trails. Alternatively, traversing the ridge to Volcano summit has transportation problems.

NAMING NOTE It's claimed the name "Allsmoke" derives from its fairly recent Stoney name *Sudiktebi,* meaning "where bear was smoked to death." Apparently, one late fall after the bears had gone into hibernation, some Stoneys built a fire at the entrance of a den on the slopes of this mountain. The main protagonists were Tom Powderface (of Powderface Trail, trail, Creek and Ridge fame), and his young son Johnny, both of small stature, who were sent into the den to first check that the bear was dead and then to slip a rope over his head with which to drag him out.

It seems a plausible explanation until you know the name "Allsmoke" was coined 116 years ago in 1895 by surveyor A.O. Wheeler and his crew, who climbed it many times in September of that year. You can imagine them trudging up the long ridge (no roads, trails or

cutlines then) to the open summit and discovering Kananaskis Country's secret waterfall, which they marked on their map. Constantly dodging rain and snow squalls, they either named it for its persistent cloud cover or, more likely, from fires seen burning on the mountain earlier in the year.

58A Usual route

Unofficial trails, route
Distance 7.4 km from trailhead
Height gain 707 m (2320 ft.)

The normal route up Allsmoke follows Ware Creek meadows and then a long southeast to east ridge direct to the summit. The going is unexpectedly pleasing via an easy-angled trail; my friends liked it so much they went and did it again the next weekend!

To southeast ridge 3 km
Read the first paragraph of #57 the Ware Creek connector.

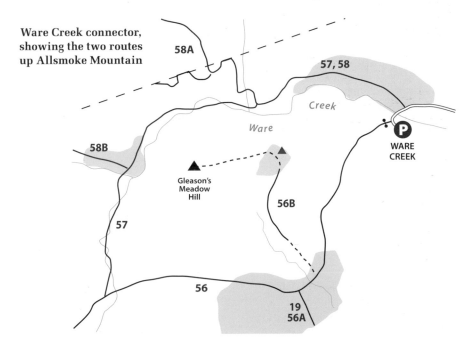

Ware Creek connector, showing the two routes up Allsmoke Mountain

In the pine forest. Photo Alf Skrastins

At the junction of sorts at 2.1 km, turn right with the track. Shortly the track crosses the side creek and heads up the left side of it to intersect a NE–SW cutline at 673227. Turn left onto the cutline.

Where the cutline rears up, as cutlines are wont to do, go left on the cutline access road. Count berms. At no. 3 turn right up a short, steep, grassed track to intersect the cutline at the top of the hill. Go straight on a narrow trail, the start of the southeast ridge section. (Meanwhile the cutline access road dipsy-doodles along the east flank of the mountain.)

Southeast ridge to summit 4.4 km.

Fast time can be made up the easy-angled ridge on a soft, needle-strewn trail. When you hit another NE–SW cutline, jog left a short distance before continuing on up the ridge. Thus far there has been little understorey, but higher up there is none at all, which makes tracing the trail a little tricky. At a flat area at 649231 you should run into a cairn with a branch poking out. Here you go left, descending slightly, in two minutes or less emerging onto south-facing meadows. This important waypoint at 648230 is marked by a cairn.

Resume the uphill climb on intermittent trail, following the meadow below the ridge crest. After sidling below a minor top get back on the ridge for the final climb through pines. The trail is obvious along the edge of the northern escarpment and soon you're on the summit marked by two survey markers, a cairn and a pole.

It's important to descend a short distance onto a grassy terrace, the start of a ridge winging out to the northwest. It's a great place to eat your lunch while perusing a fabulous view that encompasses everything from Calgary to Mount Rae to the mountains of the Ghost. Laid out at your feet are the complexities of the country between Quirk Creek and Forgetmenot. Only Threepoint Creek Gorge is out of the picture, though you can spot the top half of Kananaskis Country's secret waterfall.

Looking back down the upper ridge.

#58B On the shoulder of the east ridge.

58B East ridge

Unofficial trails, route, creek crossings
Distance 5.1 km from Ware connector
Height gain 640 m (2100 ft.) to summit

Access Via #57 Ware Creek connector at the side creek 662218.

This route requires you hike the Ware Creek connector for a longer distance before climbing a relatively short east ridge onto the summit ridge connecting Allsmoke to Volcano. There is a trail most of the way; only the last bit is route. Nevertheless, finding the end of the trail on the return is tricky without a GPS, so the electronically challenged might prefer using this route as an ascent route if doing a loop with A.

East ridge to the summit ridge 3.6 km
The track follows the tributary's right bank for 1 km. At a split take the left-hand option, which crosses a northwest fork. Climb up the fledgling east ridge in the angle of the two creeks to where the track turns left and levels.

At this spot transfer to a good trail that continues up the east ridge. The angle gradually steepens and you endure a stiff pull just before reaching a shale and bunchgrass shoulder. This is a good place from which to view the upper ridge.

The trail picks up again in the trees, climbing at a reasonable gradient toward the broad summit ridge. Nearly there, it splits. For our purposes go right and climb a little farther to about 630223 where the trail quits in shaley pine forest.

To summit 1.5 km
Steer north along the summit ridge through alternating bands of pine forest and meadows of the short grass kind mixed with greeny-gray lichen. At the rocky knob go around the left side and down shale steps. Ahead the ground is finally rising to Allsmoke's summit, which is enclosed in pines with meadow down the left side. Choose the more direct route through the pines, the going easy on stones of pinkish-coloured sandstone. Nearing the top, veer left to reach the summit.

58C Traverse to Volcano

Route
Distance 4.8 km
Height gain N–S 344 m (1130 ft.)
Height loss N–S 296 m (970 ft.)

Connecting Allsmoke to Volcano summit is a broad ridge of alternating meadow and pine forest called Volcano Ridge on the maps. The hiking is easy, but making a point to point between trailheads got a whole lot more difficult after the 2005 closure of Gorge Creek Road. Nowadays, if you want to leave a vehicle at each end (Ware Creek and Gorge Creek trailheads) it requires driving all around the boonies between Hwy. 546 and Hwy. 549. Ouch!

GEOLOGY NOTE The connecting ridge was described by geologist D.D. Cairns in 1914 as "a very irregular block of country." Why Allsmoke should be any more irregular than Missinglink is due to something called "the double fold." Apparently the thrust fault to the north, exemplified by Forgetmenot Ridge, is here displaced by the double fold, which accounts for Allsmoke's precipitous rise out of Threepoint Creek gorge. It also means the formations are upside down and the pinkish-coloured sandstone you walk on initially are of the Kootenay formation. Interestingly, by the time you get to Volcano summit the same formations appear the right way up.

NORTH TO SOUTH

From Allsmoke's summit head a short way east, then south down an easy, treed slope of pinkish-coloured sandstones into the meadows. As mentioned, all the excitement is taking place underground, because there is absolutely nothing dramatic to be seen up on top. You plod up a rise, bypass a rocky nubbin and then a shaley top by staying right, then walk down a long gentle slope with alternating belts of meadow and pine forest.

Two-thirds along at 626209 is a considerable hump. On the final steep approach to its rocky top look for an open avenue between trees with a trail up the middle. Getting off the other side can be tricky. It's a case of not being able to see the ridge for the pines, small though they are.

At the low point following is a west-facing meadow crossed by a NE–SW cutline. Cheaters can follow the cutline to the right to connect with route #51. Purists will press on past conglomerate outcrops to the base of the final steep rise where Volcano makes a decisive end to the traverse.

Get onto the left skyline ridge (the east ridge) and follow it up to the summit. Open slopes on the left side reveal a new panorama to the south of Front Range peaks. The rocky knob closer in is the high point of South Volcano Ridge.

Typical view looking back from the half-way point of the traverse to Allsmoke Mtn.

59 NORTH FORK TRAIL — map 6

Day hike
Official trail, signposts & red markers
Distance 5.4 km
Height gain S–N 229 m (750 ft.)
Height loss S–N 198 m (650 ft.)
High point 1615 m (5300 ft.)
Maps 82 J/10 Mount Rae,
82 J/15 Bragg Creek

South access #56 Ware Creek trail.
Usual highway access from the south Ware Creek Road. At 698224 is a small pullout on the south side of the road about 500 m northeast of the bridge over Ware Creek. NOTE This road is closed Dec 1–May 14.
North access Via #65 Threepoint Creek.

This trail connects Ware Creek to Threepoint Creek via a low pass and is based on the old telephone trail between Bighorn Ranger Station at Nash Meadow on Hwy. 546 and the North Fork Cabin that was located near North Fork campground

The south side meadows near the high point, looking west to Missinglink Mountain and the mountains of the Highwood Range.

on Hwy. 549. Since earlier editions, a section of the southern half has been completely rerouted to avoid mud, and now takes in even more of the lovely meadow country below Death's Head.

From campgrounds on Hwy. 549, an 18.5 km loop incorporating Threepoint Creek, North Fork, Ware Creek and 9999 trails has become popular, the loop best hiked in an anticlockwise direction so you can admire the views without turning around all the time. However, because of ease of access from Ware Creek Road and because most people just enjoy a stroll up to the high point and back through the meadows, I am describing the trail from south to north.

ACCESS NOTE When Ware Creek Road is closed you can still access this trail from Hwy. 549 via #65 Threepoint Creek.

Death's Head from just south of the watershed.

SOUTH TO NORTH

Ware Creek to high point 3.1 km

Officially the trail leaves Ware Creek trail on the north bank of Ware Creek and heads north to a pullout on the south side of the Ware Creek Road. This is the usual hwy. access with room for a couple of vehicles.

The trail crosses the road and wends right, initially sticking within earshot of cars changing gear to get up the hill. Then it turns left into the first large meadow. From here it's a steady uphill grind to the high point. En route you cross a drift fence before entering meadow no. 2, which is distinguished by a line of dead trees and an intersecting NE–SW cutline. Keep looking back for views of Front Range peaks, perhaps snow capped as in the photo on the previous page, rising above blue forested foothills.

At the trail's high point is a T-junction with the third edition trail. To your right rises Death's Head, which presents its boldest front from this direction. While the summit is more easily gained from Ware Creek Road via #60, it's kind of fun wandering up to the sandstone rockband below the top and searching for easy ways through. The farther right you go, the smaller the band.

To Threepoint Creek 2.3 km

At the T-junction below Death's Head turn left on the newer trail and wind down through meadow and aspens to a NE–SW cutline. Turn left and walk along the cutline into a third meadow equipped with horse rail—absolutely the last place to get a view of the Front Ranges. Between editions the bench has disappeared.

A little downhill of here, come to the low point in the watershed at 683254. Here you join with the telephone trail for the twisty descent down the cool, forested north slope, the gradient easing off before you arrive in the valley bottom at a T-junction of Threepoint Creek with Threepoint Creek trail.

Next to the signpost is an old wood sign tacked to a tree indicating "Threepoint Trail" to the left. Turn right for Hwy. 549, Mesa Butte equestrian campground, 9999 and Curley Sand trails and the North Fork campground.

Opposite: Looking northwest from Death's Head. You can distinguish Allsmoke Mountain (left), Forgetmenot Mountain and Nihahi Ridge.

60 DEATH'S HEAD (MESA BUTTE) — map 6

Half-day hike
Unofficial trail
Distance 3.3 km return
Height gain 219 m (720 ft.)
High point 1722 m (5650 ft.)
Maps 82 J/10 Mount Rae,
82 J/15 Bragg Creek

Access Ware Creek Road 4.2 km south of Hwy. 549. At 702239 park on the east side of the road in a small pullout. NOTE This road is closed Dec. 1–May 14.

An easy forest walk to a summit viewpoint.

NAMING NOTE In 1895/6/7, surveyors used this little summit as a camera station recorded on A.O. Wheeler's 1895 map as Death's Head, the name likely stemming from the shape in profile of its sandstone escarpment. In official circles the hill is called Mesa Butte, a name it inherited when Mesa Butte across the highway (marked on maps as "Mesa" since 1895) was changed to Square Butte to match the name of the community hall on Hwy. 762. Locals call it the Big Hill, referring to the steep pull of Ware Creek Road up its eastern flank.

Cross the road and at the sign "No Motorized Vehicles," head up a cutline access road. On reaching a NW–SE cutline, turn left. At a cairn turn right off the cutline onto a trail.

The trail follows the gently inclined southeast ridge through pine forest to a lower top. A flat stretch follows, with views between scraggy willow bushes of the real Mesa Butte across Threepoint Creek, its western slopes revealed as a checkerboard of cutblocks and well sites. A short climb up bunchgrass leads to the summit (no cairn, no view). The trail continues, heading down left to a terrace above the craggy western escarpment. Among the rocks grow saxifrages, chickweeds, daisies and cranberry bushes.

The far-reaching view catches you unawares: Calgary to the northeast; to the west Allsmoke Mountain, Mts. Cornwall and Glasgow, Nihahi Ridge, Moose Mountain; to the south Bluerock Mountain, Mount Rae and the pointy peaks of the Highwood Range. Across Threepoint Creek you're treated to a comprehensive view of the south slope of Mount Barwell showing most of the routes.

61 ASPEN VIEWPOINT — map 6

Half-day, day hike in combination
Unofficial trail
Distance to viewpoint 1.7 km
Height gain 76 m (250 ft.)
Height loss 46 m (150 ft.)
High point 1570 m (5150 ft.)
Map 82 J/10 Mount Rae

Access Ware Creek Road at the top of the big hill at 712243. Park on the east side of the road in a small pullout. NOTE This road is closed Dec. 1–May 14.
Also accessible from #62 9999 trail in two places.

This along-the-ridge trail offers a short there and back stroll from Ware Creek Road to a viewpoint that I like to visit in gaudy fall. Know that in its present state, the trail suffers from a surfeit of side trails and alternatives that can be puzzling. When in doubt, stay on the ridgeline.

From the viewpoint you can carry on and connect via cutlines with 9999 trail in two ways, but then what? FUTURE NOTE This trail is due to be upgraded and made official, part of a connector between 9999 trail and North Fork trail that will extend northwards along the east flank of Death's Head—so making possible a loop.

To the viewpoint 1.7 km
The trail heads southeast along a broad, treed ridge. (Near the start watch for a large "A"—for aspen perhaps—carved on a tree.) Go either way at a split on an uphill, then descend to a vague junction. Keep straight. At a well-defined 4-way, go left, deke around some deadfall, then keep left up a hill and traverse below the ridge crest. Descend and follow the main trail through a maze of splits and side trails to a willowy semi-open area which offers more of the same confusion. Back in trees, keep left at splits, this relatively straightforward section ending with a long, gradual descent to the low point under dark mature spruce.

The final leg climbs into aspen woodlands above bunchgrass meadows sweeping down the right flank. Continue to the ridge's far point at 725233.

Look across Ware Creek and Death Creek Valleys to Gleason's Ridge, seen in its entirety—that's Windy Point Ridge at its left end. Farther to the north, you can spot the long ridge of Volcano bounded by Allsmoke Mountain at its right end. Farthest right is Death's Head. While Front Range peaks are spread across the horizon, the view is mainly of pine-covered ridges and aspen-filled valleys that in spring appear a drab, hazy grey. Come the end of September, though, the forest magically transforms into a blaze of colour.

GOING FARTHER

61A Connecting with 9999

Who knows where the official trail will go, but in the meantime try these routes. Just before the viewpoint, go left on a side trail that leads to the high point of a NW–SE cutline just below the brow of the ridge on the northeast side. Turn right.

Follow the cutline down a long hill, twice using grassy access roads on the left side to cut out two steep hills. Ahead are views across the pass crossed by 9999 trail to the open slopes of Sinnot Ridge. At an intersecting NE–SW cutline you have two options.

1. 1.1 km from viewpoint Continue ahead up a small rise on the NW–SE cutline that soon resumes its downward direction and, after crossing a side valley creek, meets 9999 trail at 729225 Y-junction. This is not far above the Ware Creek Valley bottom.

2. 1.5 km from viewpoint Turn right and follow the rolling NE–SW cutline (two steep downhills) into Ware Creek meadows at 720224.

Viewpoint in fall, looking down onto Ware Creek Valley.

62 9999 TRAIL—map 6

9999 trail in Ware Creek Valley. Above rises Aspen Viewpoint ridge.

Day hike
Official trail with signposts & red markers, river crossing
Distance 7.6 km
Height gain and loss 90 m (300 ft.)
Maps 82 J/15 Bragg Creek,
82 J/10 Mount Rae

North access Hwy. 549 (McLean Creek Trail) at Mesa Butte equestrian campground entrance.
South access The junction of #56 Ware Creek and #14 Death Valley trails in Ware Creek.
Usual east access Hwy. 549 (McLean Creek Trail). Just after crossing the KC boundary, turn left on a track that heads for Threepoint Creek. Park just before a fence and walk through a gap in the fence to Threepoint Creek crossing where you join Curley Sand trail. Wade the creek and climb the bank to the T-junction with 9999 trail in the longitudinal meadow. NOTE Unfortunately here is no official trail access from North Fork Campground.
Middle access Ware Creek Road. The trail crosses the road 800 m west of Hwy. 549 at

724253. I prefer to park a little closer, near the Esso installation on the powerline right-of-way.
Also accessible from #61 Aspen Viewpoint at the viewpoint.

This two-part trail connects trails in Threepoint Creek to those in Ware Creek via a low, wooded pass. The equestrian muddiness of the north slope is forgotten when you pass over the watershed into aspen meadows at their most beautiful.

Obviously, a 19 km loop can be made with #56 Ware Creek, #59 North Fork and #65 Threepoint Creek trails. Most people, though, end the trip in Ware Creek meadows and return the same way. Another option, sure to become popular, is to climb to the pass, then head southeast to Sinnot Hill viewpoint (OPTION A).

ACCESS NOTE The usual east access involves paddling Threepoint Creek near the campground—even in fall. To avoid the crossing, use the middle access.

NAMING NOTE If you had been around this area between 1885 and 1902 you would have discovered that cattle grazing the upper reaches of Ware Creek and Threepoint Creek all bore the brand "9999." This was the registered brand of John Ware, the celebrated Negro cowboy renowned for his strength and horsemanship, who homesteaded just east of the forest reserve near the fork of the two rivers.

To find his memorial plaque, start from the 4-way junction of Hwy. 762 and 549. Head south on 320 St. W. At the T-junction turn right onto 370 Ave. W. After the road bends left look for a large rock with plaque in a field on the left side just before the bridge over Ware Creek. Incidentally, after the Ware family left, the land was taken over by the Basilici family, whose most famous member was daughter Elizabeth Rummel.

NORTH TO SOUTH

North access to Curley Sand trail 3.1 km

From the campground entrance Four Nines trail follows the verge between the campground fence and Hwy. 549. At a sign it heads right, into the trees, then curves down left into a small meadow bordering Threepoint Creek. Wade across. Shortly keep right (red marker) and climb high above the riverbank. Descend steeply and join a track that has arisen from the river. Follow it up to the right to Ware Creek Road (middle access).

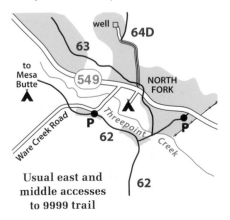

Usual east and middle accesses to 9999 trail

Cross the road. Shortly turn left onto the powerline right-of-way. At the Esso installation (also middle access) the trail leaves the right-of-way and heads to the right into forest for a muddy stint. This is followed by a longitudinal meadow, at the far end of which is a signpost signalling the T-junction with Curley Sand trail at 737248.

To the pass 1.8 km

Turn right. Or left if arriving via Curley Sand trail from east access. The trail (old road) climbs gradually up the forested north slope of the watershed, initially through spruce, where, in an effort to stem ever-widening mud, the trail was rehabilitated with culverts and ditches in 2007/8. After a brief interlude of aspen woodlands, a steeper haul through spruce brings you to the pass—a small meadow ringed by aspens with little in the way of views, but pleasant nevertheless with fallen aspens for seats. Keep straight. (Side trail to left is OPTION A to Sinnot Hill.)

To Ware Creek 2.7 km

On the sunny downslope, tall, graceful aspens arch over the trail and a side creek develops on your right. At a T-junction with a well-used horse trail to a hunting camp, keep right and descend alongside the side creek, en route crossing a NW–SE cutline at 729225 (route from #61A). Nearing Ware Creek Valley bottom, hop across the side creek and turn right into flat meadows. When we first came here eons ago, the main channel of the river ran farther south and a string of beaver ponds occupied the present river channel. Frogs croaked in tiny pools and red-winged blackbirds fought for nesting sites in the willows.

On old road (sometimes trails in triplicate) walk upstream through a string of lovely meadows sweeping up aspen hillsides to Aspen Viewpoint ridge. After intersecting a NE–SW cutline (#61.3) you come to a T-junction with signpost at 715224. Crossing Ware Creek to left is Death Valley trail; straight ahead is Ware Creek trail.

OPTION

62A Sinnot Hill

Unofficial trail
Distance 3 km return from pass
Extra height gain 100 m (330 ft.)
High point 1539 m (5050 ft.)

Instead of descending to Ware Creek, enjoy a short jaunt to the high point of a ridge lying east of the pass at 738227. The going is easy on trail to a hilltop meadow with views. Doable in spring, but at its most enjoyable in flowery summer and gaudy fall.

HISTORY NOTE The hill was named camera station Sinnot 2 when first climbed on September 23, 1895, during the Irrigation Survey, and renamed Sinnot Hill in 1914 when D.D. Cairnes wrote his memoir for the geological survey.

At the pass turn left (southeast) and on good narrow trail traverse grassy aspen woodlands on the right side of the first hill. In meadow, curve left to a col beyond the hill. (From here the first top is an easy hike up grass.)

Summit view across the foothills.

At the col the trail turns right and follows the ridgeline through spruce and pine forest. After passing a willow copse, the trail divides. Turn left (straight is the traversing return trail).

The trail winds uphill to the lower point of the highest hill, which is open to the southwest and sprinkled with a few rocks. Follow the wide ridge through a few aspens to the high point where grass sweeps down on two sides. Down below is Ware Creek Valley where Harry Sinnot obtained title to a homestead near to today's Death Valley Ranch. Beyond the valley, waves of blue forested ridges roll ever higher toward recognizable Front Range peaks.

Descend the long grass of the southeast ridge to a col. There pick up the traversing trail, turn right and follow it back to the pass.

NOTE It's tempting to continue along the ridge trail to the K Country boundary fence and drop down into the Ware Creek Valley bottom. Getting back to 9999 trail is a little messy. For one thing, the valley game trail at this point is on the opposite bank, so you're looking at two creek crossings minimum. On reaching a hunter's camp you can return via the NW–SE cutline and the horse trail.

63 CURLEY SAND TRAIL — map 6

Half-day hike
Official trail, signposts & red markers,
creek crossing
Distance 4 km
Height gain 137 m (450 ft.)
Height loss 174 m (570 ft.)
High point 1509 m (4950 ft.)
Maps 82 J/15 Bragg Creek,
82 J/10 Mount Rae

Access Hwy. 549 (McLean Creek Trail).
1. Mesa Butte equestrian campground entrance.
2. North Fork Recreation Area. Walk up the access road to the highway and turn right (east) at the 4-way junction. The trail intersects Hwy. 549 just beyond the fence. NOTE There is no official connector from North Fork Campground.
3. K Country boundary at the texas gate. Just after crossing the KC boundary, turn left on a track that heads for Threepoint Creek. Park just before a fence and walk through a gap in the fence to Threepoint Creek crossing where you join Curley Sand trail.

Also accessible from the eastern terminus of #65 Threepoint Creek, from #62 9999 trail in two places, and from #64 Mesa Butte trails C and D.

This lovely ridge trail connects Mesa Butte equestrian campground to North Fork Recreation area, then carries on across Threepoint Creek to a junction with 9999 trail on the southwest bank. Dismayingly, the creek crossing is still a paddle in late October.

NAMING NOTE The trail is named after George William (Curley) Sand of Minnesota, who came to the area about 1946, hired by the North Sheep Stock Association to track with his hounds cougars and grizzlies that were killing yearlings up in The Muskeg. "In two years he killed 11 grizzlies and many black bear beside." At his funeral "Curley never let the truth spoil a good story" said the minister, so I hope the numbers are exaggerated.

Access 1 to access 2, 2.9 km
The trail starts opposite Mesa Butte equestrian campground entrance, and after a preliminary stretch alongside Hwy. 549, winds uphill, climbing toward a gap in the ridge to the east. Before quite reaching the gap the trail keeps right at a Y-junction at 718265. (The trail ahead is #64C, the ridge route to Mesa Butte.)

Continue winding and climbing through spruce forest, then aspens onto the ridge crest. The high point is a small meadow allowing a view to the west across Threepoint Creek Valley to Death's Head and the tips of Front Range peaks.

Descending now, walk south along the ridge between aspens to the south end viewpoint — the trail's highlight — where meadows sweep down to Hwy. 549, sages lending a silvery-blue cast to long, waving grasses. Descend more steeply off the end of the ridge and down into trees. Cross a logging road which may or may not have been rehabilitated. On reaching a flat roadside meadow where the trail disappears, just aim for a post, then cross a well road to a gate in a fence. The well road lies opposite the entrance to North Fork Recreation Area on Hwy. 549, which is access 2.

Access 2 to 9999 trail 1.1 km
Straightaway after the gate, the trail crosses Hwy. 549 and runs parallel to the recreation area fence in meadow. The meadow farther south was the site of the North Fork Ranger Station, a home for assistant rangers in the days before K Country. Until about 20 years ago, the corral was still standing.

Pass through another gate, and on the bank of Threepoint Creek join an old road that has come in from the highway at the K Country boundary (access 3).

Ford Threepoint Creek. The old road climbs the bank into a longitudinal meadow where a signpost marks the junction with 9999 trail (straight and right).

#63 Curley Sand. Climbing the south end meadows onto the ridge.

#64A The south ridge of Mesa Butte, the usual ascent route.

64 MESA (SQUARE) BUTTE—map 6

The summit.

Half-day, short-day hikes
Unofficial trails
High point 1682 m (5520 ft.)
Map 82 J/15 Bragg Creek

Accesses Hwy. 549 (McLean Creek Trail)
1. Shortest 4.3 km north of the K Country boundary turn right onto a gas well access road. At a left-hand bend near the well pad, turn right and park on a grassy swath.
2. Alternative start to A 4.1 km north of the K Country boundary turn right onto a gas well access road. Park off-road just before the well pad.
3. Ridge route. 3 km north of the K Country boundary, park off-road opposite the Mesa Butte Recreation Area entrance.
4. Longest 750 m north of the K Country boundary, park off-road at a 4-way intersection. Or use North Fork Recreation Area access road to left.
Also accessible from #63 Curley Sand trail.

There are three main routes to the top of this big grassy hill—all unofficial. Regardless, the climb to its summit is quite simply the best half-day hike from the campgrounds.

Loops can be made by using the trails in various permutations in conjunction with #63 Curley Sand, #62 9999 and the highway, where the greatest danger is speeding pickups spitting gravel.

"The girls are pretty
The boys are cute
Oh thank Heaven
I made it to Mesa Butte"

This hill is incredibly popular! People of all ages climb it on foot, on horse, on bike, and even sleep on the top. There are school kids on official outings, the Moonlight Hikers from Millarville, and Germans and Aussies taking part in Neil MacLaine's Palliser Challenge. On Thanksgiving night another group plods up with food, wine and candles for a little "Beethoven on the Butte." This is all true! You can spend hours reading the summit register book originally put up there by Jim McLuskey, whose house can be seen from the summit. Nowadays, the task has been taken over by Peter Irwin.

NAMING NOTE Its true name is Mesa Hill, coined by A.O. Wheeler in 1895

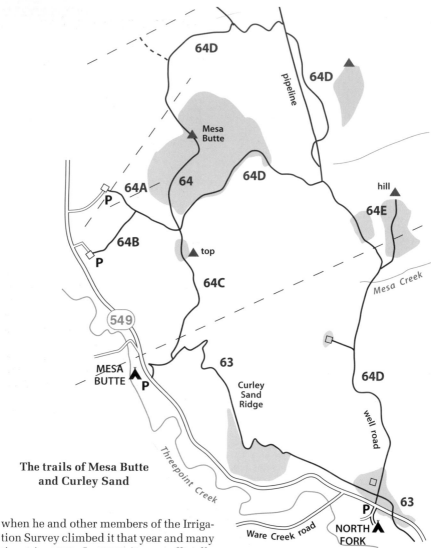

The trails of Mesa Butte and Curley Sand

when he and other members of the Irrigation Survey climbed it that year and many times in 1897. In 1949 it was officially named Mesa Butte. So naturally, after 99 years of being called Mesa on successive maps, it was disturbing when in 1994 the hill was suddenly officially renamed Square Butte, it being deemed easier to change the name of the hill than the name of the community hall on Hwy. 762. To make things worse, the name "Mesa" was transposed willy-nilly across the valley to Death's Head.

The Stoneys call it *Baha Bazo Tîda Wathte*, meaning "beautiful forested hill with open patches." Sadly, today's open patches now include cutblocks, well pads and pipeline rights-of-way. However, four different areas of prayer flags on the hill indicate it is still a special place for First Nations people.

64A Shortest

Distance 1.4 km
Height gain 204 m (670 ft.)
Access 1

Continue up the grass. Near the top turn right onto a trail that traverses right slightly uphill. At a T-junction with the trail from access 2, keep left and curve around left to the pass at 719276 (small meadow) where you meet C and D at a 4-way junction.

Turn left (north) and climb much more steeply up the south ridge, through trees initially, then along a wide grassy ridge to the summit plateau. Just before the top, look for the summit canister under a lone pine on the left side of the trail. The actual summit lies at the demarcation of trees which are handy for sheltering under when the west wind is howling (rustic benches available).

Otherwise, loll around on the grass, a heavenly sun-bathing spot facing south. One summiter described the view as "so lovely it hurts." It's certainly extensive: above a heaving sea of foothills you can identify the higher peaks of the Highwood and Fisher ranges, while nearer at hand Threepoint Creek leads the eye to Forgetmenot Mountain. And, of course, directly across the valley rises the official Mesa Butte, alias Death's Head.

64B Alternative to A

Distance 1.4 km
Height gain add on 30 m (100 ft.)
Access 2

An obvious trail leaves the left side of the access road near the well pad and climbs through meadow and open pine forest to the T-junction with A. Go right.

64C Ridge route

Distance 2.4 km
Height gain 320 m (1050 ft.)
Access 3

Follow #63 Curley Sand trail to the Y-junction at 718265 and turn left. The trail alternately climbs and traverses a grassy slope onto the south ridge of Mesa Butte. Turning north, it continues uphill through meadows and aspens toward top 720271. A direct line to the summit is thwarted by deadfall and the trail is forced to descend and circle around it on grass to the left. On the far side of the top a short steep descent leads to the pass 719276 at a 4-way junction with A and D in a meadow. Go straight for the summit.

View of the ridge route taken by #64C. Ridge at far end is traversed by Curley Sand trail.

64D Longest

#64D Nearing the point where you traverse left below the east face of the butte.

Distance 5.1 km one way
Height gain 320 m (1050 ft.)
Access 4

Head north on the well road for 1.2 km. Just before the road turns left into the well site, transfer right to a much older dirt road (track) identified a little way in by four rocks spaced across the track. Beyond a gate the track descends to Mesa Creek and crosses it on boardwalk. On the far bank is a junction. Keep left on the track. (Trail to right is SIDE TRIP E.)

Travel through a mix of woods and meadows to the pipeline right-of-way at 718273 with line block valves on both sides. Cross the right-of-way. Behind a large fallen tree starts a trail that climbs out of the trees into extensive meadows below the butte's east face. Here the trail traverses left, through waist-high timothy and a few trees to the pass at 719276. At the 4-way junction with A and C turn right for the summit.

The most interesting way back to your starting point is along the ridges via C and #63 Curley Sand trail.

Optional return 3.3 km + 2.8 km
Find the trail starting on the west side of the plateau in the pines. It runs above the west escarpment, eventually crossing over to the eastern escarpment where you inter-

cept a better trail and turn left. (If you are coming in the other direction, this junction occurs just after you step over deadfall.)

Follow the trail to a T-junction near the north edge. Turn right on a cutline access road that descends steeply into sunnier country of aspens and meadows at an easing. An even steeper descent back into pines ends at a T-junction of roads at 724289. Total steep drop is 152 m (500 ft.)

Turn right and continue more easily downhill to the pipeline right-of-way. Either follow the right-of-way to the right, or continue on the access road that crosses the right-of way and twines about it back to D at the line block valves at 718273.

Return the way you came.

SIDE TRIP

64E Hill 736276

Distance 650 m one way
Height gain 110 m (360 ft.)
High point 1509 m (4950 ft.)
Access 4

On D cross Mesa Creek to a T-junction. Turn right and follow the trail up the grassy south ridge to the summit. Not only is it a fine viewpoint for Mesa Butte, this hill is the place to look for first spring flowers.

*#64E Looking across to Mesa Butte from Hill 736276.
South ridge on the left skyline.*

#65 The Hog's Back on Threepoint Creek trail.

65 THREEPOINT CREEK TRAIL — map 6

The first section of the Hog's Back in the trees.

Day hike, backpack, bike 'n' hike
Official trail with signposts & red markers, river crossings
Distance 12.3 km via fire road, 11.8 km via the Hog's Back
Height gain 381 m (1250 ft.) fire road, 375 m (1230 ft.) Hog's Back from start 3
High point 1753 m (5750 ft.) on fire road
Map 82 J/15 Bragg Creek

Access Hwy. 549 (McLean Creek Trail).
1. Official start Entrance to Mesa Butte equestrian campground.
2. Hiker's official start 200 m north of Mesa Butte equestrian campground turn west onto a well access road. Cross the bridge over Threepoint Creek and drive 1.7 km to a road junction. Keep left. Park at the end of the road on the verge.
3. Unofficial hiker's start 200 m north of Mesa Butte Equestrian Campground turn west onto a well access road. Cross the bridge over Threepoint Creek and drive 1.7 km to a road junction. Keep right. Drive another 500 m across Threepoint Creek bridge to the former Forgetmenot Mountain fire road on the left side of the road at an orange sign "Barricade Ahead."

Also accessible from the northern terminus of #59 North Fork trail, the northern terminus of #66 Volcano Creek trail, the southern terminus of Wildhorse trail (Volume 2) and the southern end of #70 Muskeg Creek.

The route—an eclectic mix of telephone trail, fire road and historic pack trail—follows Threepoint Creek from Hwy. 549 to Quirk Creek where it meets Wildhorse and Volcano Creek trails at their southern and northern terminuses. About two-thirds of the way along there's a choice of route: the fire road or the scenic Hog's Back, the latter a name in use since the 1920s when Anderson's pack trail came this way between North Fork Ranger Station and the Elbow River. It's here that the trail reaches its dramatic conclusion above spectacular Threepoint Creek gorge.

RIVER NOTE Three unbridged crossings of Threepoint Creek are impossible when the river is in spate. The first can be avoided by starting from access 3. The other two require off-trail shenanigans.

ACCESS NOTE The trail officially starts at Mesa Butte equestrian campground. Unless you are making a loop with North Fork, Ware Creek and 9999 trails, use either access 2 or 3. I prefer the unofficial 3, which is more scenic and a tad less muddy despite recent horse use.

Trails accessed from Threepoint are North Fork and Muskeg Creek.

OFFICIAL START
Start 1 to start 2, 2.1 km
This section has changed since the third edition, owing to a new well road and a 2006 blowdown.

Walk 200 m north and turn left onto the well road that descends to Threepoint Creek bridge. Shortly after the bridge, turn right at a red marker onto a trail that parallels the road. Rejoin the road and turn right. Keep straight (new well road to left). Just before valves on both sides of the road, turn right onto a trail that descends into a big meadow at a red marker.

The trail heads northwest, paralleling the road through meadows and woods. En route you pass under a powerline and cross a few tracks. Near its end, it runs along the banktop above Threepoint Creek and emerges on another well road used by access 3.

Prior to a big blowdown, the trail continued in the same way between the first well road and the creek to the well pad. Nowadays you turn left and walk a few metres to a road junction where you turn right onto the first well road (red marker). Follow this to the well pad.

Start 2 to North Fork trail 1.6 km
Walk anticlockwise around the well pad fence. At its far end, a wide trail—the old telephone trail—heads into the forest. The trail is muddy and mainly flat to the uphill junction with North Fork trail. Turn right.

To the junction with start 3, 680 m
Gradually descend above eroding banks to Threepoint Creek. Wade across to the north bank, pass through a gate in the drift fence and climb to Y-junction 677264 in a meadow with the former Forgetmenot Lookout fire road. (See start 3.) Turn left and skip the next paragraph.

UNOFFICIAL HIKER'S START
Start 3 to the official trail, 2.4 km
The north bank route uses the reclaimed Forgetmenot Lookout fire road, which can be identified a little way in by a concrete barrier and a rusted gate. Most of the way it undulates across sunny aspen terraces high above Threepoint, only once dropping down to river level at a stony side creek crossing. On the final descent, you cross a drift fence and continue down into a flat meadow where the official trail (no signpost) joins in from the left at Y-junction 677264. Keep straight.

To Hog's Back junction 2.5 km
The fire road runs alongside Threepoint Creek out of the trees and across steep, flowery banks. At a signpost there is a choice of routes. If you're headed for Muskeg Creek, continue ahead on fire road. Otherwise turn left down the much more interesting Hog's Back trail.

The three starts to the trail

The fire road above Muskeg Creek. The Hog's Back at left.

Fire road to Muskeg Creek 2.4 km

The fire road meanders along to a high point above the Threepoint Creek-Muskeg Creek confluence, then descends into Muskeg Creek Valley. In the narrows where high, forested ridges rise up on both sides, you cross the small creek four times in quick succession. A longer stretch on the east bank leads to the fifth crossing. Soon after, the fainter Muskeg Creek track drops down the bank to your right and heads north (see #70). This point can be identified by a red marker on the fire road.

To Quirk Creek 3 km

From this junction the fire road turns west and climbs a gruelling 213 m (700 ft.) over a shaley ridge covered in pine forest allowing no views.

On descent the road turns south and you catch your first glimpse of Allsmoke Mountain up ahead. The Hog's Back finish joins in from the left just before the junction with Wildhorse and Volcano Creek trails in Quirk Creek Valley.

Turn right for Wildhorse trail. Turn left for Volcano Creek and a peek into Threepoint Creek gorge.

RECOMMENDED FINISH

65A Hog's Back

Distance 4.5 km
Height gain ~268 m (880 ft.)

The trail zigs down to a meadow and on down to Threepoint Creek. Two river crossings in quick succession give access to the narrow ridge between Threepoint and Muskeg creeks called the Hog's Back. Both crossings can be avoided by picking your way along the rocky north bank next to the river and jumping Muskeg Creek. (NOTE At high water none of this may be possible. At such times continue along the fire road to 650260 and descend easy meadow to Muskeg Creek. Cross and follow a trail along the west bank back to Threepoint Creek and Hog's Back trail.)

Climbing onto the Hog's Back is the main challenge of the day. After the initial steep rise, the ridge levels and narrows surprisingly, a shale slope on the left falling away to Threepoint Creek. Resume climbing through trees, then along a grassy ridge to a hilltop sliced clean down the middle by the eroding action of the river now over 100 m (330 ft.) below you. A grassy promontory with a cross made from horseshoes makes a perfect lunch stop.

Back down in trees, the trail undulates along to a muddy side creek crossing. This heralds a longer uphill haul to airy meadows high above the full-fledged Threepoint Creek gorge. Across the gulf rises Allsmoke Mountain, whose alternating rings of cliffs and shale postholed by wandering sheep comes as a huge surprise if you're only familiar with its tamer east side. This is the place to explore a lower terrace overlooking the inner gorge. Far too soon you come to the final, classic viewpoint that looks south to the even wilder Volcano Creek gorge beyond.

Reluctantly turn your back on all this drama and descend to the fire road. Turn left and soon reach the junction with Wildhorse and Volcano Creek trails.

#65A The trail entering meadows above the gorge. Allsmoke Mountain at left. Photo Derek Ryder

#65A The final view up Threepoint Creek gorge (which turns right at the cliffs),
and the Volcano Creek gorge beyond. Photo Derek Ryder

66 VOLCANO CREEK—map 5

Above and right: Two views (not quite joining) of Threepoint Creek gorge and Allsmoke Mountain. Note the hiker at far left.

Backpack
Official trail, signposts & red markers, creek crossing
Distance 13.2 km
Height gain N–S 268 m (880 ft.)
High point 1951 m (6400 ft.)
Map 82 J/10 Mount Rae

North access Quirk Creek Valley at the junction of #65 Threepoint Creek and Wildhorse trail (Volume 2) at 619258.
South access Via #43 Gorge Creek at the junction with Threepoint Mountain trail (Volume 2).
Also accessible from #67 Forgetmenot Lookout trail, #68 Upper Threepoint Creek pack trail and #53 Volcano South trail.

This is an easy trail, interesting at both ends, but rather mundane in the middle. Most notably the north end offers a remarkable view into Threepoint Creek canyon. Travel is via fire road, cutlines, their access roads and, finally, a grade 7 cow trail through meadows.

It connects with five other trails offering ways on toward the Elbow and the Gorge Creek area of the Sheep. At the southwest end lies Threepoint backcountry campground that is due for refurbishing in 2012.

TRAIL NOTE Since the last edition the trail has acquired the northern section of the old Volcano Ridge trail.

NORTH TO SOUTHWEST

To Forgetmenot Lookout trail 2.6 km
Straight off, from the meadow at the head of Quirk Creek Valley, you ogle the black shale gorge of Threepoint Creek, which, coupled with Volcano Creek gorge, is the grandest of all the gorges in the Sheep. Continuing along the track (Forgetmenot fire road), you cross a drift fence and, enclosed in pine forest, follow the banktop around to the right into upper Threepoint Creek Valley. At 602243 is a T-junction. Turn left. (The fire road ahead is route #67 up Forgetmenot Mountain, and also the approach to #68 Upper Threepoint Creek pack trail.)

To Black Cow Hill junction 4.1 km

The trail winds downhill to Threepoint Creek, here idling in a shallow trough, and crosses it. Who would guess that in half a kilometre it would cascade over a cliff in a spectacular fall hidden from any trail. It is not amenable to a direct approach from the gorge bottom (I've tried); you either have to push through trees from the trail to the gorge edge, or follow the creek downstream to the drop-off. A few years ago it had its first winter ascent by X and friends who rapped off the top. They nearly made it up a seep on Allsmoke as well, but lacked "One More Screw."

After the crossing you climb past coal seams around a bend and up right, to a T-junction with a NE–SW cutline cum access road. Turn left.

Now you're heading due south in the pines, and too far away from exciting Volcano Creek gorge for easy detours. Not a lot goes on in this stretch: a detour left on a shortcut trail preceding a dip to cross a small side creek just about sums up the interest. At 602214 come to an unnamed tributary. On the near (north) bank an old road heads upstream to "Black Cow Hill." (See OPTION A.)

Threepoint Creek waterfall from above. Lower down is another fall that stops you from climbing up to this one from the gorge below.

To Volcano South trail 1.9 km

Semicircling to the right, the access road crosses the creek, then gets back to its straight line. Next, cross Rock Creek, an even longer tributary, that in its upper reaches is crossed by Threepoint Mountain trail. Again semicircling to the right, descend to the T-junction at 602197 with Volcano South trail (sign). Turn right. (The cutline access road continuing south and crossing the main fork of Volcano Creek is Volcano South trail, which follows the smaller south fork to the Volcano–Gorge watershed.)

Upper Volcano Creek 3.7 km

The trail follows the main fork of Volcano Creek to the west, keeping to (mainly) dry pasture and pine forest on the north side of the valley. About halfway along, Bluerock Mountain comes into view, framed by forested side slopes. Farther on is a confusing fork. Go right up a hill with red marker. (The tempting left-hand trail, though appearing to cut out the hill, is eventually forced up a steep bank by the meandering creek.) At a signpost at 572181 the trail forks, going either side of a small round hill. You have reached the "Volcano Creek Triangle."

1. NW fork 760 m Take this if headed north on Threepoint Mountain Trail or use the shortcut to Mount Rose meadows.

The trail ahead follows the right bank of Volcano Creek throughout. Mount Rose and Threepoint Mountain appear through the gap as you approach Threepoint Mountain trail at a signpost with no junction. Keep right for all points north and west.

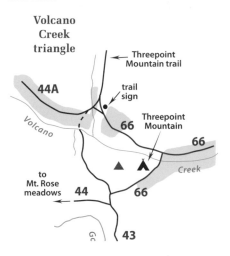

Volcano Creek triangle

Volcano Creek and Bluerock Mountain, showing the final slope climbed by #45.

Summit ridge of Black Cow Hill. Forgetmenot Mountain in the background.

2. SW fork 900 m Take this if headed for Threepoint backcountry campground, Gorge Creek trail and Mount Rose meadows main trail.

Turn left across Volcano Creek on the official Volcano Creek trail. On the right side among a few trees is Threepoint backcountry campground.

Continue on a well-used trail to the 4-way junction with Gorge Creek trail (left), Threepoint Mountain trail (right) and Mount Rose Meadows trail (straight).

OPTION

66A Black Cow Hill

Unofficial trail
Distance 4.6 km one way
Height gain 472 m (1550 ft.)
High point 2270 m (7450 ft.)

If you hunger for windswept hilltops with 360-degree views, try this easy trip on exploration road to the summit at 580219.

The old road (track) leaves Volcano Creek trail on the north bank of the nameless creek at 602214 and heads west, straightaway climbing up a hill into scattered meadows. After this, the track is gently angled to the very end. Pass a pond on the right, then opposite a line of crags on the opposite bank ignore a good game trail headed for the creek. Gradually the track and creek curve around to the northwest, the track faint where it crosses three meadows. You would think this a fairly remote

place, but this is where you might meet the black Angus, contentedly munching grass. The final half kilometre of track turns east and ends on the north side of your objective's broad west ridge.

From here it's an easy walk over short-cropped grass to two summits. The farther top has a cairn. As mentioned, the view is extensive, taking in a large number of Front Range peaks, including Bluerock, Banded, Outlaw, Cornwall and Glasgow. Directly north is Forgetmenot Mountain, separated from the hill by the deep gulf of Upper Threepoint Creek.

OPTIONAL DESCENT

2.3 km to #68, 4 km back to #66
A loop is available for adventurous bushwhackers who can pick a way down to Upper Threepoint Creek. Everyone else will have a longer walk back the same way they came.

From the first summit descend north onto the grassy northern outlier. Turn right and descend a broad ridge above a steepish grass slope bordering a creek. Lower down, where the gradient moderates, move closer to the creek and follow it down into Threepoint Creek Valley bottom. Pick up a trail heading to the right along the bank. It intersects #68 at the one place where that trail is on the south bank, at about 589235.

Go straight on #68, THEN cross the creek and climb and traverse up the far bank to the T-junction with Forgetmenot Mountain fire road. Go straight. The next T-junction is with Volcano Creek trail.

67 FORGETMENOT LOOKOUT TRAIL—map 5

Looking toward the summit ridge from Nichi.

Long-day hike, backpack
Unofficial trail
Distance 7.8 km
Height gain 631 m (2070 ft.)
High point 2338 m (7,670 ft.)
Maps 82 J/10 Mount Rae,
82 J/15 Bragg Creek

Usual access #66 Volcano Creek at 602243.
Also accessible from #68 Upper Threepoint Creek, #69 South Forgetmenot, Forgetmenot Ridge (Volume 2).

A gently graded and enjoyable trail up a reclaimed fire road leads to the summit of Forgetmenot Mountain.

HISTORY NOTE The mountain has been distinguished with the name Forgetmenot since it was *possibly* first climbed in 1895 by A.O. Wheeler's Irrigation Survey party and used as a primary triangulation station. It was positively climbed in September 1896 when the party approached it from the Quirk Creek side and in deep snow were forced to cut a trail onto the open east shoulder they called Nichi.

All was quiet on the mountain until 1952 when a lookout was erected on its summit, with a 25-km-long fire road to service it from the forest boundary. It was during this time that 80-m-deep Forgetmenot Pot was discovered on its eastern slopes in 1969 by Dave Doze. The golden age of Forgetmenot passed away with the decommissioning of the lookout in 1975, its burning down in 1977 and the demotion of Forgetmenot Pot as Alberta's deepest pothole. The fire road has since become part of Hwy. 549, Threepoint Creek and Volcano Creek trails.

To South Forgetmenot 6.3 km
On flat fire road head west, passing cutlines. At "road" junction 593237 at 1.2 km turn right. (Straight on is Upper Threepoint Creek pack trail.)

In a few minutes reach a NE–SW cutline. Turn left on the fire road. Shortly it swings right and, reduced to trail width, heads north. Three short zigs signal an even longer sweep across the entire eastern escarpment of Nichi, which is very steep and forested. On reaching a col, it sweeps back left (south) to gain the summit of Nichi. (NOTE On descent, it's easy to miss the acute bend at the col and go careening off eastwards down another trail.) Nichi slopes gently to the west, and from its grassy slopes you look toward the summit.

Climbing again, you head northwest along the broad southeast ridge of the mountain through pine and spruce forest. Go either way at a split. Just past 575253 the trail turns left (south) and crosses the ridge to the southern escarpment. Look down on a lush meadow that slopes to the noonday sun. Here is the junction with South Forgetmenot trail. Well, there's not actually a junction, because at this point both trails are missing in long grasses. All you need to know is that South Forgetmenot descends the meadow, and the lookout trail turns sharp right, following flat ground at the top of the meadow.

To summit 1.5 km

The trail soon becomes obvious as an avenue between trees, passing below ruinous red crags and areas of scree. A couple of long zigs lead onto open slopes above the flat castle top. Coming up is the steepest part of the route, most people forgoing the faint suggestion of more zigs for a straight-up bash to the summit ridge.

Here, either follow the rocky ridge crest, which undulates like the Loch Ness monster, or the resurrected trail on its right side, that extends onto flat ground beyond the rocky ridge before curling back to the summit bump. There are in fact several summit bumps, the highest marked by a cairn, remnants of supporting walls on two sides, a concrete pad and a few other undecipherable mementoes of the lookout. Naturally, the view is extensive in every direction.

The summit. Allsmoke Mountain to right.

A trail continues westwards, descending past a metal post, then curving left onto the south face, aiming for a spring at treeline where lookouts supposedly got water. In August we couldn't find any.

SIDE TRIP

67A Forgetmenot Pot

Distance 2 km return

At 575253 head right along the grassy side ridge extending northwards. A series of depressions marked by small spruce end at the pot right at the very end of the ridge at 574263. Look for a smallish hole partially covered by a large sandstone slab.

Forgetmenot Pot. Photo Jon Rollins

68 UPPER THREEPOINT CREEK PACK TRAIL — map 5

Stony section above the canyon.

Long-day hike, backpack
Unofficial trail, then route,
creek crossings
Distance 3.1 km
Height gain E–W 229 m (750 ft.)
Height loss E–W 91 m (300 ft.)
High point 1935 m (6350 ft.)
Map 82 J/10 Mount Rae

East access #67 Forgetmenot Lookout trail at 593237.
West access #69 South Forgetmenot trail at 568232.

This scenic, sometimes stony trail connects the trails of the Sheep to those of the Elbow via the canyon of Upper Threepoint Creek.

TRAIL HISTORY NOTE, or why the trail ends so abruptly. For a 1920s pack trail used in pre-Forgetmenot Lookout days and marked on maps of the era, it remains in remarkably good shape. Only a small area of shifting scree has put it beyond the scope of today's equestrians, which is why this trail was never seriously considered for official K Country status. A second scrutiny a few years ago also came to naught, which is unfortunate because this historic trail badly needs fixing up at the other, west, end where there is a 1-km-long gap. Why DOES this trail come to a complete halt between a rockband and a side valley?

I blame it on the exploration road coming from the west that was pushed over the top of the pack trail until it neared the side valley, and then it took a very much higher line across the creekbed to its end at a gully. Since then, backpackers and outfitters also coming mainly from the west have naturally followed the better trail — the road — which soon became the ONLY trail (the pack trail having faded out from disuse), and from its end either continued up the mountain (#69) or muddled a way back down to the pack trail by various routes.

So we've inherited the disconnect and have to deal with it. Connecting E–W is reasonably easy; W–E less so. See the sketch map on the next page.

Descending to side creek 583232.

EAST TO WEST

At the "road" junction where Forgetmenot Lookout trail turns right, continue straight on a grassy track, that runs along a terrace above Threepoint Creek. After downgrading to trail, it descends part way down the bank. Keep right at a junction, even ascend slightly, then descend to Threepoint Creek. Cross to the south bank.

In only a short distance the trail recrosses the creek. (A trail carrying on along the south bank is the return loop from Black Cow Hill.)

At a cairn, keep right and climb diagonally left across a steep side slope into easy-angled forest. A very pleasant section ends with a short uphill climb and a sharp right turn up a small stony ridge. From the top the trail zigs down the other side into the side creek 583232. The initial descent is on those shifting orange screes mentioned in the introduction.

At the bottom, cross the side creek and climb up and left above a crag onto the canyon traverse between Forgetmenot Mountain and the unexpectedly rugged north face of "Black Cow Hill." You're crossing a wide scree slope on a bench, the situation on the edge of a steeper drop thoroughly enjoyable. The only danger here is of tripping over rocks strewn across the trail.

Gradually the trail descends, the side slope becoming increasingly less steep, less stony and more verdant as you descend all the way to the valley bottom. Ahead you can see a long diagonal rockband blocking the way.

The trail meanders along above the creek to the rockband and crosses it low down on a wide, slabby ledge. Next, pass under a small crag. You have arrived at the disconnect. At this point #69 is about 60 m (200 ft.) higher up the slope.

Starting you off is a recently made trail that climbs uphill and zigs right, then left into a traverse of a grass–shale slope. After it fades to scrapes, continue traversing, then just head uphill on grass, weaving around a few trees. At some point you're going to intersect the last section of road (now trail) to the gully. Turn left.

Shortly, reach T-junction 568232. Go straight for Threepoint Mountain trail, right uphill for South Forgetmenot.

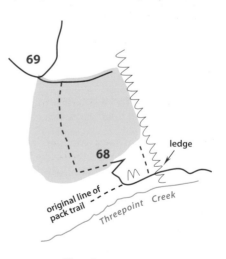

**How to connect to
South Forgetmenot trail**

69 SOUTH FORGETMENOT TRAIL — map 5

Long-day hike, backpack
Unofficial trail & route
Distance 4.9 km
Height gain 259 m (850 ft.)
Height loss 61 m (200 ft.)
High point 2164 m (7100 ft.)
Maps 82 J/10 Mount Rae,
82 J/15 Bragg Creek

The tall rock you aim for on the south ridge.
The rock castle and Forgetmenot Mountain in
the background.

West access Via Threepoint Mountain trail at Threepoint Creek crossing (Volume 2).
North access Via #67 Forgetmenot Lookout trail at 574248.
Also accessible from the west end of #68 Upper Threepoint Creek pack trail.

This trail, well used by outfitters, connects Threepoint Mountain trail to Forgetmenot Mountain lookout trail via Threepoint Creek and a south ridge of Forgetmenot Mountain. Only the middle section is at all steep; the rest is easy, with lots of meadows to delight in.

Most obviously it can be used to access Forgetmenot Mountain. It also makes available loops. The first time I used this trail was in combination with Big Elbow, Threepoint Mountain and Forgetmenot Ridge trails (all in Volume 2). On such mammoth one-day expeditions it's essential to check your party beforehand to ensure no one has a dinner date in Calgary at 5 pm!

TRAIL HISTORY The route is a combination of new and old trails. The section in Threepoint Creek was once a 1920s pack trail (continuation of #68 Upper Threepoint Creek pack trail), overlaid in the 1940s by an exploration road that ends at a gully. The road has since reverted to trail and from near its end outfitters made an ongoing trail.

WEST TO NORTHEAST
Upper Threepoint Creek 2.9 km
Leave Threepoint Mountain Trail on the north bank of Threepoint Creek crossing at a post. (See Volume 2.)

On trail (old road) head east down Threepoint Creek, the stream bubbling alongside the trail in a wide valley of grass and small willow brush. Shortly the SW fork joins in from the right. At a bend, either cross a pesky shale bank or paddle. Farther on, the trail undulates a little, crosses a couple of side creeks and is faint in the long grasses of the valley bottom. Throughout this section keep looking back for fine views of Threepoint Mountain framed in the vee.

Where the valley starts to close in a little, the trail rises onto a treed bench (note the falls in the creek below), then turns left and circles around a side valley. Just after it pulls out of the trees is a T-junction at 568232. Turn up left on the good trail. (The lesser trail continuing ahead soon ends at a gully with a perpendicular rock wall that extends all the way down to the valley bottom. To connect with #68, head down the hillside shortly after the junction.)

South Ridge section 2 km

The climb up a forested rib is moderately strenuous with the odd patch of deadfall to detour around. Near treeline keep left. Flagging marks the entry into meadow at 568239—an essential waypoint if you're hiking the trail in reverse, because there is no trail in the meadow leading to it.

The broad south ridge of Forgetmenot is lovely, covered in grasses waving about on windy summer days amid glittery little tarns. Ahead rises the summit ridge of Forgetmenot Mountain and to its right the flat-topped rock castle that overlooks the south ridge.

As mentioned, there is no trail. Just make your way northeasterly, aiming for the castle. Below it is a belt of forest. And in front of the forest is a tall rock. Delve into the forest belt nearest the rock (flag-ging). The trail starts up again and continues northeasterly, passing below the castle and descending slightly off the south ridge into a large south-facing meadow at the head of a side creek. Sheltered from west winds, this meadow grows luxuriant grasses and a myriad of flowers. Where the trail peters out, pick your own line (as the horses do) to the TOP of the slope, where you meet the lookout trail on the bench at 574248. Okay, so you have to use your imagination to envisage both trails and the junction.

Turn left for the summit 1.5 km distant; go straight if heading east and look for flagging as you enter the trees.

Top: A tarn on the south ridge. Behind are Bluerock Mtn., Mt. Rose and Threepoint Mtn.

Bottom: The south-facing meadow. The route aims for the top edge of the meadow at top right.

70 MUSKEG CREEK — maps 5 & 6

One of the shale banks rising up from the creek.

Long-day hike, backpack
Unofficial trail, creek crossings
Distance 3.4 km
Height gain S–N 61 m (200 ft.)
High point 1615 m (5300 ft.)
Map 82 J/15 Bragg Creek

South access Via #65 Threepoint Creek fire road at ~638271.
North access Via #72 Fisher Creek at 621295.

Muskeg is an unusual valley, characterized by meadows and high shale banks rising straight out of the creek. A track used by ATVs runs all the way down it, so the trail is good, though a little nebulous in places at the south end. Luckily the 16 creek crossings are the sort can be jumped except when swelled by rain.

The trail can be used in a variety of ways: aside from being a connector trail between #65 and #72, it offers a shortcut between Threepoint and Quirk creeks without you having to climb over that forested ridge on Threepoint.

NAMING NOTE This attractive valley is burdened with an off-putting name that once belonged to Quirk Creek. There's absolutely nothing muskeggy about it. Unfortunately, its Stoney name, *Horrokta pa usnabi*, "where a whiskeyjack's head was plucked clean," is even worse. I believe it was once called Holden Creek.

SOUTH TO NORTH

Just before the red marker at about 638271, turn right off the fire road and descend the bank to Muskeg Creek. Straight off jump the creek. During the next six crossings, try to ignore motorbike trails shooting up the hillside to the right, and pass below the first of the shale banks.

An uphill leads into a longish stretch along the east bank where the track is very distinct. After crossing no. 8, pass through a drift fence into a small copse of spruce with a muddy floor. Across the valley at this point is shale bank no. 2.

Two crossings a few minutes apart and you're back on the west bank. Go either way at a split and soon enter a really long meadow below shale bank no. 3. After crossing no. 11, keep right on a shale path to avoid crossings 12 and 13. Is anyone still counting?

Cross a side creek and climb into another large meadow. Three crossings in quick succession and you are on a west bank meadow, veering left to the T-junction with #72 at 621295. (Left leads to Quirk Creek, straight on to Fisher Creek.)

71 MOUNT BARWELL — map 6

Half-day, day hikes
Official trails with signs, some
unofficial trails
Map 82 J/15 Bragg Creek

Access Hwy. 549 (McLean Creek Trail).
NOTE Hwy. 549 is closed Dec 1–April 30
between McLean Creek campground access
road in the north and Fisher OHV staging area
in the south.
1. Fisher Creek OHV staging area and campground. Start from the far end of the right-hand
loop near the info board.
2. Just north of Mesa Butte equestrian campground, turn west onto a well road that crosses
Threepoint Creek. At the junction keep right
and recross the creek. Drive up the hill to a
3-way junction of roads at 694273 and park.
3. Just north of Mesa Butte equestrian campground, turn west onto a well road that crosses
Threepoint Creek. At the junction keep right
and recross the creek. Drive up the hill to a
3-way junction at 694273. Take the middle
fork up a steep hill. Just after the road bends
left to the well, park below the obvious pipeline
right-of-way at ~689279.
Also accessible from #72 Fisher Creek on the
watershed and from the staging area.

Barwell is a large, sprawling hill shaped
like a comb with three tops and five ridges
extending southwards. Running along
these ridges are trails built by K Country
for motorbikes. Still with me?

These trails differ only a little from
regular hiking trails, being more undulating, narrower and drier underfoot. They
make perfect spring training walks when
snow still mantles the Front Ranges to the
west. Though you'll be walking mainly
through pine forest, there are also flowery
meadows and cutblocks on south-facing
slopes and craggy outcrops.

Trails can be combined in various permutations to suit all levels of effort. The
best all-day loop (18.5 km with a considerable height gain) is Barwell Summit trail to
the main summit and a return via Moonrocks, Second Ridge and East Ridge from
access 1. The best half-day loop (6.5 km)
is East Ridge, Barwell Summit trail and
First Ridge from access 2.

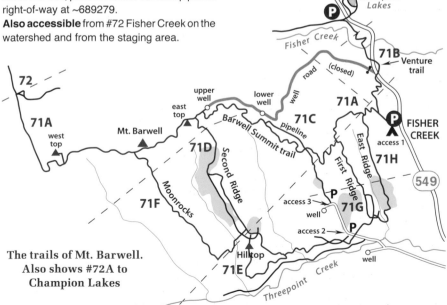

The trails of Mt. Barwell.
Also shows #72A to
Champion Lakes

Allsmoke Mountain from the west summit.

HISTORY NOTE Barwell's various tops were first climbed in 1895 and 1896 by members of the Irrigation Survey, and named after A.O. Wheeler's chief assistant, C.S.W. Barwell.

71A Barwell Summit trail

Distance 11.6 km
Height gain E–W 728 m (2390 ft.)
Height loss E–W 491 m (1610 ft.)
High point 1905 m (6250 ft.)
Access 1

The main trail of Barwell follows the east ridge over the east, main and west summits to the low point in the ridge between mts. Barwell and Quirk where it meets Fisher Creek trail. Though an easy, winding forest trail, it is long and unnecessarily undulating—a great route for people trying to get fit in the spring.

Most obviously, use it to gain the highest summit, at 653287 (15.2 km; height gain 789 m [2590 ft.] return). Or loop with Moonrocks, Second Ridge and East Ridge trails to bring the height gain up to 914m (3000 ft.). A longer loop takes in #72

Fisher Creek trail and B back to access 1. An even longer loop exists for runners like Bob Walker over Mount Quirk.

To Venture trail 440 m
Start left of the info board, heading northwest on a NW–SE cutline. At a junction at 698297 keep straight. (The old well road to right is Venture trail to Fisher Creek.)

To East Ridge trail 710 m
Just before intersecting a NE–SW cutline turn left onto a trail that makes easy zigs up the eastern escarpment to a T-junction with East Ridge trail at 695297. Turn right.

To First Ridge trail 1 km
Cross the NE–SW cutline. The trail then wends left, following the broad, slightly undulating east ridge. A steeper rise signals a recrossing of the cutline and the junction with First Ridge trail at 690292. Turn right.

To Pipeline 1.3 km
The trail descends to a col. Cross the NW–SE cutline and climb steeply up left onto the main summit ridge. Turn sharp right

and follow the edge a way before turning left onto the grassy swath of the pipeline right-of-way at 684290.

To second ridge 3.5 km
Cross the pipeline right-of-way into the trees of the south slope where the trail rock and rolls. Shortly after crossing the top of a cutblock offering a view to the southwest of Junction Mountain, an escape trail (sign) heads rightward to the well road just below the lower well.

The trail parallels the well road down below on the south slope, but goes twice the distance. It's a killer to hike: short, steep ups and downs following one on top of the other, finally ending with uphill zigs onto the summit ridge just west of the upper well. The well is in sight and the connecting trail is useful if you decided to miss out this section and walk up the well road! Turn left along the ridge crest and wind uphill to the junction with Second Ridge trail at 662296. Keep right.

To main summit 640 m
Walk over the broad east summit and down the other side to a col. A steeper, twisting climb leads to the main summit cairn and views to the north and west of Front Range peaks.

To Moonrocks trail 380 m
The trail turns left and pushes through a few trees to the edge of Moonrocks (danger sign), where it turns sharp right. This is where I peer over the edge to check for smashed dirt bikes and bodies. A rocky descent down the south side of the summit ridge brings you to the junction with Moonrocks trail at 650289. Go straight.

To west summit 1.5 km
The trail undulates along the ridge, steeply at times, then starts climbing toward the west summit, but misses it out completely by contouring around the south slopes. To reach the nicest summit of the three, take the second side trail to the right up a rib to a treed dip, then turn left. The rocky top

was used as a camera station in 1895 by the Irrigation Survey, who named it Long Muskeg Cairn for the view of Quirk Creek.

To Fisher Creek trail 2.1 km
Return to the trail that winds down the west flank and along the watershed ridge between Fisher and Muskeg creeks to the 5-way junction at 628300. Go second right for Fisher Creek; straight on for Muskeg Creek, Quirk Creek and the escarpment route up Mount Quirk.

71B Venture trail

Distance 1.3 km
Height gain N–S ~122 m (400 ft.)
Height loss N–S ~40 m (130 ft.)
High point 1518 m (4980 ft.)

North access #72 Fisher Creek at Hwy. 549.
South access Via #71A Barwell Summit trail 500 m distant from access 1.

A hilly trail connects Fisher Creek trail near Hwy. 549 to Barwell Summit trail near access 1, thus making possible the long loop with A and #72 without walking along Hwy. 549.

NORTH TO SOUTH
The trail leaves the south side of Fisher Creek trail near Hwy. 549 and runs between the highway and Fisher Creek, undulating madly along the banktop high above the creek. This section ends with downhill zigs to a crossing of Fisher Creek via a bridge. Climb gradually to the highway and cross it. Shortly, recross the highway (sign) just south of the well access road.

Straightaway, turn left at a T-junction. Soon the trail climbs, turns left and crosses a NE–SW cutline into a reclaimed meadow—former well site. Pick up the well access road on the far side and follow to a junction with a NW–SE cutline which is Barwell Summit trail at 698297. Turn left and in 440 m reach Fisher Staging area.

#71A *View from the main summit of Barwell, looking west across Forgetmenot Ridge to Mount Glasgow.*

#71F *Moonrocks trail, the final stretch under the moon rocks to the main axis of the mountain.*

71C Pipeline

Distance 2.1 km
Height gain S–N 137 m (450 ft.)
Height loss S–N 37 m (120 ft.)
High point 1692 m (5550 ft.)
Access 3

From access 3, the pipeline right-of-way climbs to the well road on the summit ridge and is the fastest, shortest route to the summit.

Simply put, you just follow the pipeline right-of-way—a sinuous, grassy ribbon imprinted with a trail. The route rises, steeply at first, to the summit ridge, where you cross Barwell Summit trail at 684290. An unexpected drop and re-ascent over another bump in the ridge gains you the well road just below the lower well. Either use the short connector to Barwell Summit trail, or walk up the well road to the upper well and continuing trail.

#71C Pipeline.

71D Second Ridge

Distance 5.7 km
Height gain S–N 375 m (1230 ft.)
Height loss S–N 24 m (80 ft.)
High point 1814 m (5950 ft.)
Access 2

A fairly easy forest and cutblock trail that links with Barwell Summit trail between the upper well and the east summit.

To Moonrocks trail 2.7 km
Straight off you can cheat! The trail starts back down the road at the sign, but why not just head along the left-hand logging road and wait for it to come in? The trail crosses the logging road. Again, stay on the logging road and only when the trail crosses the road for the second time, do you head off left into the bush.

A lovely section through aspen meadows ends with a side creek crossing (bridge) in a deep dip. Climb up the other side to a T-junction at 1.7 km. Keep right. (To left is Hilltop.)

Wander through lush open forest with smelly cow parsley onto a south ridge. Climb dry pine forest to a logging road, cross it and arrive shortly after at a second junction with Hilltop. Go straight. A few metres on, intersect a NE–SW cutline where Moonrocks trail officially turns left. (NOTE the logging road you crossed is the alternative meadow route into the upper cutblock.)

To Barwell Summit trail 3 km
Go straight up the ridge, the trail undulating over little tops, pines to the right, a cutblock to the left. Eventually you join the logging road and head up right into the upper cutblock. Keep an eye out for red markers. At logs laid across the road turn left onto a trail with red markers on both sides. The final stretch is gently uphill in pines, en route crossing a NE–SW cutline. Join Barwell Summit trail just east of the east summit at 662296.

#71E Hilltop

71F Moonrocks trail

Distance 3.9 km
Height gain S–N 378 m (1240 ft.)
Height loss S–N 113 m (370 ft.)
High point 1850 m (6070 ft.)
Access Via Second Ridge trail at 673274.

This trail runs from Second Ridge trail to Barwell Summit trail between main and west summits. If you can hack the very steep start, the rest is a rather beautiful walk along a south ridge. Seriously consider using this trail in reverse direction in combination with Second Ridge.

Follow Second Ridge trail to the cutline 673274 at 2.7 km and turn left. Alternatively, walk left along the logging road you crossed earlier until you intersect the cutline, THEN turn left.

Descend the grassy cutline to a side creek crossing (no bridge). The cutline winging up the ridge opposite is 122 m (400 ft.) high and appears vertical. Initially use the cutline access road that swings around to the left and joins the cutline above the first rise. After that you just have to knuckle down and plod up its loose, stony floor that serves as a test piece for extreme motorbikers. Just get ready to dive into the bush should you hear a bike coming up, because they ain't going to stop for you.

Now for the good bit. On gaining the ridge, turn right on a trail that climbs gently to a top, then undulates over many smaller tops in the pines. Here and there are views west toward the Glasgow massif. Cross a little rock ridge and on shale intersect a NE–SW cutline. Below a rockband blocking the way the trail turns left and traverses below the Moonrocks at the edge of talus. Suddenly — this is a glitch for hikers — the trail turns left, drops steeply, then very gradually regains height as it climbs to the main summit ridge, meeting Barwell Summit trail at 650289, 380 m west of the main summit.

71E Hilltop trail

Distance 2.1 km
Height gain 186 m (610 ft.)
High point 1620 m (5310 ft.)
Access Via Second Ridge trail in two places.

A short trail that can be combined with Second Ridge trail to make a half-day walk in the woods.

CLOCKWISE
Follow Second Ridge trail for 1.7 km to the T-junction after the side creek crossing with bridge. Turn left.

The trail climbs to an area of alder, then descends and crosses a wee side creek. At this point you are very close to Threepoint Creek fire road at the drift fence. Begin a long, gentle climb (one short, steep hill, one small cow parsley meadow) up onto a stony hilltop under the pines at 674266. Gradually descend, then climb to a logging road. Cross the road to the higher T-junction with Second Ridge.

Turn left if headed for Barwell Summit trail. Turn right if returning to access 2. (You can also just follow the logging road around to the right to where it intersects Second Ridge.)

71G First Ridge

Distance 2.4 km
Height gain 204 m (670 ft.)
High point 1661 m (5450 ft.)
Access 2

An easy-angled climb up a south ridge to Barwell Summit trail east of the east summit.

Walk back down the road a bit to an intersecting trail at signs and turn left (east). The trail wanders a damp dark forest below a cutblock (ignore an unmarked trail heading left after the bridge), then rises to cross a logging road at 698275. (For East Ridge turn right on the road.)

At the junction with East Ridge trail proper, a few metres on, keep left and undulate along the right side of the developing ridge, finally swinging up and left onto its crest. Climb the ridge above a large cutblock to left. Descend slightly to cross a ENE–WSW cutline, after which it's fairly level going through pine forest to the junction with Barwell Summit trail at 690292.

#71H East Ridge view of Allsmoke Mountain.

71H East Ridge

Distance 3.1 km
Height gain S–N 186 m (610 ft.)
Height loss S–N 30 m (100 ft.)
High point 1615 m (5300 ft.)
Access 2

The easternmost of the south ridges shares the same start with First Ridge trail, so it's logical to combine the two plus a small section of Barwell Summit trail to make a half-day loop of 6.5 km. This one has meadows (cutblocks) and in summer a dazzling assortment of prairie flowers.

Follow First Ridge to the logging road. Turn right on the road, in a minute intersecting East Ridge trail proper.

Turn right, descending ever more steeply to a side creek crossing with bridge. The trail heads up-creek, then cuts right and up the ridge on open slopes so well grassed you'd never guess you're in a cutblock until you try going walkabout. Cross a ENE–WSW cutline into pine forest and walk the edge of the eastern escarpment to the Y-junction with Barwell Summit trail at 695297.

72 FISHER CREEK—map 6
(Fisher Creek to Quirk Creek)

Day hike, bike 'n' hike, backpack
Official OHV trails with signs, unofficial
trail, easy creek crossings
Distance 11.3 km
Height gain 350 m (1150 ft.) from hwy.
Height loss 171 m (560 ft.) from hwy.
High point 1774 m (5820 ft.)
Map 82 J/15 Bragg Creek

East highway access Hwy. 549 (McLean Creek Trail) at Fisher Creek West staging area. This is where a well road cum logging road heads west up Fisher Creek. Any 4-wheel drive vehicle can drive the road to just past the 5 km mark (the road has kilometre signs), at the division of well road and cutline access road. Permanent puddles have solid bases. NOTE This section of Hwy. 549 is closed Dec 1– to Apr 30.

West access Quirk Creek trail just east of the unbridged crossing of Quirk Creek at 611290 (Volume 2).

Also accessible from #70 Muskeg Creek, #71A Barwell Summit trail.

Dave's Ridge rises above Fisher Creek Valley and gives a good view of the north slopes of Barwell.

This is a very useful connector between Fisher Creek on Hwy. 549 and Quirk Creek. For the most part the route uses well, cutline access and logging roads travelled by OHVs, specifically Fisher Trail West. Grades are easy except for the mid section climb up over the watershed ridge between Fisher and Muskeg creeks. Both sides are bikeable to the bottom of the big hills. Then leave the bikes or push them.

The route serves as access to #73 Mount Quirk and to #71A Barwell Summit trail from the watershed ridge.

ACCESS & CAMPING NOTE In 2005, floods washed out the well road in Fisher Creek at the entrance to the camping meadows. In 2007 a new logging road bypassed the washout AND the camping area, which is now reached by backtracking from the meadow below Dave's Ridge. While no longer available for rowdy high school grad parties, the increasingly muddy camping area is popular with OHV enthusiasts whose idea of "leave no trace camping" is to stuff beer cans into a Safeway bag and leave it hanging off a branch for someone else to remove. Oh well... it's a start.

EAST TO WEST
To road junction 4.9 km
On foot, on bike or in a vehicle, head west along the well road/logging road that is Fisher Trail West OHV trail up Fisher Creek. The road is flat; to your left are old beaver ponds and dams, to your right a series of interlocking cutblocks. Just before crossing a NW–SE cutline, turn right onto the latest logging road. (Ahead, the old road ends at a barrier above the wayward creek.)

The logging road arches through forest, crossing a bridge en route to the meadow below Dave's Ridge, where you meet up again with the well road. Keep right. (Turn left to reach the camping area.)

To your right rises a steep grassy ridge that serves as a "destination slope," and is criss-crossed by more cutlines and OHV trails per square inch than any other ridge in the foothills. Nevertheless, it's worth plodding up for the view of Mount Barwell through to Mount Quirk, the mountain foursome of Banded, Outlaw, Cornwall and Glasgow seen rising above the col in between the two. On the first top is a cairn and cross dedicated to David John Moore.

But back to the road, which remains obvious in the midst of assorted side tracks and cutlines, as it veers left and starts to undulate. Just past the 5 km marker is a Y-junction with a cutline access road. Park the car and continue on foot or by bike.

Turn left down the narrower road. (The better road ahead climbs to a well site and is the route taken by #73A up Mount Quirk.)

To the watershed 3.4 km
The cutline access road (also used as a log hauling road in the past) closely follows the right (north) bank of Fisher Creek in the forest. Note two side roads crossing the creek into a logged area. In 740 m opposite the second side road, Show and Shine trail (#73C) turns off to the right.

Beyond this junction the road gets rougher, stonier and more undulating. A narrowing of the valley signals the start of a 152 m (500 ft.) climb up onto the watershed ridge between Barwell and Quirk. After an initial up-down, the climb is relentlessly steep on stones continually rearranged by spinning wheels. Near the top is a junction. Straight on is the steep direct route. I prefer traversing right to a NE–SW cutline, turning left and finishing up the cutline. Top out at an unsigned 5-way junction with the road at 628300. Turn right. (Trail to left is #71A Barwell Summit trail.)

Follow the road along the watershed ridge, descending a little to a Y-junction at 626306. Hereabouts, clearings allow views of Muskeg Creek and Forgetmenot Ridge to the west. Keep left. (Ahead is #73B, Mount Quirk's escarpment trail.)

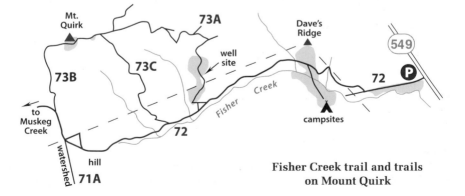

Fisher Creek trail and trails on Mount Quirk

Muskeg–Quirk meadows, looking southwest to Forgetmenot Mountain.

To Muskeg Creek trail junction 1.7 km
The road zigzags steeply down the west flank of the ridge to Muskeg Creek—a drop of 107 m (350 ft.). Cross. On the far bank is a T-junction. ATVs follow the road ahead that climbs up a hill. You turn left down the valley.

The dirt track heads downstream along the grassy west bank of Muskeg Creek. At 621295 the track turns sharp right. (The trail ahead at the bend is #70 Muskeg Creek from Threepoint Creek Trail.)

To Quirk Creek 1.3 km
Head west again through a wide gap between low ridges, keeping right, crossing a NW–SE cutline and climbing a little. To left, the lush meadows of Muskeg Creek meld imperceptibly with those of Quirk Creek. The track rounds the bottom of the ridge to the right and rejoins Fisher Trail West at a newer edition of the logging road.

Turn left and follow the road up a slight hill. The road then descends, curving left

to signed junction 611290 just east of the unbridged Quirk Creek crossing. The trail ahead and the road to right is Quirk Creek trail (see Volume 2). Go straight for Wildhorse trail and Threepoint Creek Gorge, right for Cobble Flats and Hwy. 66.

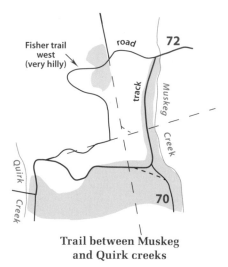

Trail between Muskeg and Quirk creeks

OPTION

72A Champion Lakes

**Interpretive trail, unofficial trails
Distance 1.5 km loop**

A short trip from the trailhead to two popular fly-fishing lakes named after John and Dexter Champion.

From the east side of Hwy. 549 at the junction with Fisher Creek trail, head north on a grassy track through meadow. At an interpretive sign turn right and climb steeply onto a small ridge to the east. The trail heads left and down into the small valley holding the lakes, the main trail making for the upper lake to left.

Starting between lakes, rough trails run on either side of the deeper lower lake to its far end. Here starts a draw that can be followed out to the meadow from which you started. See the map on page 219.

73 MOUNT QUIRK — map 6

Day hikes, bike 'n' hike
Official trails with red dirt bike signs
High point at summit 1899 m (6230 ft.)
Map 82 J/15 Bragg Creek

Mt. Quirk and the western escarpment.

Access Hwy. 549 (McLean Creek Trail) via #72 Fisher Creek at three places.
Usual east At the Y-junction with the cutline access road at 651306, 4.9 km from Hwy. 549.
West At 626306 on the watershed ridge.
Middle At 645303 in mid valley.
Also accessible from #71A Barwell Summit trail on the watershed.

Since my first visit, when there were no trails to the summit, this large, forested hill has been officially infiltrated by a network of quad and dirt-bike trails that now double as hiking trails.

ACCESS NOTE The summit can be reached comfortably in one day if you bike or drive the Fisher Creek section of #72 to the 4.9 km junction. If making a loop with descent options, leave the bike or car here. If going to the summit and back the same way, you can continue driving or pushing the bike up the well road to the well site at 650313. It's a little steep and stony in places, so use your own judgement. If you make it, subtract 1.1 km from the distance and 113 m (370 ft.) from the height gain. See the sketch map on page 227.

HISTORY NOTE Initially, the mountain was called Rock Point by the Irrigation Survey who climbed it on September 29, 1896. It describes the rockband at the northwest point.

73A Quirk Mountain trail

Distance to top 4.7 km from Y-junction
Height gain from #72, 411 m (1350 ft.)

The Quirk Mountain trail — a moderately easy forest trail with one really steep hill — follows the broad east ridge of the mountain to the summit, where a great view awaits you.

FROM USUAL EAST ACCESS
To the well site 1.1 km
Walking? At the Y-junction keep straight on the good well road. A few easy windings lead into a cutblock. The road then steepens and climbs around to the right of a forested knoll. Shortly after the gradient eases off, you cross a NE–SW cutline and reach the well site in a large, lush meadow, née cutblock, spread across a saddle behind the knoll. Leave the car here at 650313.

To Show and Shine 2.9 km
A trail carries on up the meadow to the right of a pond, for decades the resting place of a rusted-out car. On entering pine forest, it twists ever more steeply uphill to a T-junction. Turn left.

The next section is an easy, enjoyable traverse through open trees a little way down the south slope of the broad east ridge. En route at another junction keep left. The traverse ends with a short downhill in duplicate. Use the left-hand trail.

The summit cairn, looking west.

Continue traversing, then climb to the ridge crest with T-junction. Again keep left. (Trail to right peters out.)

Not long after, you come to the steep uphill which splits higher up into three shaley chutes, each as gruelling as the other. I advise starting up this hill from farther back on the trail at some flagging, and heading diagonal up left, following scuff marks in the vegetation. While dirt bike trails always feature one steep hill as a matter of principle, it's good to know there is often an easier route made by wimps.

At the top the trail turns left and splits. Keep straight up a steep bit of cutline. The following easy section ends with a short climb to the rocky lower summit. Head down the other side. Viagra Ridge trail turns off to the right. A little farther down the hill at 634319, OPTIONAL DESCENT C turns off to the left at some flagging.

To the summit 710 m

Start the final climb. High up, go straight at a T-junction. (Bypass trail descending left misses out the top.) Happily, the summit trail misses out the summit nubbin, which has a cairn perched on top. Sited above the northern escarpment, Quirk's summit is a satisfying viewpoint taking in a large number of foothills and peaks in the Front Ranges. The very pointy peak to the southwest is Mount Rose.

OPTIONAL DESCENTS

73B Via the escarpment

Distance 5 km to usual east access
Height gain 30 m (100 ft.)
Height loss 177 m (580 ft.)

A pleasant walk along the rim of the northwest and western escarpments is combined with #72 to return you to your starting point. Some steep downhills.

Escarpment 1.6 km

Continue west on the summit trail. Shortly, turn left, then right onto the bypass trail that descends steep grass to a saddle. Back in pine forest, head slightly uphill to a barbecue built out of rocks. Three lawn chairs were leaning against a tree when last we looked. From this point on, a wide track, made by Hummers before they were kicked off this trail, takes over and heads out to the northwest corner of the mountain above a colourful rockband. As you turn south, the rocks are replaced by meadows sweeping down the hillside to Muskeg Pass. Look west across OHV lands to Forgetmenot Ridge.

Far too soon you start the steep, twisty descent to Fisher Creek trail. Reach the cutline access road at 626306.

Fisher Creek 3.4 km

Go straight (south) on the road that more or less follows the watershed ridge. At the 5-way junction turn left down the NE–SW cutline. At the next junction turn right, then left back onto the cutline access road. Endure a long, stony descent into Fisher Creek Valley.

Continue to follow the cutline access road along the left (north) bank of the creek to the junction with the well road.

73C Show and Shine

Distance 2.6 km
Height gain 18 m (60 ft.)
Height loss 290 m (950 ft.)

A Jekyll and Hyde trail that follows a southeast ridge between Quirk Mountain trail and Fisher Creek trail in the valley bottom. Not so good in reverse direction.

The trail leaves Quirk Mountain trail just west of the lower summit at 634319 at some flagging.

It starts out really well: "Hey, this is a really nice dirt bike trail!" Then it takes a down-step in the ridge direct. Luckily, the forest is open with lots of grass underfoot, so you can zig down anywhere. After a brief traverse in the open, pick your way down a shorter, rockier downhill that ends with a groove where the ground has been worn to slippery bedrock. So narrow is it that you can hardly put one leg in front of the other without tying them in a knot.

Another nice section follows, ending on an open rise offering views to the west. At one time the route continued on down the ridge (perhaps still worth taking), but now it takes a nose-dive off the right side in duplicate. Look for a zigzag trail on the left side, which is possibly the dirt bike riders' attempts to climb UP this thing. At the bottom, the trail turns left and roller coasters—the show and shine bit.

The next downhill to a cutline marks the start of the final approach to Fisher Creek Valley, a sort of descending traverse between the ridge and a deep side creek to your right. There's still the odd steep descent, but overall the going is much easier. It ends with a flat walk across grass to the cutline access road at 645303, directly opposite a logging road crossing the creek.

Turn left and walk 650 m to the usual east access.

Left top: #73B The northwestern escarpment.

Left bottom: #73C The upper part of Show and Shine on the ridge.

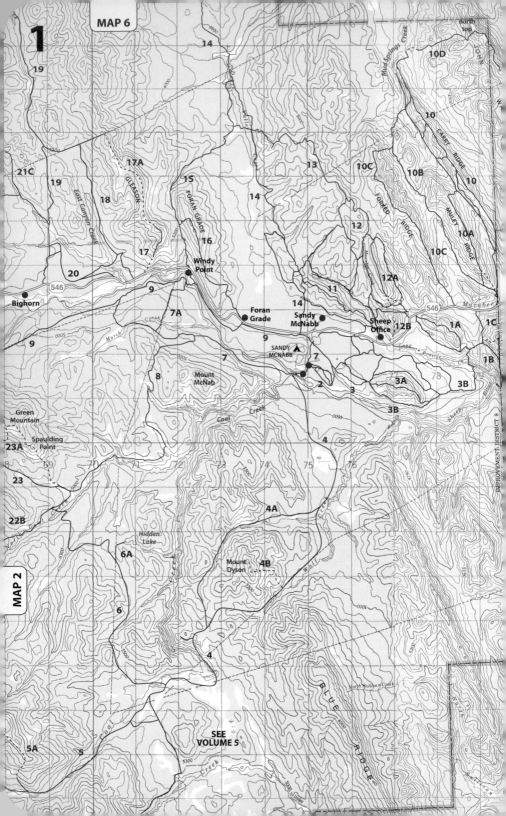

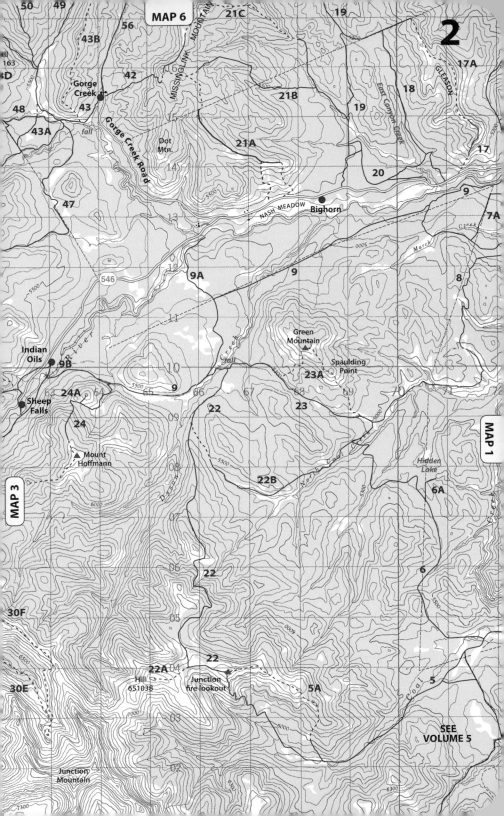

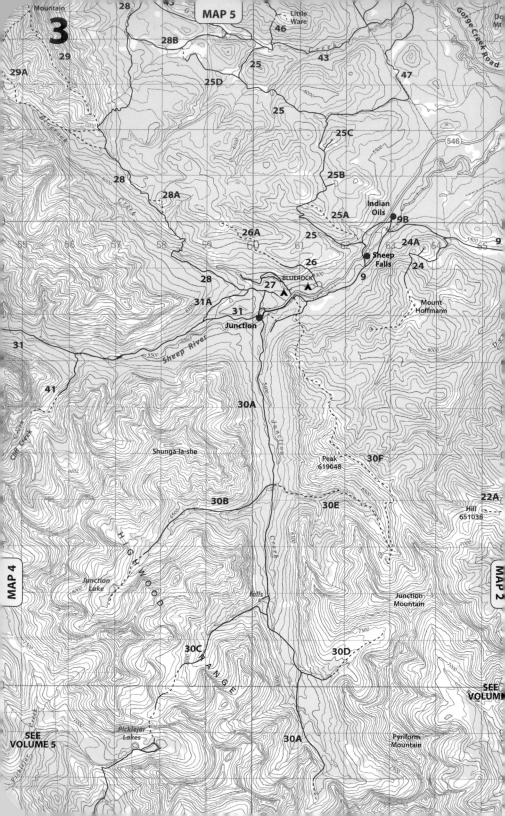

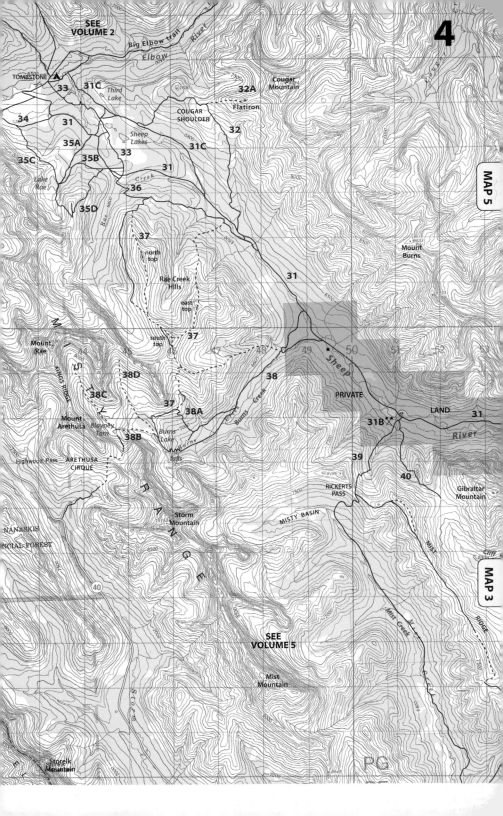

542

Dave's
Ridge

Champion
Lakes
72A

73A

Mount
Quirk

73B

73C
72

72
Fisher   Creek
72

71B

72

upper
well   well
71A
71A

71A
71B

Mount
Barwell
71A

FISHER
CREEK

Mesa
Butte
64D

71D

64A
64E

70
71C   71G   71H
well

64B
64C
64D

71F

71E

65
well

65
well
MESA
BUTTE

65
65A
Three point
65   MeSA
BUTTE
63

66
59
Death's
Head
62

60
Ware Creek Road
NORTH FORK

59
62

Allsmoke
Mountain
61
viewpoint

62A

58A
57
56
Sinnot
Hill

MAP 5
58C   58B
56B   56
Ware
Creek
62

57
56

56
14

Volcano
51   52A   49
56A   19

52
52
56
15

3   50   43B
MAP 2
MAP 1

INDEX

CONTACT NUMBERS

For government establishments use the toll-free line 310-0000, which is available from 8 am–6 pm on weekdays only.

Kananaskis Country Head Office
(Alberta Tourism, Parks & Recreation) in Canmore 403-678-5508

Alberta Sustainable Resource Development in Calgary 403-297-8800

The Friends of Kananaskis Country
403-678-5500 ext. 288
www.kananaskis.org

On-line info
Kananaskis Country and trail reports
www.Kananaskis-Country.ca

Gillean and Tony Daffern's blog site
KananaskisTrails.com.

Information Centres
Sheep River Provincial Park office
403-933-7172

Elbow Valley Visitor Centre 403-949-4261

Campground Reservations
Kananaskis Country Campgrounds
403-949-3132

Government of Alberta
reserve.albertaparks.ca

Backcountry Campground Permits
403-678-3136

In an emergency DIAL 911 and tell the operator you have an emergency in Kananaskis Country. Or contact Kananaskis Country Emergency Services at 403-591-7755.